Zion
Devotions

Zion
Devotions

Cleris Christian

XULON PRESS

Xulon Press
2301 Lucien Way #415
Maitland, FL 32751
407.339.4217
www.xulonpress.com

Paperback ISBN-13: 978-1-6628-0409-0

Ebook ISBN-13: 978-1-6628-0410-6

Acknowledgement

"He must increase, but I must decrease". John 3:30

All glory and honor belong only to my LORD and Savior Jesus Christ for His perfect timing and provision for this book according His promise, "At the right time, I, the LORD, will make it happen" (Isaiah 60:22, NLT). A heartfelt thank you to my dear husband Jodrejoy, who took the initiative for this book and stood by me every step of the way. I praise God for my beautiful children, godly parents, family, friends and well-wishers for their tremendous support and encouragement for the writing of these devotions. May God bless those who read this book and I pray that it will stir a heart to come a step closer to God through these messages.

With a grateful heart,
Cleris Christian

How beautiful upon the mountains are the feet of him who brings good news, who publishes peace, who brings good news of happiness, who publishes salvation, who says to Zion, "Your God reigns." Isaiah 52:7

Table of Contents

For I know the plans I have for you," declares the LORD, "plans to prosper you and not to harm you, plans to give you hope and a future.
Jeremiah 29:11

January

New Beginning - January 1

Therefore, if anyone is in Christ, he is a new creation. The old has passed away; behold, the new has come. 2 Corinthians 5:17

Waking up on the first morning of the New Year, we all woke up with an expectation of some change. We expect to have a change in us, others, and in our lives. Yes, life will change and move on as it has for centuries but, overall, it remains the same day to day and we too continue as usual. Only the date on the calendar has changed but it really does not mean anything significant for us unless we have a change of heart. The change of date, year or decade can move forward but if we remain the same, we will not see a difference in our growth.

If we desire a change, it starts with us. We must learn to be disciplined, self-controlled and spiritually focused every day and in every matter in order to move forward to being a better person.

Just because the year has changed and we have a desire to be better, it will not happen automatically or miraculously until we ourselves do something about it. It takes effort and change of attitude from our part also for God to help us. We cannot remain in the same stubborn attitude and live the same lifestyle and expect God to change us.

Therefore, as we move ahead in the new year, let us remember that the "new" will only happen when we ourselves have a new outlook on life and ourselves. Only when we put away our old self and put on a new self, we will see a difference in the coming years.

Dear LORD, thank you for the past year and now as we move into the new year, please help me to make the necessary change I need in order to be a better person in You. We pray for Your blessing, guidance and protection throughout our days. In Jesus' name, Amen!

Next right thing - January 2

A man who makes a vow to the Lord or makes a pledge under oath must never break it. He must do exactly what he said he would do. Numbers 30:2

We often make a promise of "always" or "never" to do something again. Long term promises are hard to keep and that is the reason why yearly resolutions do not work out and we end up breaking them in many cases.

Instead of making long-term promises, daily commitments seem to work effectively. Before getting out of bed in the morning, we can make a promise to do or to not do something which is needed. Then make a commitment to the LORD about it for that day alone and make every effort to fulfill it. We do not need to think of how we failed at it yesterday or worry about keeping it again tomorrow, just be focused on keeping the commitment for this day. And when we make specific commitments to do only for today, it becomes easier to remember and keep the promise.

God gives us what we need in increments of one day at time. He gives us His grace, strength and ability to accomplish our goal one step at a time. And we too ought to live one day at a time. Therefore, let us not jump ahead of ourselves lest we fail. Doing something for just one day sounds achievable versus doing it always, so let us work on our commitment one day at time and see what a day's worth of difference it makes.

Dear LORD, help me understand the meaning of a commitment and how to fulfill it. Help me not be the one to fail at it but follow through on it. Teach me to work on it step by step and not be in rush to finish it, hence I fail. May I do the next right thing and slowly achieve the goal which we have set up. In Jesus' name, Amen!

Somebody prayed - January 3

Then the Lord said to Moses, "Write this on a scroll as something to be remembered and make sure that Joshua hears it... Exodus 17:14

As Joshua led the battle against their enemy, Moses sat on the mountain praying with his hands lifted to the throne of God. As long as Moses' hands stayed up, the Israelites won but if the hands came down, the enemy would win. So, for his hands to remain up, Aaron and Hur held them up when Moses felt weary. After the victory, God told Moses to record this event for memory and to make sure that Joshua knows about how the battle was won so that he doesn't think he did it by his own strength and become puffed up with pride. It was because of Moses' intercession; Joshua won the victory through the LORD.

Often, we give credit to ourselves when we accomplish something. We think that we did it by our own might and knowledge. But do we ever consider that maybe somebody was praying for us? We think of such things lightly but all the blessings that we encounter in life are a result of prayers that are made on behalf of us by others such as our parents, grandparents and faithful friends. It is because the lift us up to the throne of God, we can fight and win the wars of life that we face.

Therefore, let us make sure that we know and remember that it is due to the prayer that someone prayed, we are blessed. And we too need to pray for others as our prayers give someone else the strength to overcome their struggles.

Dear LORD, I thank you for those people in my life who faithfully pray for me. Because somebody prayed for me and lifted me up to Your throne when I could not do it for myself, I am saved. Please help me to stand in the gap and pray for someone else when they are too weak to pray. Let my prayers be so full of faith that You will look at my faith and save the one whom I am praying for. In Jesus' name, Amen!

"Martha, Martha," the Lord answered, "you are worried and upset about many things. There is only one thing worth being concerned about. Mary has discovered it, and it will not be taken away from her." Luke 10: 41-42

I had been too busy to pray lately. With so much going on and with sleep deprivation, I really did not have much time and motivation to pray or even think about writing my devotions. Like Martha from the Bible, I was "busy" trying to get things done while I should have been like her sister Mary, who chose to sit with Jesus first and let all else be secondary.

In this fast-paced world, all of us are just too busy living our lives that we do not even have a spare moment for God. We go about frantically from one place to another, doing something or the other and try to figure out solutions to problems on our own. Although our intention may not be do so, we end up putting God as our last priority and other people or activities first. We burn ourselves out with no energy left to sit and focus on prayer or God's word.

We may even say that God understands, sees what we are going through and so we decide to catch up with Him later. But what a wrong perception to have! If anything, we need to go to God foremost with everything. He absolutely understands the craziness of life and the things we need to do in our day but all of it would be so much better if we consult with God first before we go running around. When we go in our own strength, we end being stressed out and may even cause more of a mess but if we take it to God first, He helps us through it by giving us the strength, wisdom, patience, and skills to handle whatever we need to do.

So as busy as we may be, let us not put God secondary to all other things instead give Him the priority over all. Everything else can wait and will get done somehow if we bring it to God's attention and seek Him first.

Dear LORD, my main purpose in life is to have fellowship with You and then do what You have called me for so please help me to not become so busy doing the things of the world that I miss my purpose of being who I am in You. Help me to seek Your kingdom first and know that everything else will fall into its place. May You always be my priority above all. In Jesus' name, Amen!

Hidden Sins - January 5

Would not God have discovered it, since he knows the secrets of the heart?
Psalm 44:21

I came to realize over the weekend that we are afraid of people more than we fear God. Therefore, we commit sins in our mind and heart more than we do from outside. Because we are concerned about our self-image and reputation in society, most of us are well-behaved outwardly. We commit sin inwardly through our thoughts, imaginations, eyes and feelings, we just do not act on them. We ensure that our name and status are in right standing with people, so we allow ourselves to commit certain acts only in our heads or in secret but not publicly. Instead of worrying about our inner self which God is concerned about, we focus more on our outer image which goes to show that we care more about what people think rather than God.

Many are broad-minded about everything and have pretty "free" lifestyle. They are genuine inside out and open about who they are and what they do, including their sins. But there are many of us who are more concerned about the society and afraid of what others think so are done in secret and because we have not physically acted upon it, we consider ourselves innocent. We often look down on others when we can see them commit the "sin". But since our sins are hidden from people's eyes, we downplay ours. When we do this, we are worse because not only are we guilty of committing the sin itself but also of deception. We fool others by portraying ourselves clean and holy while our true self is totally the opposite. We carry ourselves so perfectly in front of others that no one can find any fault in us but if what is done inside would be exposed on the outside, we would be willing to tie a millstone around our neck and drown in shame.

We might be innocent till proven guilty in the sight of people, but we are already convicted in God's eyes. We cannot hide anything from God who knows all, sees all and searches the motive behind it all. So, we need to fear God first and try to be clean in His sight rather than others.

Dear LORD, thank you for the conviction of Your Holy Spirit which shows me my secret faults. In your eyes a sin is a sin whether it is thought of or acted on, so please help me to not commit sin even in my heart or mind. Please help me to guard my thoughts and motives so that in all that I think and feel, I remain pure from inside out. In Jesus' name, Amen!

Recognize God's voice - January 6

My sheep hear My voice, and I know them, and they follow Me. John 10:27

When we went to the airport to pick up my husband who was coming to America for the first time after we got married, I had a little difficulty recognizing him right away because I hadn't seen him for a few months. Although we were married, we had not spent much time together and were parted for a few months, therefore it was a little hard for me to pick out my own in the crowd.

Similarly, we may be tied to Jesus Christ religiously and be known by His name as Christians but until we have that close relationship with Him, we truly are not able to relate to Jesus. In order to know someone intimately, its crucial to spend time together to know each other well. Until we are close to God and know His voice, we cannot recognize Him readily in the midst of others and surrounding noises. I was almost deceived a couple of times by "look alike" of my husband until he came closer. I recognized his voice right away because although we were physically apart, we had stayed in constant touch through phone calls during our separation. In the same way, we must recognize our Savior's voice when He speaks to us. Many look-alikes may come our way to deceive us from God but when we know our own, we cannot be fooled. The devil himself is the wolf who comes in sheep's clothing in many shapes and forms to deceive us but when we know our God, we can recognize who is not.

We need to minimize the distant between us and God and stay in close contact with Him by praying, reading His word regularly so that we recognize and know Him well. The more time we spend with God, the stronger our intimacy.

Dear LORD, I ask for discernment to separate the truth from evil. Please help me to spend more time with You so that I know You intimately and can recognize Your voice amongst those who come to deceive me. May I only follow the voice of my shepherd, Jesus Christ who leads me in the path of righteousness. In Jesus' name, Amen!

Phone Addiction - January 7

For you are a slave to whatever controls you. 2 Peter 2:19

An addiction is a dependency, craving, habit, weakness, or compulsion of using or doing something to the point that it basically takes over life. When we think of addiction, drugs or alcohol normally come to mind. But there are many other less thought-of addictions which we take lightly but can equally dangerous to ruin one's life. One of them is the addiction to phone. We may laugh at it but many of us are addicted to our phones. We have become so dependent on the smartphone that we cannot live without it for a moment. The phone is smart, but people are becoming dumb as we rely on it more and more. We are losing the ability to think for ourselves and run to the phone for every little matter.

It is the first thing we reach for in the morning and the last thing that we put down. And throughout the day our hands just reach for the phone automatically every few minutes, if not seconds, to text or check what is going on Facebook, WhatsApp, Instagram, etc. It has become a compulsion of staying in constant contact with people but mostly with those who have no added value to our lives. We easily ignore the people around us and do not make an effort to have a simple conversation with them, but we can chat away for hours on the phone with others who are insignificant.

Satan is using this technology to steer us away from having personal relationships with each other and with God. He is using this tactic in subtle ways that we do not even realize it is the underlying source of our struggling marriages, families, finances and education. The devil feeds our mind with worldly pleasures that we find enjoyment in the stuff that the little black screen shows us instead of those who are in front of us. We can become too busy when it comes to praying, reading Bible, spending time with family or doing some chores but we sure have more than enough time to waste, entertaining with outsiders. Satan has messed up the order of priorities for us and we have given into it and not even aware of it. We have replaced God and our significant ones with the phone and socializing with outer circle.

It is time to examine ourselves and acknowledge this issue as an addiction for many of us. Break this chain of slavery to the phone and be freed in Jesus name!

Dear LORD, it is true that something as innocent as a phone can be the source of separation between You and I, and myself with my loved ones. So please give me the wisdom to draw a limit on how much I allow myself to socialize through the phone before it becomes an idol and I start to worship it more than I worship You. Please break me free from the bondage of this social slave master. In Jesus' name, Amen!

God-given talents - January 8

Each of you should use whatever gift you have received to serve others, as faithful stewards of God's grace in its various forms. 1 Peter 4:10

At our Women's Ministries group, we learnt how to crochet. There were some women who have a passion for it and are pros to make a bag or blankets within a matter of hours. There were some like my daughter who grasped crocheting in a matter of minutes and picked it so well that she was able to make a scarf overnight. Then there was someone like me, who struggled to even hold the hook correctly and no matter how much I tried, I just could not get it. I watched the others in awe how quickly and beautifully they could do this while I fought to get the yarn through the loop each time. I realized that this is not my skill set and let it go.

It did make me think about how God has given us different skills as individuals. We all do not have the same ability to do the same things. I can write a book if I need to, but crocheting is not my cup of tea. When we see someone carry out a skill flawlessly, we may wish we could be like them and try to do the same thing. But their ability does not necessarily mean it is ours also. And what they may not be so good at, we could do it with our eyes closed.

God needs diverse talents and therefore He equips each one of us with different abilities to do our part and execute His purpose on earth. We as individuals need only to be concerned about our role and passionately give our best so that God can use it as a part of His big picture. If we worry about what others are doing, compare ourselves to each other or try to be like someone else, we go out of God's will and cannot not fulfill His purpose.

Therefore, we need to figure out what our God-given ability is and use it, whatever it may be for Him. In God's sight nothing is insignificant and not one person's talent is better than the other. He has chosen each one of us to do a specific task, so we need to do it with God's purpose in mind without comparing our work to someone else's.

Dear LORD, please help me to understand that I cannot take someone else's talents and make them mine. Thank you for giving me the specific abilities that I can utilize for Your kingdom. Please help me to recognize it and give You my best. In Jesus' name, Amen!

God's endorsement - January 9

Whatever you do, work heartily, as for the Lord and not for men. Colossians 3:23

Any time we begin to do something, what we normally think about is People! We wonder what people will think or who will notice what we do. Whether it is good or bad, we are more concerned about what people think! We basically seek approval of men first over God and put our hands in everything, even if it is not our calling, just because we desire the praise and approval of people.

But we need to know that when it comes to doing something, particularly for God's work, it is about the anointing and not endorsing! It is God who chooses a person or group for a specific purpose. David was the future King, anointed by God, not his brothers. He was just a shepherd boy considered insignificant compared to his brothers who may have been endorsed and impressive to people, but they were not the chosen ones.

When God chooses, no person can disapprove. If God calls us for a specific task, He puts His favor on us and equips us in every way to accomplish what He has called us to do. We may consider ourselves little or incapable of doing something compared to what others can do but if God's anointing is over us, there is no need for men's endorsement. If we keep our eyes on the Lord, only seek His approval and do what He wants us to do, our work is blessed and multiplied. But if we do it for people to notice, our work "For the Lord" is not acceptable or worth anything in God's sight. Men may be pleased by us but if God's hand is not in it, it is all in vain and falls apart.

Dear LORD, as I work for You, my family, job, church and community, help me to do it to seek Your approval over any person. May I not do it for prestige or praises from people but only from You. Teach me to work at it humbly to receive Your "Well done, my good and faithful servant". In Jesus' name, Amen!

Consult God first - January 10

But Jehoshaphat also said to the king of Israel, "First seek the counsel of the Lord."
2 Chronicles 18:4

God has given us a mind to think and make decisions. However, we often make decisions solely based on our own knowledge. We may consult with some trusted loved ones, but we forget to check with God. In our hurry and own wisdom, we do not take the time to ask or hear what God has to say. Or we might think that our issue is too small for God's attention, so we do not bother Him with our every little problem.

But God is a God of details. He knows our every thought, concern and fear but also desires that we seek His will and help. Just how we feel privileged when someone asks and takes our advice, God too feels honored when we look up to Him.

The King of Israel asked King Jehoshaphat of Judah to go with him to fight against his enemy, and Jehoshaphat did not give him an answer right away but told him to seek the counsel of the LORD first. Although both kings were powerful, Jehoshaphat feared God and did not want to make a move until he consulted with God and got His blessing.

We too need to consult God first before we make any move in life, big or small. Many companies pay large amounts of money to professional consultants to guide them in decision making for the company's benefit. But we have free access to the best consultant in the universe. He is at our service, only one prayer away. His advice is never wrong, and we will never be disappointed if we trust His leading in our lives. So, let us take advantage of this privilege and seek God's counsel first before we make a move.

Dear LORD, please help me to keep You first in everything that I do. Help me to seek Your counsel and follow Your advice. Please speak to me clearly and say, "This is the way, walk in it". Let me not move if You will not bless me in it. May I recognize Your voice and walk where You lead me. In Jesus' name, Amen!

Not by might nor by power, but by my Spirit,' says the Lord Almighty.
Zechariah 4:6

We generally ask "what is the secret behind your success" when we see someone achieve something great. Oftentimes we give credit to our family and friends for their support or even to ourselves for our own ability or intelligence. It is true that we need each other's help and prayers in order to get something done but the biggest role played in our success is through God. We may have man's favor, the intellect, finances and passion for something but unless we have God's Spirit in us, we cannot succeed. We can try our hardest to please others, to fit in, or satisfy our own need but if it is not what God wants us to do, we will not get too far. It is God who gives us the vision, ability, strength and wisdom to carry out a task. Therefore, it is essential that we recognize God's will first before we start something. And our prayer should be like Moses' who said, if God will not go with us, then we will not move either. It is about doing things God's way rather than by our own might and will.

When we are in alignment with God and His favor rests on us, everything falls into place. God examines our heart to see the reason behind why we would like to do a certain thing, and when He sees it as selfless and only for His glory, God comes through for us. He brings the right people and things in order; He pours out His Holy Spirit on us who guides our path and makes us able. The task may be difficult but all we need to do is to trust God more than we trust people or our self. Once we submit to God, we can be assured that He who began a good work in us, will carry it on to completion without fail.

Dear LORD, please help me to understand and accept that I am who I am because of who You are in me. It is not through my own ability or wisdom that I can do anything, but it is only by Your power in me. By Your strength in me alone, I can do everything. Help me to be available for Your work and allow You to make me able. In Jesus' name, Amen!

Restoration - January 12

Forget the former things; do not dwell on the pasts. Isaiah 43:18

While doing the dishes, I broke a glass. It shattered into a few pieces, so I just picked up the broken glass along with the pieces and threw it right away in the trash. I did not even hesitate or think twice about fixing it, I knew it was beyond repair so just threw it out. Thank God that He does not think like that towards me. No matter how many times I have broken down into pieces in my sins, God does not throw me out. When I consider myself useless and unworthy of restoration, God sees it as an opportunity to make something new out of my brokenness.

What we perceive as useless, God calls it priceless. He takes our shattered pieces and brings them back together in a more beautiful way. The Chinese use a gold or silver colored glue to stick broken things back together so that joint pieces make a stunning new design. It also serves as a memory to one who broke and glued it back together of how bad it was previously and how pretty it looks now. In the same way, God does not waste or throw any of our past sins or experiences but uses them to restore us into a better and stronger person. The memory of our sin may remain, but not to taunt us though, rather to remind us of God's grace and restoration. Therefore, let us not allow the devil to make us feel guilty and unworthy due to our past sins. Instead remember how God has restored us anew into a more beautiful way, better than what we were.

Dear LORD, please forgive my sin and restore me back to You. I bring to You my broken pieces of hopes, dreams and purposes that You have for me. Thank you for taking my mess and turning it in my message. Help me to always remember Your goodness and mercy upon me. May I go about declaring Your mighty work in me as I display Your love and forgiveness. In Jesus' name, Amen!

No shortage – January 13

Give us this day our daily bread. Matthew 6:11

God provided Manna "heavenly food" for the Israelites each morning as they journeyed through the wilderness. He gave specific instructions to only gather as much as needed for only one day at a time for each family. However, some tried to take more than needed and it only resulted in rotten food that had to be thrown out.

Some of us tend to collect more than what we need, especially food. If an opportunity is presented for taking left-overs or free food, we pack as if it is the last food that we will ever get. We may eat some of it for a couple of times but the rest of it usually sits around getting spoiled and eventually thrown out. But still we just do not let go any opportunity where we can have something for free, even if it turns out useless later. This human tendency proves two things – selfishness and doubt about God's provisions.

Although we have enough of what we need, we tend to want more. There is a difference between need and want which we fail to differentiate. A need is something that is necessary for our survival, but a want is just a desire to have it, regardless of its necessity in life. God provides for our necessities and gives us what is essential, but we do not get satisfied with just enough, we desire more than enough. We also fear that we may not get it again and might miss out on an opportunity, therefore we gather more than what we need.

By doing this, we indirectly doubt in God's ability to provide and collect more than what is needed. God knows our needs and there is never a shortage in His storeroom so let us not worry about our tomorrow but only ask for and enjoy what He gives us one day at a time.

Dear LORD, thank you for Your provision according to what I need. You are my Jehovah Jireh, my provider whom I trust to meet my daily needs. So please help me to keep my focus on heavenly blessings and not worry about the possessions of the world. In Jesus' name, Amen!

It's about Passion - January 14

For where your treasure is, there your heart will be also. Matthew 6:21

In a single day, we were able to attend two magnificent praise and worship concerts at two different locations with two different, anointed artists. We felt a taste of heaven on this side of heaven as we just worshipped God from the bottom of our hearts. In addition, to praise songs, we were blessed by the messages that were shared by these artists which seemed like God spoke to us directly through His word.

As I looked around though, I noticed the absence of so many local people who missed out on this wonderful opportunity. Understandably, there were folks who could not be there for genuine reasons, but I could not understand why so many just chose not to come although they were invited, capable and available to be a part of this. This question haunted me through the night and God gave me the answer in one word "Passion".

When we have true passion for God, we do not allow other priorities, distance, convenience, status, or anything come in between us and God. We seize every opportunity to be with Him and serve Him whenever and wherever we can. We do not worry about situations and circumstances but gladly look for a chance to offer our praise to Him in return for His blessings and provision. Our hearts yearn to be with God and amongst sincere believers with whom we can whole-heartedly lift the name of Jesus.

We may gladly accept an invitation to a party and usually make every effort to attend because we like to enjoy the fellowship with others, the food, and entertainment. But why do we decline the invitation to a praise party for God? It boils down to our passion for spiritual food and fellowship with God.

Dear LORD, please help me to cease every occasion to be a part of fellowship where we can gather and worship Your name together. You are in the midst where two or more are gathered so please help me not miss out an opportunity to meet with You. Create in me a passion for You and Your works so that I praise You and serve You with a glad heart. In Jesus' name, Amen!

Credit belongs to God - January 15

But by the grace of God I am what I am, and his grace to me was not without effect.
1 Corinthians 15:10

I read a Facebook post which said, "When God put a calling on your life, He already factored in your stupidity". As funny as it sounds, it is so comforting to know that God does not require perfection before He calls us to do something. He knows our weakness, failure and shortcomings, yet He does not hold it against us. He does not wait for us to get the right education, status or skillset to use us. Instead He factors in our weaknesses and works around our limitations to empower us to carry out our calling.

If we can accomplish something despite of our foolishness, people may wonder how we did it. But when we cannot take credit for ourselves, the credit goes to God and He gets the glory. So, like Paul said, we need to be glad about our weakness because when we are feeble, God's power is displayed through us. Our spiritual stupidity turns out to be our spiritual strength if we rely on God to work in us.

Many hesitate to admit their fault or things done in foolishness because of pride, fear or embarrassment but if we can recognize our deficiencies, it is a sign of God's power already at work in us. God knows that we are sinful and will continue to prove our stupidity over and over, but He continues to prove His faithfulness by giving us a chance over and over. He does not consider our level of smartness or maturity but only our availability and sincerity.

Therefore, let us not wait to become spiritually mature before we respond to His calling; our immaturity has already been accounted for and God still has a use for us, just the way we are!

Dear LORD, thank you for loving me, despite of me being unlovable. Thank you for forgiving me, despite of being unforgivable. Thank you for using me, despite of being incapable. Please help me to understand that You are not waiting for me to become strong and worthy prior to being accepted rather You want me just as I am so that in my weakness, Your strength can be displayed in me. In Jesus' name, Amen!

United - January 16

Though one may be overpowered, two can defend themselves, but a cord of three strands is not quickly broken. Ecclesiastes 4:12

Our Wedding Anniversary is the day of remembrance of the ceremony of our vows that united us legally as a husband and wife. But our real Marriage anniversary is about six months after, when we truly began the sharing of our lives together and our married life journey started. We have come a long way together, two strangers getting to know each other after marriage, adapting to each other's likes, dislikes and to each other's personalities. I cannot think of more opposite personalities than what my husband and I are, yet we have managed to make our marriage work through prayer, love and sacrifice.

As different as we might be as individuals, we have a common ground, a special bond that holds us together and that is none other than God. We each have a love for God, and it is our top priority to bring Him glory through our lives as individuals, couple, and as a family. We stand by each other but at the same time we are each other's biggest critics too. We want to see each other make it through the gates of heaven so we hold each other accountable in our Christian walk.

We may be opposite in personality, taste or attitudes but I am so thankful that we are united in our faith. One of the things that brings me joy about my husband, is when I see our closet door closed. I know then that he is in there praying and consulting God. We tackle our battles on our knees praying, which is the source of our strength for our family.

As individuals we may be weak on our own, but together and with God in the center, we can accomplish anything by HIS strength.

Dear LORD, thank you for being the cornerstone of our marriage and family. May we remain intertwined with You that our marital bond becomes stronger by the moment. Help us to continue to walk in unity with You and with each other and be who You have called us to be. In Jesus' name, Amen!

Their faith - January 17

When Jesus saw their faith, He said, "Friend, your sins are forgiven." Luke 5:20

When we pray for a particular person or situation, we often base our faith according to the condition of that individual or the situation itself. If it looks out of control or hopeless, our faith also diminishes. We feel as if our prayer is not effective since the person or our situation does not look promising to us.

When the friends carried the paralyzed man on top of the roof and lowered him down to Jesus, I am certain that the paralyzed person himself felt hopeless or perhaps resilient while he was being carried up and then down. He might have been afraid, fighting to get off and probably did not understand what his friends were doing to him. But while the paralyzed man was not able to bring himself to Jesus, his friends knew exactly what they were doing and did not allow the rebellion or doubt of the man to stop them from taking him to Jesus.

In the same way, while we are lifting someone in the stretcher of prayer and if they are still in rebellion and resistance, it should not stop us from losing our faith or bringing them to Jesus. We need to fervently pray for them whether they are ready or not to meet Jesus. After all, Jesus was not looking for faith in the paralyzed man first before he healed him. Jesus saw "their" faith, the faith of the people, who lifted him there. And because of their faith, Jesus forgave and healed the man.

If our situation looks hopeless or an individual whom we are praying for seems to be resisting God, do not let that stop you from losing hope. It is not the faith of the individual only that will save them but since we are the ones lifting them up to Jesus, He is looking at us and will deliver according to our faith. So, the result of deliverance for someone is in our hands – how much faith do we have?

Dear LORD, as I carry my loved one in prayer to You for healing and forgive-ness, help me to remember that it is my faith that you are looking at. No matter the condition of the individual, please help me to keep my eyes on You as I pray and believe. Thank you for answering my prayer and making me a channel through which someone else can get saved. In Jesus' name, Amen!

Run towards, not run away - January 18

The thief does not come except to steal, and to kill, and to destroy. I have come that they may have life, and that they may have it more abundantly. John 10:10

Often when I fail at something, I am afraid to bring it to God in prayer and ask for His help because I feel like I am the root cause of the failure to begin with. How can I ask for forgiveness when I am the one who made the poor choices and led myself in trouble? I feel embarrassed and scared to pray about it. I imagine that God would not want to speak to a sinner like me after what I have done. But this perception of mine is from a human standpoint. We can accept this kind of attitude from each other, but we forget that God is not like us. He does not hold grudges against us nor does He cast us out when we turn to Him for help. Instead He stretches His hand out and is ever ready to forgive and help us. Our God is an understanding God and He is aware of our weaknesses. He knows that our flesh is weak, and we often give into temptation and pressure without much resistance. God sees when our Spirit is willing but overpowered by the flesh, and so He does not hold it against us.

Despite our own shortcomings, God desires that we bring to Him whatever we have left. Even if it is just broken pieces, filthy rags, hurt and shame, God asks us to bring them to Him and cry out "Abba, Father" for help. He never looks down on us or judges us due to our failures. Just as how a parent does not judge, gets embarrassed or gives up on a child who is learning how to walk, God does not forsake us no matter how many times we fall and fail. He encourages us instead and gives us the strength to get up and try again and again.

Therefore, whatever it is, we should not allow the devil to stop us from running back to God. The devil's goal is to kill and ruin our peace, but our God's goal is to free us so that we can live a full, abundant life in Jesus.

Dear LORD, thank you for the reminder that You love me and accept me no matter what I have done. We cannot forgive and forget easily but thank you that You are not like us. You remain faithful to us regardless of our unfaithfulness to You. Please help me to remember this and never run away from You, instead teach me to run to You with all my sin and shame. In Jesus' name, Amen!

Spotlight on God, not me - January 19

For it is not ourselves that we preach; we preach Jesus Christ as Lord, and ourselves as your servants for Jesus' sake. 2 Corinthians 4:5

A Pulpit is a raised stand for preachers to deliver their sermon from in a church. It was designed simply as a place for the preachers to place their Bible and notes on while being slightly raised to higher elevation so that the congregation can see the speaker clearly. The honor to preach from the pulpit is often only given to certain clergy in most churches. So, many seek the honor of being called clergy and to have the right to stand elevated on the pulpit. The pulpit has become so exclusive that many consider preaching only if it is done from inside the church and from the pulpit alone. Sadly, in many churches today, to preach from a pulpit has gained more importance than the scripture itself.

While preaching during a Sunday service from behind the pulpit is sacred and important for church, but simply talking to someone about Jesus from no matter where we are, is no less of significance. God's spiritual pulpit is placed in front of us whenever we are in front of an individual with whom we have a conversation which involves Jesus' name. We all are God's clergy and wherever He places us, we have the sacred duty to spread His love through our actions and words. We do not necessarily have to be behind a church pulpit, have the clergy status, eloquent in speech or highly educated about the Bible to preach God's word; we just need to be available for God to use our mouths to talk about Him.

And while we stand in front of others to speak, we need to remember that the elevation is not for our glory but for God. The spotlight should be on the scripture, not the speaker on the stage as the power is in the word, not in the power of the pulpit.

Dear LORD, please help me to take up every opportunity to talk about You no matter where I am. Help me not to worry about my personality, speech or education but come out of my comfort zone and declare You boldly as You put Your words and courage in me. Teach me not to focus on making myself rise higher for accolades from people but may my purpose be to lift Your name higher. Thank you for using me as a vessel for Your kingdom. In Jesus' name, Amen!

"Well done, my good servant!' his master replied. 'Because you have been trust-worthy in a very small matter, take charge of ten cities.". Luke 19:17

During checkout at a store, the cashier forgot to ring in one of the items. She did not realize it, but we did, and I told her about it. She was grateful for my honesty, but my child questioned why I did that. She laughed and said we would have gotten a free item if I did not say anything. More important than the free item, my daughter witnessed my integrity which is far more valuable, and it opened a conversation between us about being faithful in little things.

It was a perfect opportunity to explain that while we may have skipped the eye of a person, we can never get away with God. He sees everything we do and sometimes puts us to test to check how faithful we are. We often neglect little things and do not consider it a big deal if we cheat in little matters. But I have experienced it many times that I end up losing twice as much, if not more, over little things that I have been unfaithful about. In God's sight there is no scale of big vs small. Everything is measured according to our faithfulness. And if God sees our faithfulness in little things, then He trusts us with bigger things.

And while we are being examined by God, we are also being watched by others around us. People do keep an eye on us and test our integrity in different ways. So, in all circumstances we ought to leave a godly example for those in our influence. Actions speak louder than words and so it is by our behavior and faithfulness in every little matter, we demonstrate how serious we are about God and following His example.

Dear LORD, thank you for demonstrating to us how to live a godly life. Please help me to be sincere in every little thing. I may be able to escape the eye of people but can never hide from You so teach me not to do anything that can compromise our relationship. When you test my integrity, may I be always be found faithful in everything. In Jesus name, Amen!

Sun & Son - January 21

Jesus Christ is the same yesterday and today and forever. Hebrews 13:8

As I sat on the shore, waiting for the sun to rise, I realized that there is really no sunrise or sunset. The sun does not rise nor does it go down. It remains in its place, the same place where God set it from the beginning of its creation. It is the earth which rotates and makes it seem like to us that the sun comes up and goes down each day. We think of God by the same method. We think that it is God that comes in and out of our lives. We see Him rising in us at certain times and feel His absence during our dark times. But it is us who change as we pass through different seasons of life and our perception of God is determined by the course of our circumstances we encounter as we journey through life. There are times when we feel His light and heat on us strongly while on some days, He seems to be hiding behind the clouds. But God is the same yesterday, today, and forever. He has set himself in a steady state for us from the beginning. He has promised to never leave us nor forsake us. No matter what our days are like, His light never ceases to shine on us even on gloomy days. His faithfulness towards us does not rise nor set each day, it remains constant and unchanging regardless of our faithfulness to Him.

The sun may seem to rise and set each day, but the Son remains steadfast through it all. Seasons come and go, people and time may change for us, but the Son will never change. He is has risen once and is here to stay till the end of times.

So as we experience the rising and setting of the sun each day, let's remember that the sun is in its steady place as its been set and so is the Son, Jesus Christ, who will continue to be constant no matter how our lives rotate.

Dear LORD, thank you for Your constant presence in my life. Please help me to always remember that You are here with me, regardless of how I feel or what I go through. May Your light always shine upon me and make me radiant in You. In Jesus' name, Amen!

Authority of Jesus' name - January 22

Then Jesus came to them and said, "All authority in heaven and on earth has been given to me. Matthew 28:18

The Centurion whose servant was deathly sick knew what it meant to be a person of authority. He had the power to tell his soldiers and servants what to do and they would do it right away. So, when Jesus came by him, the Centurion knew Jesus' power and acknowledged His authority right away. He requested Jesus to just say a word of healing for his servant right from where He was, and the Centurion was so confident that whatever Jesus said would be done right away. Even Jesus was astonished at the type of faith the Centurion had in Jesus.

Although we may say we have faith in Jesus, we still have some doubts given the circumstance we are in. We often submit to the authority of what is against us rather than who is for us. Only if we open our spiritual eyes and see with eyes of faith, we will realize that if we have Jesus, there is no need to fear anything else. Simply Jesus' word has the power to heal and move mountains. There is no higher name that we can call to deliver us. There is no sickness that Jesus cannot heal, no bondage that Jesus cannot free, no addiction which Jesus cannot break, no marriage or prodigals who Jesus cannot restore and no circumstance which Jesus cannot change. He is above all and His word is good as done the moment we call out to Him for help with a humble heart and a contrite spirit.

We ought to be like the Centurion and acknowledge Jesus' authority. We need to understand that Jesus' name is no ordinary name but realize how powerful He is. Even if our condition seems more powerful for us to overcome, still, let us learn to have faith like the Centurion by which even Jesus gets amazed to see our trust in Him.

Dear LORD, help me to understand how beautiful and wonderful is in the name of Jesus. May I use Your name with honor and trembling for there is no other name under heaven given to us by which we can be saved. Thank you for giving me authority to use Your powerful name and break free from bondages of sin and sickness. In Jesus' name, Amen!

Devil's methods - January 23

Put on the whole armor of God, that you may be able to stand against the wiles of the devil. Ephesians 6:11

It is known that the mind is the biggest battlefield of our lives. It is the mind that plans and executes the choices that we make. Majority of spiritual attacks occur in the mind and often the battle is lost due to lack of self-control over it. Our mind is the primary ground that Satan uses to destroy our life, marriage, family, finances, etc. He studies us well to get to know our weaknesses and takes control of these areas to hurt ourselves and others.

The word "Wile" is taken from the Greek word methodos which translates into English as methods. Wiles are tricks or manipulations designed to deceive someone. The devil uses specific methods against us to cause us to fall. He plans a roadmap on how he will attack us. He travels closely along with us and seeks every opportunity to hurt us. He pays attention to our every word and action and ceases the opportunity to use it against us. The devil starts off with putting subtle, "innocent" ideas, things and people in front of us that make it difficult to resist and grows bigger and bigger if we do not shut them out. If we are not vigilant, we most likely would fall in his trap that he sets up in our minds.

Therefore, it is essential that we learn to watch out for the wiles of the devil and not allow him to play mind games with us. Just the way the devil has a method, we too need to have a strategy to fight against him. We need to discuss our plan of attack against the devil with God in prayer every day and gear up with God's armor to fight back.

Dear LORD, thank you for the spiritual weapons you have given me to fight against the enemy. Please help me to put on the full armor so that I do not leave any unprotected part for the devil to enter in. May I always be vigilant and be prepared to act using the powerful weapons of prayer and Your word when I am attacked. In Jesus' name, Amen!

Faith-filled prayer - January 24

Therefore, I tell you, whatever you ask for in prayer, believe that you have received it, and it will be yours. Mark 11:24

Most often our prayer time is faith-filled. During prayer, we acknowledge God as mighty to accomplish our request and believe that we have received whatever we asked for. But in no time soon, as we finish our prayer and come back down to the valley from our mountain top conversation with God, we face the reality of life and our faith turns into doubt. The same mouth that had just proclaimed trust in God now starts to say doubtful things. We contradict ourselves and cancel out our prayer when we start to speak negative over the situation or a person for whom we were praying for. Our prayers are not effective because doubt overrides faith. We cannot have faith and fear in us at the same time. These do not go together, and we can only have either or. If we pray with faith then whatever we have asked for, we must claim it in the name of Jesus. Afterwards our mouth should not utter any negative words, nor our mind think any doubtful thoughts once our trust in God has been proclaimed. Satan immediately catches us the moment we show any sign of doubt or unbelief and infiltrates our mind against God's sovereignty.

Therefore, when we pray, we ought to believe and thank God that He has already heard and met our need. We must leave it to God to figure out and not worry ourselves about how and what. If the request has been brought to Jesus and we have claimed victory over it, then we cannot go back and surrender to defeat. We need to continue to speak God's goodness over our circumstance rather than Satan's lies filled with doubt and fear.

Dear LORD, please help me to release my concerns into your hands once I have committed them to You. Help me to hand them over to You as if it is Your problem and not mine anymore. May I be at peace knowing You are able to meet my needs and will do what is good for me as You have the best planned for me. In Jesus' name, Amen!

Godly example - January 25

In the same way, let your light shine before others, that they may see your good deeds and glorify your Father in heaven. Matthew 5:16

We try to stay away from someone who we know is not good for us. Because of their behavior or for the things they do, we feel threatened by them as if they will bring us down and so we keep our distance. We often pray to God to remove them from our lives as they could be the primary reason for our certain sins. Yes, there are those folks whom we do not need to associate with as they pose a danger to our lives and certainly do not need to be around them. But in non-threatening ways, before we cast someone out of our lives, do we ever wonder that maybe God brought them into our lives purposefully? He placed them there to either teach us a lesson or for us to be a teacher to them. Instead of us being influenced by their negativity, God may want us to influence them by our godly example. Bad company does corrupt good character, but it can also work the opposite way where good company leads to good character.

I've been praying for a certain individual to be removed from my life as they pull me down spiritually but God taught me that instead of me being weighed down by them, I need to pull them up and lead them to Christ. They are the ones with a spiritual need and so God has placed me in their life to shed God's light and teach them the truth with God's word.

No matter if others try to pull us down or influence in doing wrong, if we are firm in Christ, we can be immovable. We need to be the godly role models to the people around us so that by observing our behavior and way of life, they may see Christ in us and turn from their ways. We must remain intact and be the godly example which others will want Jesus the way we have Him. So instead of being fearful of being corrupted and hiding, cease it as an opportunity to display Christ in you!

Dear LORD, I thank you for sending folks in my life whom I can minister to and by whom I need to be ministered. Increase my patience and help me to continue to do good regardless of how they treat me. Please help me to remain who I am in You no matter how much others try to break me. In Jesus' name, Amen!

Sponsored by God - January 26

Commit your work to the LORD, and your plans will be established. Proverbs 16:3

For every project assigned at work, we need sponsorship from our boss or higher management. Only with their agreement on the proposed plan for our project, we get the green signal to proceed. Since they have sponsored it and have their name tied to our project, our boss supports and promotes our plan till completion and implementation.

Similarly, God allows us to have ideas and plans but if we are to succeed in it, we need God's sponsorship. Only if we have God's blessing over it and if our will aligns with God's, then only will our plans succeed. Otherwise no matter how bright our ideas or plans may be, eventually they will fall apart as we go against God's will when we do our own thing.

God has given us a free will to decide for ourselves what we want to do, however if we have His stamp of approval on it, our plans will succeed. When God is pleased with our ways, He comes alongside us to guide, provide and promote us all the way to completion.

So as God's children, it is important that we seek God's sponsorship in every little thing we do. Every morning before we go about our day or make any plans, we need to lay them in His presence and pursue God's approval by consulting with Him in prayer and wait on Him to approve or reject our proposed ideas. If God is not in it, we should not be either but if God is for us, who can be against us?

Dear LORD, in every plan that I make and in all that I do, please help me to seek Your counsel and acknowledge Your will. If You will bless it and go with me, then only let me take the next step otherwise I dare not move. Your plans are always better for me so may I not rest in my own understanding but trust You with all my heart and do what only You would want me to. In Jesus' name, Amen!

Moving along - January 27

So, we fix our eyes not on what is seen, but on what is unseen, since what is seen is temporary, but what is unseen is eternal. 2 Corinthians 4:18

Certain things are just easier said than done. It is simple to say we have faith but to have it is difficult. That is why Jesus said that all we need is faith as small as a mustard seed in order to move mountains in our lives that stand against us. And faith is not a one-time deal where we believe in it once and think it is sufficient to fulfill what we believed in. In the Bible verse above, Faith is an action word which means that we cannot stand in one place and wait for circumstances to change. Rather we need to have faith as we continue to walk. It is easier to remain in one spot and hope that all will just pass by. But life is about us moving along on a path unknown to us but trusting in an all-knowing God. As we begin our journey in any phase of life, God starts us off by giving us a promise to never leave nor forsake us and that He is with us through it all. So, as we walk step by step, we take God's promise with us and trust Him to get us through it despite of what we face.

We may not have a clear vision nor know what to expect on the way but still trusting God and His promise over us is what faith is about. As we walk through life, we trust God regardless of what is in front of us. What is in our eyesight certainly can be scary and create doubts about whether God is still with us or if His promises still stand. Our current situation may suggest a different story than what has been promised but even then, by faith, we need to refuse to accept it and trust God through it all. Once God has promised, He will remain faithful to it. Our faith in Him may falter but God will never let us down.

Therefore, it does not matter what circumstances we see in front of us, we need to look beyond it and see ourselves through God's eyes and at our fulfilled destination.

Dear LORD, although things around me may look dark and gloomy right now, please open my eyes to see beyond it and look with the eyes of faith the bright and wonderful future You have for me. Help me to not look at this side of the mountain only and feel discouraged as I climb up the rough and steep slope but understand that there is a beautiful other side waiting for me. So please give me the courage to keep moving and know that You are with me and we can get through this together. In Jesus' name, Amen!

Pose of Prayer - January 28

Pray in the Spirit at all times and on every occasion. Ephesians 6:18

When we pray, often it is us just sitting in a certain pose with our eyes closed and basically emptying out our brains of the thoughts that are racing in our mind. We usually feel better after we have "prayed" as we think we talked to God but honestly, we were probably just speaking to ourselves and unloading our mind.

Prayer time is not just about closing our eyes and saying words to make ourselves feel better. It is to stand at the throne of King of the Universe and present our praise and requests by our spirit, not mind. As we pray, God gives us His undivided attention but if we are not focused on Him and just pray for the sake of praying, God pulls away. He is not interested in our mere words if they are not accompanied by our heart and soul.

If we were given an opportunity to meet with the CEO or President, we would present ourselves in the most respectful manner, choose our words wisely and give our undivided attention to ensure we have a meaningful conversation. In the same manner when we pray, we need to lift our hearts, spiritually stand in awe front of God and truly sense His presence. And when we are in God's presence, we stand on Holy ground, so we need to ensure that we offer ourselves humbly before Him. It is our one-on-one time with God, so it is not just about us speaking but we need to be quiet and give God a chance to talk back to us.

Whether we pray individually, collectively, in public or in secret, our hearts are to be aligned and in one accord, only speaking to the Audience of One – Jesus! When our prayers are offered unto Jesus and not to ourselves indirectly, we truly feel at peace as God takes the burden off us and takes it upon himself.

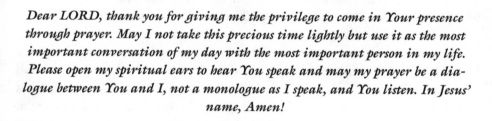

Dear LORD, thank you for giving me the privilege to come in Your presence through prayer. May I not take this precious time lightly but use it as the most important conversation of my day with the most important person in my life. Please open my spiritual ears to hear You speak and may my prayer be a dialogue between You and I, not a monologue as I speak, and You listen. In Jesus' name, Amen!

Season of Silence - January 29

There is a time for everything, and a season for every activity under the heavens. A time to be quiet and a time to speak. Ecclesiastes 3:1,7b

When the Israelites were ordered by God to march around the walls of Jericho for seven days, in the first six days they were to go around the city quietly without saying a word. Only on the seventh day, they were to make a sound. The reason for silence is that God wanted the Israelites to ponder upon what He is up to and trust Him even when it did not make sense about what they were asked to do. If they talked, chances are that the conversations amongst themselves would be nothing more than complaining and grumbling towards God. So, they simply had to follow God's instructions and be silent until the right time to speak out. And while they walked around in silence, fear gripped their enemies as they too wondered what will happen next.

God takes us through seasons of silence and isolation in our lives. He builds our trust in Him as we march about silently. We may not understand the reason for doing what we are doing but during this time of quietness and obedience, God works to prepare us for the battle and give us the victory He has in store for us. We may look foolish in people's eyes as they may wonder what we are up to but we need to just remain mum and watch and wait until the appointed time for God to reveal His power in and through us.

If we start paying attention to the jeers and start to talk back before our time, our words most likely could be negative and filled with doubt and fear. Satan undoubtedly grips this opportunity and fills our mind with doubtful thoughts and mouth with fearful words that hinder us from doing what God has purposed for us.

Therefore, if God is asking us to be quiet now, we need to accept our season of silence and let God do His work behind the scene until He is ready for us to make noise and break down walls for His kingdom.

Dear LORD, please help me to trust in You and do what You have called me to do even if it does not make sense to me or others. Help me not to complain about or doubt the plan that You are about to fulfill in my life. So, teach me to walk silently now as You lead me around the walls that need to breakdown, and then shout to the LORD and declare His power with the loudest praises. In Jesus' name, Amen!

Hate my sin - January 30

...Hate what is evil; cling to what is good. Romans 12:9

Passion is necessary for any successful outcome. Only if we have a true desire for something, we can give it our best to accomplish it. Otherwise it does not produce much results if our heart is not in it or we do it with a wrongful intent. This includes passion to continue in sin or passion to be freed from it. We often find pleasure in our sin and are not in a rush to get rid of it. We may pray casually for God to help us overcome it but if we enjoy it, God does not move. If we are serious about our sin habit and have a desire to be freed, then only until we come to the point of hating our sin and abhor what we are doing with passion, God will not deliver us out of it.

God has the power to deliver but our stubbornness keeps us in the wrong we are doing. And when things go bad, we end up blaming God for it as if He did not help us. But is not God that did not, it is us who refused His help to rescue us. Our desire to continue in sin overpowers God's power as God does not force us out of our own will. He is ever ready to help but if we do not want to be helped, then we are at fault. If we still have a taste for sin or do not mind being in it here and there, it will not be removed from us. Rather it gets bigger and worse as we continue to indulge in it.

Therefore, if we genuinely want to be rescued from sin, we must hate our sin first. We need to realize a need for repentance and cry out to God with a passion for forgiveness. Only when we cannot stand our sin and hate it with all our heart, will we see God's deliverance from it. So, pray for a passion for hatred of sin and to be delivered out of it!

Dear LORD, thank you for offering Your forgiveness and deliverance from my sin. Please search my heart and point me those things that are displeasing to You. Create in me a will to turn from my sinful ways and may I pay attention to Your conviction and repent of my sin. In Jesus' name, Amen!

Appetite for God - January 31

Taste and see that the LORD is good. Psalm 34:8

One of the symptoms of the Coronavirus is the loss of the taste buds. Some folks who tested positive reported that they did not have sense of taste in their mouth. Since they could not taste the food, it led to loss of appetite which in turn caused weakness and low immunity. During the sickness, though the taste buds of the mouth may have been dead, many reported that their taste buds for God increased as their physical vulnerability awakened their spiritual hunger.

It is mostly in our weak moments we find ourselves seeking God more for strength. We meditate on God's word further and pray often. We seem to not get enough of Him, and the more time we spend with God, the more we want of Him. Our physical appetite may decrease but our appetite for God increases. We hold on to the hope and recall those times where we have tasted God's goodness earlier and know that He will come through for us again.

When we dine at a good restaurant and like their food, we often rave about it to others and promote the restaurant. In the same manner when we have tasted God and seen how good He is to us; we go out and tell others and encourage them to give Jesus a try. As we are witnesses ourselves, greater testimonies will continue to be proclaimed as folks get a taste of God during these trying times.

So while the virus may have made our mouth tasteless, we can get spiritually nourished by the heavenly food that comes from God and share that food with others so that they too can taste and see how good God is.

Dear LORD, thank you for the wonderful flavors of blessings that You have bestowed on me. Please help me to remember Your goodness and use it as a testimony to inspire others to taste You also and experience Your goodness for themselves. Please increase my appetite for You so that I want more and more of You in my life. In Jesus' name, Amen!

February

Better Parent - February 1

Can a woman forget her nursing child and have no compassion on the son of her womb? Even these may forget, but I will not forget you. Isaiah 49:15

The most prized possession for parents is their children. There is nothing more precious or anyone that can take place of the children in the parents' hearts. They love them dearly and go to any extent to give their children the best of everything. They make sacrifices for themselves so that their kids will not lack anything. Parents are constantly concerned for their children and always try to protect them from all harm and danger. The love is unique and there is no comparison to any other kind of love.

If we as parents have such love for our children, can we imagine how much our Heavenly Father loves us! Just the way we care for our children, God cares even more for them and for us, as we are all God's children and His love for each one of us individually is unique. There is nothing we can do that would take away His love for us. No matter who we are or what we have done, God's love never ceases. He loves us unconditionally, cares for us, provides the best for us, and looks out for our good in everything in much better ways than we can ever.

If we are concerned for our children's safety and wellbeing, just remember that God is the better parent to our children than we can ever be. We may not have the ability or capacity to provide and protect our children in every aspect, but God's hand is not too short to save. He can reach where we cannot, and He can deliver from where we are powerless. We may lack and fail at some point in our parental duty, but God never fails.

Therefore, rest in the assurance that God's got His children in the palm of His hands and He is mighty to save!

Dear LORD, thank you for loving my children more than I could ever love them. Please help me to be at peace knowing that You are with them where I cannot be. I may reach my limit but there is no end to how far You can reach so please go with them and watch over our children. Put a tight hedge of protection over them with the blood of Jesus so that they cannot try to escape from You nor no evil that tries to come against can prosper. In Jesus' name, Amen!

Control myself - February 2

A person without self-control is like a city with broken-down walls. Proverbs 25:28

Out of many spiritual battles that we face daily, to battle against impulse is probably the strongest to fight against. Impulse is the strong urge to say or do something in the heat of the moment. It comes in such a strong force that many of us give into it instantaneously without giving much thought. Impulse causes us to overreact or become overexcited and we end up doing things we would regret later. It overrides wisdom, discernment, experience and common sense and we blurt out words which we should not say, go where we should not and do something which we know is not good for us.

Self-control is a huge struggle for all of us but if we can master it, we can avoid falling into many sins. To have self-control is about training the mind to say no and it begins with having a proper understanding of God's word and knowing what is good and bad. It is the determination to do what is right according to God's teaching. The world teaches us one thing and God's word teaches us the truth, so it is imperative that we recognize the difference and set our heart on doing what is right in God's sight. Once we know the truth, our desire should be to only please God and make every effort to do what is right according to God.

The devil studies us very well and knows who and what our weak point is. He then uses every situation, person or place to jump at his impulse and cause us to sin. If we are not watchful and let our guard down, he enters and attack us our mind. We are sinful by nature so doing wrong comes naturally but by God's help we can overcome it. To subdue it, we need God's grace to help us stop in the heated moment and think before we act. We make it worse and prove ourselves no better when we act on impulse and react to it. So, let us guard ourselves and pray for self-control, to be wise and slow in our reaction to any matter.

Dear LORD, please help me to have self-control and think twice before I say or do anything. Help me not to jump to conclusions, overreact, become over excited and act on impulse. Instead teach me to pause, seek Your advice and only act according to Your leading. May all my actions reflect Your presence and will in my life. In Jesus' name, Amen!

Right into future - February 3

The righteous keep moving forward, and those with clean hands become stronger and stronger. Job 17:9

I was in for a shock when I visited my college with my son who is ready for college. It hit me hard and realized how fast time has flown by and how I have grown. The auditorium looked as is when I used to sit there for classes years ago but me and my life has changed so much since then.

When we are in our youth, we stand still as if time is frozen and think that we will remain young forever. We do not think seriously about our future or see ourselves as grown up adults. As much as we like to live in the present, time keeps moving forward and we keep moving with it "into the future" we never imagined to be in. God has designed us with a perfect plan that leads us through phases of the life we have been given. One phase affects the other and either through success or failure, we continue to move through life. The decisions and choices we make do have their consequences and those lead us into the next phase of our life. We only get one chance in each phase of life to make or destroy our future. Real life is not like a refresh button where we get a chance to start all over again from the beginning. We must continue forward from where we left off. Our God is a God of second chance, but it does not mean that He places us back into our past and let us live again to give it another shot from the beginning. God does not operate that way. There is no reverse button in life. Instead God resets our life and gives us new beginning from where we stopped.

When we see our life in hindsight, we see the full picture and purpose for everything. We often realize our mistakes and wish we could go back, undo some of our past and re-live again. We can never erase our past, but God can reset our life and give us another chance to try again. We only have one life to live so let us not leave room for regrets but learn from our past mistakes and move forward as a better person in Christ.

Dear LORD, thank you for giving me another chance to make it right with You. Although I may have deviated from the path You have mapped out for me, thank you for bringing me back. Moving forward, please help me to stay close to You and in every choice that I make, may it be aligned with You so that I continue to live in the good plan and hopeful future You have in store for me. In Jesus' name, Amen!

Not curiosity, but expectancy - February 4

But Jesus said, "Someone touched me; I know that power has gone out from me." Then he said to her, "Daughter, your faith has healed you. Go in peace."
Luke 8: 46, 48

It is difficult to not touch people when we are amid a crowd. Because of the space or number of people around us, we end up brushing up or inadvertently touching someone. Everywhere Jesus went, crowds followed Him. He was like a celebrity that people came out to see and watch perform miracles. Many people brushed up on Jesus out of curiosity, trying to see if anything happened to them if they were able to touch Him. There was something about Jesus and the power that is in Him that drew the crowds towards Him. The woman who had suffered from issue of bleeding for twelve years was one of the people in the crowd who tried to touch Him. Out of all the people that must have touched Jesus then, she was the only one who received instantaneous healing the moment that she touched the hem of Jesus' cloak. The difference between the woman and the rest of the crowd was faith versus curiosity. She came with expectancy while others came with "let's see if He can" attitude.

There is power in Jesus' name and the same power is available for all us in the same way. But to receive it, this depends on us. Prayer is two-sided! Jesus' power is there and ready to flow out but for it to work, we must be willing to receive it. Many of us receive answers to our prayer because we come to Jesus with faith and expectancy. While many of us pray but it is accompanied with doubt, not with confidence in God's power. It does not matter whether we pray ourselves or have others pray for us, the power of Jesus only works when we receive it with faith. Jesus does not force His power on us if we are not willing to accept it.

Therefore, when we pray, let us not be like the ones in the crowd who come to Jesus to touch Him but have no expectancy. Rather, we need to be like the woman who purposely reached out for Jesus, fully confident that if she touched Him, she would receive it.

Dear LORD, please help my prayers to be faith-filled and not doubtful. When I approach You, may it not be out of curiosity but with expectancy, fully confident that You are able to supply all my needs according to your riches in glory. In Jesus' name, Amen!

Purging is required - February 5

Therefore, if anyone cleanses himself from what is dishonorable, he will be a vessel for honorable use, set apart as holy, useful to the master of the house, ready for every good work. 2 Timothy 2:21

Before nurses administer IV injection into the patient, they purge the line first by applying some pressure to the line so that all air bubbles and impurities are taken out so that only pure fluid flows in.

In the same manner when we desire to live a holy and righteous life, we need to purge out everything that blocks our way of holiness. The process of purging causes a lot of emotional pain as the Holy Spirit applies spiritual pressure on our wrongdoing. He reveals to us those things and people which are a hindrance to our holiness and strongly convicts us for a need of repentance and purging. Once we have identified the impurities and have a willing heart to be pure, God helps us remove these from our life so that only purity and holiness flows in and out of us. If we do not do anything about it and allow the impurities to build up, they block our connection to God, and we end up being sicker in our sin.

Therefore, purging is necessary even if it aches. It may hurt and feel uncomfortable to let go of old habits, things and relationships which we are attached to but if they are reason for our spiritual sickness, they need to be removed. Nothing unholy can stand in the presence of God so if it is due to anything or anyone that makes us unholy, it is time to recognize and purge the line! We must release the blood of Jesus to flow through us and cleanse us from all unrighteousness.

Dear LORD, I realize that only when the evil is purged out of my life and my heart is pure, I can stand in the presence of God. So, help me to allow You to purge impurities and make my life clean and clear, holy and righteous for You! Your word says, "Blessed are the pure in heart, for they will see God". I want to see You so please create in me a clean heart, O LORD! In Jesus' name, Amen!

Fight like a lion - February 6

Be strong and courageous. Do not be afraid or terrified because of them, for the Lord your God goes with you; he will never leave you nor forsake you.
Deuteronomy 31:6

We think of it as an insult when someone refers to another as a coward. A coward is a person who lacks courage in facing danger, difficulty or pain. It is a type of person who runs away from or avoids unpleasant situations out of fear. We all have fears and have genuine reasons for being discouraged. We might be afraid of the circumstances that are happening in our homes; the news that we hear about horrific situations in our community cause us to fear for our family; our finances or health may lead us to emotional or spiritual downcast. But through it all, we are called by God to not run and hide like a coward but rather face it with courage like a lion. We may think that we are alone and insufficient to fight the battle on our own, so we just run away or ignore it, hoping it will go away. Often it is the case where we run but there is nothing chasing us; it is just us blowing things out of proportion in our heads and driving ourselves insane. Regardless, the harder we run away from anything, the fiercely it chases us down.

When we try to run away or avoid confronting our fearful situation, we show that we do not trust God and His power to save us. But God has given us a promise to be with us in all circumstances which means that God does not silently just walk along and watch us struggle alone, instead He empowers us at every step with strength, wisdom, courage and ability to tackle what comes against us. He fights our battle for us, He goes in front of us, walks besides us and watches our back. Then whom shall we fear if the God of Angel armies is with us?

Dear LORD, when I face situations in life that cause me to become fearful, please give me the courage to stand against it. Increase my faith, strength and confidence in You as I face it. Help me not hide like a coward but fight like a lion who has You, the Lion of Judah by my side! In Jesus' name, Amen!

Waiting for the appointed time - February 7

The LORD is good to those who wait for him, to the soul who seeks him.
Lamentations 3:25

We know that God answers prayer in three ways – yes, no, or wait. And how do we recognize these answers?

When our will or desire aligns with what God already has in mind for us, His answer comes as an immediate Yes and things work out as planned. But when we ask God for those things that might be right in our eyes but if God knows that they are not good for us, then He tells us No. He shuts the door for us that no one can open. And if we say we trust God, then we just must accept that He will provide according to His will.

Often God's answer comes as "Not yet" which is the most confusing and hardest of all. In this fast-paced world, we like things done immediately and when God tells us to wait, we find it exceedingly difficult to just do nothing and let God work. Frequently we rush God and try to help Him out by putting our two cents in every matter. While we are in the waiting period, our mind constantly races around with thoughts and we try to impose those ideas onto God. We ask God to bless our plans and thank Him for it as if He's the one who suggested it, while it maybe be only us who came up with it and God has nothing to do with our plan. We may attempt different things but when we are not successful or the process seems lengthy, we need to acknowledge that God's timing is not yet, and we need to be still.

No doubt waiting is hard and while God seems silent, our world keeps moving rapidly and we wonder why God is delaying His response. But while He may seem silent, God is on the move. He is busy getting people, things and places ready so that everything works out for our good in perfect order and time. God is very aware of our past; He knows our present needs and what lies ahead for us in the future. He knows what He is doing, and His plan and timing are exactly right so remember, if we say we trust God, then let us truly learn to wait for Him.

Dear LORD, teach me rely on You to meet all my needs according to Your timing. Help me not to rush You or force You to do something before its appointed time. As I am waiting for the door to open, may I learn to praise You in the hallway and look forward to seeing Your wonderful plans unfold for me. In Jesus' name, Amen!

"Do two walk together, unless they have agreed to meet? Amos 3:3

On a recent vacation, my husband and I sat on a hammock together. We were nicely settled in our positions and enjoyed it for a couple of minutes until I told him to move over a little. As soon as he moved a bit, we lost balance off from the center and the hammock completely flipped over. He fell first and I came tumbling down after. It was probably the most hilarious moment of our lives and we still laugh every time we think about it.

This funny experience teaches us a serious lesson though about how important balance is in a relationship. When God connects people together whether it be a husband-wife, parent-child, friends, coworkers, or church members, we are there to support and stabilize each other. We need to make up for each other's weakness and carry some of their burden on our side in order to make the relationship firm and steady. God has placed us in a certain position in someone's life so that we can build them up in some way. When we have the same goal and are ready to work in unison, we can enjoy the company and accomplish great things together. But when there is discord between us, it ruins the purpose, the relationship, and flips us towards our downfall.

God is the pivot point which balances our relationships. When our eyes are focused on Him and are in one accord with God and each other, we can do mighty things. But when it becomes one-sided and we move farther from the center, not only do we fall but bring others down with us.

Therefore, let us ensure that wherever God has placed us in another's life, that we keep our eyes on God, the center of our being and together, do great exploits for His kingdom.

Dear LORD, thank you for being the center of my life. Please help me not to move away from You and lose balance so that I fall but may I stay so close to You that we become inseparable. In all that I do, may You be the focal point of my life. In Jesus' name, Amen!

Start with Me - February 9

If my people, who are called by my name, will humble themselves and pray and seek my face and turn from their wicked ways, then I will hear from heaven, and I will forgive their sin and will heal their land. 2 Chronicles 7:14

We usually refer to this Bible verse when we pray for our nation or any other country.

But it also pertains to each individual person as we all belong to a specific piece of land which God has blessed us to live in. Our house, whether owned or rented, big or small, is our land that God has set us as the caretaker. The people who live in that particular piece of land together make it a home and call us a part of the family. Even if we are separated by distance, we associate as a family and hold each other close in our hearts. All families go through seasons of ups and down and if one person in the family is hurt, it effects the entire family. A poor choice of a single family member results in ache to the family first and then might spread outwards towards others.

For restoration and healing of our nation to take place, it must begin from our own family first. If we want to see a change, we must start from within and then circulate outwards. Our prayers are not effective as we pray generally for the entire nation to be healed, but we or our own family are not willing to repent or turn from our sinful ways. We cannot pray for revival for others when we ourselves are spiritually dead. If we consider ourselves Christians, we need to begin the circle of prayer and repentance with us individually, next our land/family, and then extend it out. Jesus told His disciples to go and make disciples of all nations, starting from Jerusalem and then everywhere else. Jesus' call is to start right where you are first!

Therefore, let us call on the name of the LORD to forgive our sins and heal our family first. As a result, all people in the entire nation will feel the ripple effect and see the transformation that God desires for the children of His family.

Dear LORD, please help me to realize that my Jerusalem is my own heart, home and loved ones first. Help me to begin where You have placed me before I go to the outside world. May my heart be humble and repentant first. In Jesus' name, Amen!

Relentless fight - February 10

I have fought the good fight, I have finished the race, I have kept the faith. 2 Timothy 4:7

When we think of a fight, we imagine two opponents having a physical fight where they beat each other up and one ends up winning and the other defeated. Most Christians are gentle and peacemakers who choose to stay out of trouble and not engage in any type of physical fights. We tend to avoid conflicts or put ourselves in certain situations that provoke such trouble. But there is also another kind of fight which we cannot circumvent and must face it.

Our life is that fight which is a never-ending struggle against evil. There is a constant battle between our physical and spiritual being. This fight is not something that we can choose to fight or avoid but need to deal with it in some way or the other. Many do not even realize that a battle is going on because they have already surrendered to the opponent, the devil, before it even started or have given up easily.

But as Christians, we should not try to run away or hide from the devil in fear. If we succumb into fear, he has already won over us so we must fight back like a pro. We must give the devil a run for his money and give him a good fight back. When he strikes a blow at us, we need to strike him back with blows of unwavering faith and trust. No matter how hard he hits us, we need to bounce back and resist him each time so that he eventually gets tired and flees. We need to be the warrior that makes the devil worry about who he is up against and who is fighting the battle on our behalf.

The fight is never easy, in fact it gets tougher as we become stronger in Christ. The devil becomes restless when he sees us training for the battle with our Master, Jesus. But when we have Jesus, the devil does not stand a chance as greater is He who is in us than who is in the world. So, when the devil strikes with blows of sickness, finances, family issues or anything else, let us not yield into defeat towards these but confidently continue to fight till our very last breath with Jesus by our side who has already won the victory.

Dear LORD, thank you for always being with me and equipping me to fight. Please help me to become stronger as You train me to fight on my knees in prayer. Help me to be a Prayer Warrior and pray in all circumstances so that it may release the power of Jesus in me against whom no one or nothing can stand. In Jesus' name, Amen!

Faith-filled words - February 11

So is my word that goes out from my mouth; It will not return to me empty but will accomplish what I desire and achieve the purpose for which I sent it.
Isaiah 55:11

God created the universe and everything in it by His spoken word. He just said it and it came into being because God spoke with authority and power. God has given us the same power over everything. Our words have tremendous power but often it is not manifested because we do not speak with the same authority as God. We would like to pray with confidence but often our confidence soon turns into fear when we look at our situations. We allow our circumstance to determine the outcome of our prayer rather than looking at God and let Him change our circumstance. We may feel that we've prayed with power and "believe" for a while but as soon as things look dim or the opposite of what we prayed for, we lose faith and start doubting which in turn cancels out our spoken word.

Although we may have initially prayed faithfully, but afterwards if we start speaking negative words over the same matter, we withdraw our prayer. Speaking with authority means seeing with eyes of faith and being confident that what we have spoken is already accomplished. Once we have declared victory with faith, we must accept it as done and Amen, and release it in the name of Jesus. From that point forward, we must submit it in God's hand and not think or speak doubtful, negative words about it.

When God speaks, not one word is void as there is power in His name to fulfill what He declares. With the same token, for our words to accomplish what we speak, we need to pray boldly and with full confidence in Jesus' name who has given us His Spirit to accomplish the impossible.

Dear LORD, thank you that Your promises are Yes and Amen! Thank you for being true to Your word. Would You please help me to be faithful and speak victory over the words that I speak in Your name? You have given me the same authority over it all so may I not allow the devil to put thoughts of doubts and cause my faith to stumble. In Jesus' name, Amen!

There is a reason - February 12

And we know that in all things God works for the good of those who love him, who have been called according to his purpose. Romans 8:28

I am a planner and I like to plan everything down to the minute. I calculate time, people, place and things in order in my head and expect it to be executed as I planned it. Many times, it works out perfectly as I had prayed, planned and intended it to be, but there are times when God throws a curve ball and throws everything off course at the last minute. Initially I may feel lost and frustrated and question God as to why it did not work out.

My daughter always reminds me that everything happens for a reason and that God has a purpose for why or why not. We just need to trust Him and allow Him to unfold His plan at the right time. While we may not understand it, God knows what He is doing and often He either blocks us from some upcoming danger and issue which we do not foresee, or He has a better plan for us that He wants to execute.

It might be different than our expectation, but God's plan is always the best. While we scramble and try to figure things out, God is already at work and reveals His plan for us in due time. We might not know a reason for why God changed things for us, but He surely does fulfill His best will for our need. And if our plans have been submitted to God and our desire is in alignment with His will, we can be assured that everything always works out somehow. God cares for every minute detail of our lives and He is interested in our happiness, so He takes care of it all, big or small. Just trust God, be still and look forward for God's unveiling of His perfect plan for our every matter.

Dear LORD please increase my patience and trust in You when my plans fall apart. Give me the ability to accept that Your thoughts are much higher than mine and You always have the best plans for me. Help me to allow You to lead me through the path which You know is good for me. I love You and trust You with all my heart. In Jesus' name, Amen!

Heart of Worship - February 13

But as for me, I will sing about your power. Each morning I will sing with joy about your unfailing love. For you have been my refuge, a place of safety when I am in distress. Psalm 59:16

One of my hidden talents is singing. I only sing when I am hiding in my closet or in room where no one can hear me. As much as I would like to sing, I have accepted that public singing is just not my thing, so I do not even try to prove it to myself or to anyone. However, I have noticed that my best singing voice comes out when I am singing in distress. It is easy to sing and whistle when all is well and good or when we are amid an atmosphere where people around us are also upbeat and accompanied by good musical instruments. But to sing when filled with sorrow and tears, specifically requires the vocal cords of the heart to tune in. And when the heart is heavy, we are focused more on the words and what they mean rather than what we sound like, who is listening to us or if we are in tune with the musical notations or not.

When we truly express our joyful or sorrowful praise, we tune in to God while tuning off the rest of the voices around us. Our attention to the words itself and being aware that we are singing to God, raises us up to the throne of God directly and we find ourselves worshipping Him with all our heart, mind and soul.

We often mistaken great praise and worship for the sound of our voice, music, or presentation but true praise comes from the heart alone. The Holy Spirit is aware of the difference with our singing casually or meaningfully. And when He sees our heart for worship, He joins in and together we lift the name of Jesus.

Praise is a one-one conversation with God and all He cares is how well we are tuned into Him. Therefore, let us sing away with our best voice of the heart filled with joy, tears and groans without worrying about the tone, tune or who to impress, besides God.

Dear LORD, thank you for the gift of sound and music. Help me to bring You my praise and sing joyfully to You without focusing on my voice or audience. Teach me to tune out all other distractions and tune into the words that my heart sings to You. May the chords of my heart be music to Your ears. In Jesus' name, Amen!

I love You – February 14

But I have this against you: You have abandoned your first love. Revelation 2:4

One day my husband shocked me said to me that he knows that I love someone else more than him. I did get what he was implying and told him yes, I do. We smiled at each other and I took it as a compliment because we both knew very well who we were talking about – our first love, Jesus! My first love is Jesus and it is evident to my family about my relationship with Him.

When we love someone, we give them our full attention, look forward to being with them, and just the thought of that person brings a smile on our face and joy to our hearts. When people look at us, they can just sense that we are in love. In the same way, when we say we love Jesus, it should be evident all over us. There should be joy in our heart and a true smile on our face because we love Jesus and He loves us too. Spending time with God through Bible reading and praying should not feel like a chore but a joy and should be something that we look forward to. He should be foremost, above anyone or anything else. When our relationship with Jesus is steady, the rest of our relationships also flourish.

The order of priorities of a Christian is Jesus first, spouse second, children next, and others afterwards. What is your order of priorities? Is Jesus your first love or have you abandoned Him for someone else?

Dear LORD, thank you for loving me and calling me Your own. Please help me to love You in return and keep You first in my life. May my love for You not be lukewarm but love You with my whole heart as You love me passionately and gave Yourself as a sacrifice for me. May I not abandon You for anything but hold on to You forever. In Jesus' name, Amen!

The real Me - February 15

Yet you know me, LORD; you see me and test my thoughts about you. Jeremiah 12:3

We often find ourselves asking this question, "Who am I?" We may think the answer lies in our beauty, dress, makeup, career, possessions, or status. These are materialistic answers which may satisfy the worldly question, but the truthful answer is that we are who we are from inside. We may talk nicely, behave well or put on good show for others but that is not who we are. The real "me" is the person who no one else sees or knows what we are thinking, feeling or doing in our heart or mind. We might compliment a person for their looks or achievements but if our heart has negativity, or if our mind is thinking something different about that individual, then the real us is the bitter person who is within. We could do all the good works but if we have resentment or selfish motives while doing it, the real us is the hateful person.

The motive of our heart and the thoughts in our mind is what God looks at. We cannot fool God by our sweet words or impress Him with an outward performance. People may never know how we behave internally or get into our minds to ever find out what our true thoughts are, but we cannot hide these from God.

When we receive a gift, we might be momentarily impressed with the way it is wrapped but our main interest is what is inside of it. The real value of the gift lies inside of the box then what is shown outside. In the same manner, it does not matter how beautiful, well-dressed or made up we are from the outside, our true worth is what we are from the inside which can be hidden from others but is fully spotlighted to God.

Dear LORD, it is a scary thought for me to see that my inward may not be so grand as my external appearance and persona. But it is the only thing that matters to You so please help me to focus on being beautiful and holy from inside out and not worry about meeting the standards of the world with outward appearance and worldly lifestyle. May the beauty of Jesus be seen in me. In Jesus' name, Amen!

No excuse for sin - February 16

But test everything; hold fast what is good. 1 Thessalonians 5:21

Sometimes we are so blinded in our sin that we do not see anything wrong in it. We have our own way of thinking and even twist God's word around to pardon our sin. Since we do not recognize it as sin and consider ourselves innocent, we sometimes even indirectly ask God to bless us in it. For example, we might ask God to be with us when we are going somewhere and bless us in everything we do while clearly where we are headed and what we are about to do is something sinful. And if we succeed in it, we give God the credit for helping us and not thinking of it as a sin committed. Satan is very smart, and he stays awfully close to us to grab any opportunity he can get to destroy us in any way possible. He pays attention to everything that we desire and often helps us to get it, misleading us to think that it must have come from God since we prayed about it. The devil encourages us in our sin and smoothens out our path for us so that we continue to walk in it and get further away from God.

We need to realize that whether we acknowledge it or not, God clearly knows what sin is and He will never bless any wrongdoing or ill intent. He is a Holy God and sin cannot stand in front of Him no matter what shape, form or excuse we may have. So instead of indulging in our sin and thinking that God is in it, we need to realize the truth that anything wrong is never from God, it only comes from the devil. We need to pray for our spiritual eyes to be opened to see sin as it is, even if it is fruitful. And instead of being deceived by Satan, we need to be wise to understand what is from God and what is from the devil.

Dear LORD, help me to not to be deceived by the devil and fall for his tactics because he is the father of lies. Teach me to recognize sin and may I not come up with reasons and excuses to commit sin. I ask for Your Spirit of Truth to penetrate my heart so that I can discern between right and wrong in Your sight. In Jesus' name, Amen!

Dust you are, to dust you will go - February 17

"Even now" declares the LORD, return to me with all your heart, with fasting and weeping and mourning. So, rend your hearts and not your garments, and return to the LORD your God". Joel 2:12-13

Ash Wednesday is the first day of Lent, the beginning of the season of preparation of the resurrection of Jesus Christ on Easter Sunday. It is also a season of self-reflection, repentance and renewal as "new life" comes forth at Springtime. On this day, we notice folks with smeared ashes on their forehead. In the Catholic Church as a ritual, the priest uses ashes which are a collection of burnt palm branches from the previous year, to mark a cross on the foreheads of the believers and says, "Thou are dust and to dust you shall return". It is basically a reminder of our mortality and the need for repentance.

During Lent, we find ourselves to be humbler and are disciplined in keeping our commitment throughout this period. But often by Easter morning, instead of resurrecting and living onwards as a "new creation in Christ", we return to our original, sinful self, defeating the purpose of lent. We observe the season of fasting, mourning and reflecting but soon forget as soon as it is over. Lent is not meant to be for a season only but should be observed each day as we reflect and renew ourselves daily.

The main reason for lent is to reflect on our sins and realize our need to turn from it. However, most of us acknowledge it but do not really make much effort to do anything about it afterwards though. True repentance is not just reflection of our sin, but it is to turn from it. While Jesus shines His light on our hearts to bring out those sinful ways which are hidden within us, they are not meant to be hidden back again once they have surfaced. A city on a hill cannot be hidden, in the same way, once Jesus brings us out of darkness into the light, our changed lives should be reflected out which people can see and notice the difference in us, not only during lent but every day.

Dear LORD, renew my mind, remove my spiritual blindness and take away my stubborn, stony heart as I open myself up to You to bring to light those things which are hidden within me. Please help me to repent and change myself in needed areas of my life, not only during this lent season but as a new creation in Christ. In Jesus' name, Amen!

I can deal with it - February 18

...And as your days, so shall your strength be. Deuteronomy 33:25

A mountain might look huge from the outside and we wonder if we would ever be able to cross it and get to the other side. But as we approach it and slowly make our way through it, it does not seem that scary, and often we do not even realize we are on a mountain. The roads are lined according to the curves of the mountain and the incline does not seem that difficult as it is a gradual rise to the top.

In the same way, when we come to a mountain of difficulty, just by looking at it, we may get nervous, lose hope and wonder if we can ever overcome it. The size and height of our mountain make us feel discouraged and want to give up without even trying to face it. In our journey of life, we all come across these mountains of hopelessness and discouragement which we cannot swerve away from but need to face it and go through it. So, as we travel through these mountains, we are never left alone to pass through on our own, but God is there to help us with every climb and every turn. He lights our path for us so that we have His direction to follow, He lines up the right people who come alongside of us to share our burden and God provides the right resources that assist us through our difficult journey. He gives us strength and builds our endurance as the moments go by so as we go higher, the incline is gradual and sustainable. And while we are in the midst, it may not be as bad or difficult that we thought it would be. Knowing that we have God and others to help us, we can climb the mountain and come off it on the other side.

Therefore, let us not become afraid by looking at the mountains that are in front of us regardless of how big and dark they may appear. Let us come closer and see that God is in the midst and He is the one who will see us through our problems and difficulty, moment by moment, day by day.

Dear LORD, as my days are so let my strength be so that when I walk up to the mountain of difficulty, I would have endurance and ability to face it. Thank you for being by my side and walking along with me, guiding my steps and stabilizing my feet as I walk through rough patches in my life's journey. In Jesus' name, Amen!

Power under control - February 19

Blessed are the meek, for they will inherit the earth. Matthew 5:5

I have often been told that I am too nice which I take as a compliment because it is the character of meekness in me. Meekness is often misunderstood as weakness. But there is a big difference between being weak and meek. A weak person is not capable of or is unable to do something due to lack of strength or courage. While a meek person is fully able to do something but chooses not to and remains submissive. For example, a Horse has the full capability to run and outdo a human but chooses to remain under the authority of a bit and bridle. In the same way, meek persons are those with power under control. They choose to control their temperament, tongue, and attitude in those moments where they too can easily retaliate, but they rather let it go and not behave similarly like those who come against them. The world may consider this as a sign of weakness or cowardice but in fact it is a sign of strength as it takes great amount of patience, self-control and discipline to remain gentle and lowly. We are taught by the world to stand up for ourselves, speak back, give like for like and boast about ourselves, but God's word teaches us to let go, not avenge and remain humble. It is not an easy thing to do because people look at it as stupid and soft and may try to take advantage of it. But meekness is not foolishness, it is wisdom at its best.

Jesus exemplified gentleness multiple times for us and if we are to be Christ-like, being meek and gentle should be our aim. There is no room for pride or arrogance in God's kingdom but reserved for those who are humble and know how to submit to God's authority rather than their own or someone else.

Dear LORD, please help me to have a humble attitude in all that I do. Regardless of what people say or behave towards me, help me never to forget who I am in You. Teach me to keep my emotions and behavior under control and may my meekness be my strength as it is Yours. In Jesus' name, Amen!

Fresh Anointing - February 20

He anoints my head with oil, my cup overflows. Psalm 23:5

While sheep are gazing in pastures, they are attacked by small flies, especially the Nasal fly, which buzz around the sheep's head in attempt to get into in the damp mucous membrane in the nose to lay their eggs in. The eggs then hatch and form little parasites that make their way up to the brain, causing severe irritation and pain to the sheep. In order to stop the pain and agitation, the poor sheep rub their head at the tree or even bang their head on a rock, sometimes even up to the point of death. The Shephard understands his sheep's struggle and rubs or anoints the sheep's head with a mixture made mostly out of olive oil and other spices. This brings relief to the sheep and repulses the flies from getting in.

Symbolically, David refers to this anointing of the oil on the sheep with what God does for us by pouring down His Holy Spirit on us to protect us from the "flies" that buzz around our head. These flies can be thoughts that make us irritated, worried, fearful, jealous, insecure and angry which try to get into our brain and make us miserable. The devil does anything to take control of our mind by constantly buzzing around and steal our peace. So in order to be relieved from these enemies that make us lose our sleep at night or cause us to bang our heads against the wall due to our worries and racing thoughts, we need to allow God, our Shephard to anoint us with His Holy Spirit to cover and protect us.

The devil can buzz around all he wants but if are anointed with the precious oil of the Holy Spirit, Satan cannot get into us. Deliverance for the sheep only comes from their Shephard who knows his sheep. In the same way, deliverance from our enemy can only come from our good Shephard, Jesus Christ.

Dear LORD, I pray for a fresh anointing of Your Holy Spirit on me to repulse the attacks of the flies of worry, fear, pride, lust and envy that are buzzing around me and trying to get into my head. Please anoint my head with oil so that I can be completely covered and find relief to lie peacefully in the green pastures You have laid out for me. In Jesus' name, Amen!

Best foot forward - February 21

If we confess our sins, he is faithful and just to forgive us our sins and to cleanse us from all unrighteousness. 1 John 1:9

To put your best foot forward is an idiom or expression which means to show oneself in the best and most positive way to make a good impression. Most of the time we put our "best foot forward" on social media such as Facebook where we only show the good and positive things about us. We like to impress people, so we show off our looks or luxuries of life that we have but we hide those not so good or negative aspects that we all deal with. The reality is that we all have our downfalls and struggles but we try to minimize these in front of others in order to look our best and outdo each other.

We try to impress God too by doing the same. We put our best foot forward to show Him how good we are with our charity, volunteering, and other religious activities that we participate in. We display all the good and focus only on the positive qualities but attempt to block and ignore our sin. We forget that God is omnipotent, which means that He is all-knowing. Whether we tell Him or not, God knows our reality and we should be aware of it too. Instead of hiding, we need to confess our sin to God so that He can help us through it. By avoiding or thinking otherwise, we deceive ourselves and the truth is not in us. God wants us to be genuine and He is most impressed when we humble ourselves in front of Him rather than hide or be fake.

In God's sight to put our best foot forward is to take our steps towards Him just as we are with all our sin and shame. It is to be real, confessing ourselves as sinners and in need for a savior.

Dear LORD, I realize that I can fool people by only displaying my good side, but I cannot fool You so please help me to be genuine inside out. Help me to be concerned more about what You think of me rather than my impression with people. I bring to You today my whole being, my sin and all, so please accept it and deal with me according to Your tender grace and mercy. In Jesus' name, Amen!

Give back what was stolen - February 22

And I will restore to you the years that the locust has eaten... Joel 2:25

What we face currently might be a result or consequence of our past choices. We may have not realized it back then but now in the present we understand our poor decisions from the past, the things that we did or didn't do, and wish we can go back and change some of it. What is done is done and we cannot return to our past to fix anything and start over. So, we stand in our present with our broken pieces from the past, regretting and mourning our mistakes.

The only thing we can do about it is bring whatever we have – our ashes, messes, brokenness and failures to God now and let Him work with it. Nothing is wasted with God; He can put it back together and make use of it in a different way. God takes whatever we give to Him and turns it into something beautiful. He allows us a fresh beginning, right from where we left off and does not hold our past against us. He takes our disasters to teach us a lesson and make us better and stronger. God replaces our failures into multiplied blessings once we bring to Him whatever leftovers of the mess we have. It adds to our testimony about God's goodness despite our disappointments.

Therefore, let us not mourn over our past mistakes but rather look it as lesson learnt and move forward anew in Christ. He promises to restore back to us in bigger and better ways what was taken away from us by the enemy. Just trust God with the mess from the past and allow Him to renew us.

Dear LORD, thank you for being a God of new beginnings and not holding my sins against me. Please help me to have learned from my mistakes and not commit the same sins again. Thank you for erasing my past failures and giving me a clean slate to start over again. I give you my mess, LORD take it and turn it into my message of deliverance to those around me and may my renewed life be lived with Christ in me. In Jesus' name, Amen!

Misinterpretation - February 23

But when he, the Spirit of truth, comes, he will guide you into all the truth....
John 16:13

We often take the words out of context in the Bible and come up with our own version to back up our thought process. For example, if we want to take revenge on someone, we quickly justify it with the Bible says, "an eye for an eye". But in order to know what it truly means; it is important that we understand the history and reasoning behind each verse. "An eye for an eye" may seem justifiable for the person who has been wronged and a fair punishment for the one who did the wrong. But this verse was not written to punish but rather protect the wrong doer. When one person was harmed, usually the entire family or the clan went out against the one who did the crime, inflicting more harm than what was done originally. Therefore, this law was given in the Old testament to only punish the person according to how much harm he had done, and not more than that; the punishment must fit the crime.

So, you see, we often take Bible verses like these out of context to fit our crime and use it with wrong intent. When we misinterpret the truth, we not only deceive ourselves but cause others to stumble along also. Therefore, it is necessary to clearly understand the meaning of the word of God before applying it. When we sit to read our Bible, we must not read it casually and leave the interpretation to our own mind but ask for the intervention of the Holy Spirit to interpret the truth.

Therefore, pray before you read the Bible and allow God to fill your mind with His truth!

Dear LORD, please open my heart to hear You speak the truth about Your word as I read it. Help me not to read the Bible for the sake of reading it but may it be my bread of life. Please help me to not interpret it in my own way to fit my cause instead let the Spirit of truth bring to light my own fault and help me turn from my sinful ways. In Jesus' name, Amen!

Way Maker - February 24

Fear not, for I am with you; Be not dismayed, for I am your God. I will strengthen you, Yes, I will help you, I will uphold you with My righteous right hand.
Isaiah 41:10

About 600 people climb Mount Everest every year and get the accolades for accomplishing such an adventure. Most climbers are western climbers and they are the ones who become famous and get the credit, but this achievement is not accomplished alone and they could not do it without Sherpas or porters who help and guide them every step of the way. The Porters are the expert, local people who lead the climbers up the mountain, carry their gear and food, affix ropes and pave the way for the climbers. They are the critical piece to the climber's success, yet they are mostly overlooked.

God is our Porter so to speak figuratively. We are the ones climbing through our journey of life and we take credit for many of the things we accomplish. But truthfully, if it is not for God, we cannot get anywhere. God is the one who helps us in our walk from beginning to end. He willingly carries our burdens too heavy for us to carry, He provides for all of needs and comes along with us every step of the way. He foresees the dangers and seasons and gives us strength to endure it, He promises to remain by our side and does not abandon us not matter what. God is the pro who knows every detail of our climb and paves our way at every step so that we can continue to climb, following in His footsteps.

Therefore, no matter how foggy, slippery, steep or dangerous our path may look, we can trust God to go ahead of us to clear our path and help us through it all. And as we reach to the top, we need to ensure our Porter is not overlooked but given the credit to whom it belongs – The Way Maker, our LORD Jesus Christ.

Dear LORD, thank you for coming alongside me and being my guide and aide. Thank you for clearing the path as we climb along rough patches in life. Without You I can do nothing but with You I can do everything, so I give You praise for being with me and helping me every step of the way. In Jesus' name, Amen!

Throw out the baggage - February 25

But now I urge you to keep up your courage, because not one of you will be lost; only the ship will be destroyed. Acts 27:22

Sometimes our life may feel like a shipwreck. We may face severe storms with no sunshine during the day nor any sign of moon or stars at night due to dark clouds glooming over us, being tossed around by big winds and waves, feeling sick to our stomach and not being able to eat or sleep. We pass days and nights just floating around on the sea of trouble, not knowing which way the shore is or if we will ever get there. When the apostle Paul and his shipmates faced this kind of wreck, God answered Paul's prayer and told him that crew of the ship would lose everything except for their lives. They would be saved but without any baggage! So, they had to toss all the cargo and everything they had one after the other into the sea in order to be saved, alone and without the ship or anything else.

When we go through our storm of life, we want to be rescued but we are not willing to throw out the heavy cargo that holds us down. We pray for deliverance but hold on to our sin, worry, fear, money, fame and whatever else that hinders us from being saved. But it is necessary to lose what binds us down in order to bind us to God. We must learn to let go anything or anyone who takes us away from God rather than bring us closer to Him. If we continue to trust in materials or people, we prove that we do not trust God fully. Therefore, we need to let go and destroy all else so that we can be rescued by God. When we have nothing, we have to depend on God and God wants us to depend on Him, so He waits patiently for us to toss everything else out of our life so that we have nothing but ourselves to give to God.

Dear LORD, search my life and point out those things in my life that I need to let go that are a hindrance to my deliverance. Please help me not to put my trust in materials and people to deliver me but put my hope in You who is mighty to save. In Jesus' name, Amen!

Prayer is effective - February 26

The prayer of a righteous person is powerful and effective. James 5:16b

The implication of this Bible verse has been misunderstood by many of us. We think that there is some order or method of praying that we must follow for our prayers to be effective. Our viewpoint according to this verse is that the first order of righteous praying is for ourselves to be righteous prior to praying. So, before we even pray about anything, we try to clean ourselves up and then go to prayer. And if our prayer does not seem to get answered, we often put the blame in our own unrighteousness for the ineffective prayer.

But the theme point of this verse is not about our righteousness but about prayer. We believe in the power of prayer and therefore we pray. Thus, being a prayerful person, itself proves our righteousness. Praying is not about how to make it powerful or effective but to be confident that prayer is effective and so we pray continuously regardless of our unrighteousness. Elijah is used as an example in the following verse after this one to prove this point. He was not any extraordinary individual that made his prayer effective. He was a man just like us, with nature like us and He prayed fervently. And God answered his prayer not because He was special in any other form but because he prayed persistently. It was not Elijah's righteous acts that caused God to answer prayer, but it was Elijah's fervent, righteous prayers that caused God to move.

Therefore, do not wait to be righteous first. Keep praying as ordinary people to an extraordinary God!

Dear LORD, thank you for giving me the privilege to pray just as I am. I acknowledge that I am a sinner who does not deserve Your goodness, but You are a gracious God who loves me and invites me to come to You with all my sin and shame. I believe there is power in the prayer prayed in Jesus' name, so I bring you my requests and look unto You to answer it according to your perfect will for my life. In Jesus' name, Amen!

I said, "This far and no farther will you come. Here your proud waves must stop!" Job 38:11

When we stand on the shore and observe the waves, we notice that the waves come with a good force from a distance but as they arrive near the shoreline, they lose their intensity and die off. God has set a boundary for the waves that they may come only up to a certain point and not cross any more. When they hit the borderline that God has established, they turn around and go back into the vast ocean. They may try over and over but must turn back around as they cannot pass over the line which God has commanded them not to pass.

We may have those waves of sickness, addiction or other issues in life where we feel that it is getting worse and worse and too late to correct. They come with such intensity that we fear it will overtake us and we will drown in it. But just the way God has set boundaries for the oceans, He can set spiritual boundaries over our illnesses and issues. When we call out to God for help, He commands it to not go any further. When we pray for our concerns with faith, God equips us to rebuke these waves in Jesus' name to not go any further than what they have come so far.

Sickness, illness, addiction, brokenness and desperation cannot cross over the limit that God sets over it and it must turn back around. It can attempt to come back again but we too must stand firm by being rooted in faith and not allow these waves to come over us.

Dear LORD, set a boundary over the sickness, addiction, worry and everything else that tries to come against me or my loved ones. I declare victory over them and rebuke these waves by faith in Your powerful name, the creator of the earth and all that resides in it. They shall not cross this limit but must turn around and return without causing further damage to me or my family. In Jesus' name, Amen!

Rooted in Christ - February 28

Blessed is the man who trusts in the Lord, and whose hope is the Lord. For he shall be like a tree planted by the waters, which spreads out its roots by the river, and will not fear when heat comes; But its leaf will be green, and will not be anxious in the year of drought, Nor will cease from yielding fruit. Jeremiah 17: 7,8

Trees need the wind to blow against them for their roots to grow. The stronger the wind, the more effort the roots must make to withstand the force of the wind otherwise the tree would just topple over. So, the wind forces the roots to become stronger and grow deeper to keep the tree to stand tall. It may appear that the wind is the enemy but in fact it is an indirect blessing for the tree.

Like the tree, we too need some hardships to come against us sometimes for us to deepen our spiritual roots in Christ. When blows of hardships come against us, we may get discouraged and try to run away but these are meant to make us stronger in God. Our hardship may seem like an enemy and we wish our life were always smooth and free of pain. But if we did not have any struggles, we would not have anything to resist which in turn would make us weak, fragile and eventually topple over. When the enemy strikes and if we are rooted in Christ, we are equipped to stand against its forces and become stronger each time it blows. The harder it comes against us, the more we find ourselves kneeling for prayer, reading God's word and relying on Him. In our difficult days we find strength in God and learn to trust Him when we are too weak to stand up for ourselves. The winds can bend us and make us sway back and forth but it cannot uproot us if we are deeply grounded in God.

Our difficulties teach us valuable lessons and make our roots grow deeper in God's love. So as hard as it feels, be grateful even for the difficulties as they are a blessing in disguise.

Dear LORD, please help me to not get discouraged when blows of heartaches come against me. Through these, I humble myself and come closer to You, so give me strength to endure them and even be grateful for the hardships. May my roots go deep down and be firmly rooted in You so that I can understand how marvelous Your love for me is. In Jesus' name, Amen!

Praying on behalf of each other - February 29

Therefore, confess your sins to one another and pray for one another, that you may be healed. James 5:16a

O ccasionally, we find ourselves involved in someone else's spiritual battle. We are unable to figure out what our place is in their situation and why we are involved. But if anything, God places us in someone else's situation to do nothing more than just pray for the individual. The battle for that person could be so fierce that they do not have the strength and ability to pray for themselves. They could be so immersed in their war of sin that they cannot think for themselves or know what to do. If left alone to find their own way to God, they would be lost and remain unrepentant.

And there is where we step in. We need to stand in their gap and pray on their behalf. We need to lift them up to the throne of God and continue to intercede so that by our prayers, they receive the deliverance.

Whether it's a spouse, child, parent, friend or an acquaintance, when God puts us in the middle of someone else's problem, let's not be upset about it or try to run away, instead use this opportunity to pray for them as they need it more than you can imagine. We randomly do not run into others' problems; God places us right in the middle of their battle purposely so that we can come alongside to fight the battle on our knees with them. So, whosever fight we are fighting, let us fight fiercely so that we can save each other by our prayers!

Dear LORD, I lift that particular person whom You have placed on my heart to pray for. I may not know the full extent of their struggles, but I do know that my place is to just pray and lift them to You. Would You please help and deliver them from whatever they are dealing with? In Jesus' name. Amen!

March

Meeting with God - March 1

Let us then approach God's throne of grace with confidence, so that we may receive mercy and find grace to help us in our time of need. Hebrews 4:16

Sometimes I wonder what I would talk about if I ever got a chance to meet the President of our country or what would I request if he asked me what I wanted from him. Of course, this is quite impossible as the President is a big deal and meeting him is rarely possible. We would need to be fairly important to have an opportunity to have a meeting with him. And if by any chance this did happen, we would be overly excited, prepared and look forward to meeting the President.

We have an open invitation to meet God, the President of the Universe personally whenever we want. Through prayer, we have a direct connection to God, and He is never too busy to meet us nor are we any less important for Him to turn us down. In fact, God feels excited when we approach Him and is always ready to hear us. However, it is us who often take our meeting with Him lightly. We often take prayer time for granted and sometimes even decline the precious opportunity to meet with God because we are busy with other things. Or we simply pray as a part of our daily routine that we must do and do not take our time with God seriously. Many times, we merely sit there with our eyes closed and say words as if we are talking to ourselves and afterwards go on to life as usual.

But when we pray, we need to realize that we are standing in the presence of the King of the Kings. We should be excited to meet Him and feel privileged that He knows us personally by name, knows everything about us, genuinely cares for us and gives us His best.

It is our privilege that God has given us to approach His throne boldly whenever we desire. Therefore, we should take prayer time seriously and never miss the opportunity to meet with God personally.

Dear LORD, thank you for giving us the honor to approach you whenever we want. Please help me to keep You as my priority and use every opportunity to meet with You through prayer and talk about anything that concerns me. Thank you for listening and allowing me to lay my burdens at Your feet as You care and willingly carry them for me. In Jesus' name, Amen!

Meeting point - March 2

Your word is a lamp to my feet and a light to my path. Psalm 119:105

Every time we go to a new place, we usually pick a meeting point to come back to in case if one of us gets lost. Whether it's in front of a particular store, street corner or a landmark, we keep that place in mind as our marker to come back to as it's easy to get distracted and lose our sense of direction when we are in a new place, having too much fun or occupied with being focused on other things.

It is also easy to get lost in our spiritual journey when we focus on the things of the world. We become busy being entertained with worldly pleasures, obtaining materialistic things, keeping our eyes on what other people are doing, and displaying our possessions and status, that we get lost in the crowd of this world and lose focus of who and where we are. Sometimes we go deeper and deeper in our sinful living that we do not know which is true north anymore. We follow people's advice or try to figure out our own way, often leading us further away.

But we need to remember that the Bible is our marker that God has set for us. He has given us the Bible as our meeting point in case we get off track or lose direction. As we go about in our life's journey, we need to keep our eyes on this marker and remember to come back to it every time we find ourselves getting away from where we need to be. It keeps us grounded in God and is the meeting point where God anxiously waits for us to bring us back home.

So, while we are busy living and enjoying this life, let us remember to return to the Bible when we find ourselves drifting away from God.

Dear LORD, You are the way, the truth and the life. Thank you for showing me the way back to return to You when I feel lost. Please help me to keep my eyes on You no matter where I go or what I do. In Jesus' name, Amen!

Gradual sin - March 3

But each person is tempted when he is lured and enticed by his own desire. Then desire when it has conceived gives birth to sin, and sin when it is fully grown brings forth death. James 1: 14. 15

hen I got the water ready to soak my feet in some Epsom salt solution, I realized that the water was too hot and could not put my feet in. So, I removed the water and replaced it with some warm water and gradually added hot water to the point where my feet were comfortable and did not feel the increasing heat.

The devil gets us to sin similarly, not suddenly but gradually. Most of us believe that we are grounded in Christ to be able to recognize a sin and not allow ourselves to fall into it. So, the devil lures us into sin slowly by adding on pressure, a little heat at a time. He starts off with putting a thought in our head which turns into a desire that we act upon and the next thing we know is that we've completely immersed ourselves in the sin and didn't even realize how or when it happened. It may start off as an innocent thought which does not hurt initially but gradually grows in a full-blown sin that causes us to burn up.

If a frog jumped into boiling water, he would jump right out but if the water is warm to begin with, he will get comfortable and not realize if the heat is turned up gradually, leading to its death. In the same way, if we let our guard down, the devil works his way into our head, heart and body to destroy us, slowly but surely.

Therefore, we must always be vigilant and guard against the devil's tactic in order to feel the heat rising and jump out instantly.

Dear LORD, please help me to recognize my sin as soon as I feel it. Help me not to play with it or give it any attention but flee from it the moment I see it coming. Give me the courage to jump out and not become comfortable in my sin. In Jesus' name, Amen!

Easier said than done - March 4

I have been crucified with Christ. It is no longer I who live, but Christ who lives in me. Galatians 2:20

I like to read bumper stickers and figure out what some unique license plates mean on cars. I also like to find cars with a fish symbol on it. Besides the cross, the symbol of the fish is also known to represent Christianity. Many know the history behind the cross but may not be aware of the fish symbol. Basically, the fish symbol is based on the Greek acronym for Jesus Christ, God's Son or Savior. The first letter of each of these words also spells "Fish". And fish is also referred several times in the Bible, relating to Jesus' ministry. In the earlier days when Christians were under persecution, they worshiped in secret places and would sketch a fish on the outside of the door to let other Christians know that they were welcomed in and are safe.

It is easy to find cars with a cross and fish symbol to represent Christianity. But not all who represent these symbols are necessarily Christians. Calling ourselves Christians does not make us one unless we genuinely believe in Jesus from our heart and accept Him as our Lord and Savior. Following Jesus involves denying our own worldly desires and desiring God; it involves forsaking our worldly treasures in return for spiritual treasures. Being a Christian requires to put to death our selfish, worldly pleasures and let God live and work in and through us.

It is easier said than done. Therefore, if we refer to ourselves as Christians, let us remember that it is not about outward show of religion but knowing and abiding by the truth of God.

Dear LORD, I choose to be a Christian, not by my name or religion but by my personal relationship with You. Please help me to follow You with my heart by denying myself and taking up my cross daily. In Jesus' name, Amen!

Clean from within - March 5

For as he thinks in his heart, so is he. Proverbs 23:7

When we look at ourselves in the mirror, we get a sense of what we look like. We get a sense of who we are as a person by how we feel about ourselves or what others have to say regarding us. So basically, our looks and personality define us a person in worldly terms.

But the real person is not what we look like or what we portray ourselves to others. The real us is who we are from the inside. The thoughts that we think, the words that we speak behind closed doors, our behavior in private vs public and our secret activities define the true person. We can say something but mean something else, we can pretend to do something while our motive is for another reason, or we can be "nice" to others but in reality, we are the total opposite.

Most of us can put on a good show and impress people with our looks, attire and act. We can have a good control over ourselves in what to say or not do in front of others, but our heart could be far away from the truth. We can impress people but cannot impress God the same way. We can refrain our tongue from saying something but if we said it in our heart, then it's as good as said in God's eyes; we can stop our body from doing something but if we did it intentionally in our heart or mind, it's as good as done to God. God's definition of real is the genuineness of our heart. True beauty is the cleanliness of our heart and what our motives are behind all that we say and do.

Therefore, it is crucial that we guard our heart above all because what we think in our heart is what makes us real.

———————————————

Dear LORD, please help me to be clean and clear from inside. Let me not put on a show for the world and have different intentions in my heart. I want to be holy and genuine so please help me to guard my heart to be true and pleasing to you first. In Jesus' name, Amen!

———————————————

Smart vs Wise - March 6

Set a guard over my mouth, Lord; keep watch over the door of my lips. Psalm 141:3

There is a difference between being smart and being wise. The best way a pastor explained the difference is that a smart person knows what to say but a wise person knows whether to say it or not.

Most of us can and will answer back when spoken to, to prove or defend ourselves, but it does not necessarily mean what we say is always right, good and builds up. If our speaking leads to breaking someone's heart or makes the matter worse, we would be better off not saying it. There is a better way to handle a situation and it often calls for silence rather than remark. A situation can always be resolved by having healthy conversations at the appropriate times than to blurt out words which we regret later and cause more damage. Some consider it being clean-hearted by saying whatever is on their mind and not holding it in but in reality, it's considered a form of selfishness as it may make them feel better about themselves but does not take into consideration the recipient's emotions or situation. Answering back readily may attest to our wittiness, but true wisdom comes from knowing when, how, what and if to say it.

So, let us put our intelligence into perspective and strive for true wisdom of knowing whether it is necessary to speak or not.

Dear Lord, please help me to hold my tongue back and be silent in those moments which may lead to breaking rather than building up through my words. You know my heart so be my defender and prove my innocence through my silence. Help me to have the wisdom of Christ rule my heart and mind. In Jesus' name, Amen!

God is certain - March 7

For I know the plans I have for you," declares the Lord, "plans to prosper you and not to harm you, plans to give you hope and a future. Jeremiah 29:11

My daughter reminded me that this is the decade where kids her age will graduate from college, get married and have families of their own. It made me realize how life is passing by so fast and like it or not, we grow up and go through different phases of life. We do not know when and how things will turn out, and it seems overwhelming sometimes when we really think about.

Although our lives change and we are on a constant move forward and even when our future seems uncertain, one thing that gives me assurance is that God is certain. He is the constant factor who remains the same as He was, is, and always will be. His faithfulness will see us through regardless of our age or phases in life.

Because He is, we can face tomorrow without fear or any worry. God holds our future in His hands and works everything out for us for our good. Therefore, life is worth the living just because He lives, and He is our God!

Dear Lord, thank you for Your promise to never leave us nor forsake us regardless of what goes on in our life. Please help me to trust in You and live life with full joy in my heart without any fear knowing You are with me now and forever. In Jesus' name, Amen!

Tuned into God's word - March 8

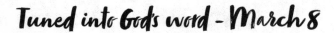

I have hidden your word in my heart, that I might not sin against you.
Psalm 119:11

I honestly do not remember how I got to work today. I do not remember turning on my car, driving or turning on certain roads. I obviously did not land here miraculously but my arrival was an automatic function of the brain. My brain has been fine-tuned after many repetitions of the same thing over and over that it knows what to do even when I am not paying attention.

In the same way, our heart needs to be tuned into God's word so much that we automatically know what to do in spiritual matters. We need to train ourselves to be godly by meditating on God's word, memorizing scriptures and putting them into practice in every situation to avoid falling into sin.

When Jesus was tempted by the devil, He responded promptly by using scriptures against the devil's attack and resisting him. For the appropriate Bible verses to come out from our mouths at the right time and right situation, we too need to study, believe and take these verses to heart. Just reading certain Bible passages in a day is not enough to combat the attacks we face. The scripture must be deeply rooted, trusted and practiced over and over so that it becomes an automatic response of the heart.

_____

Dear Lord, help me to read my Bible with diligence and not as a form of duty.
Teach me to meditate and trust Your word so that I can use it as a weapon to
fight against the devil and his temptation to sin. May the words of my mouth and
the meditation of my heart be pleasing to You and useful for my life. In Jesus'
name, Amen!

_____

Prayer is power supply - March 9

Never stop praying. 1 Thessalonians 5:17

Some do spend quality time with God in prayer diligently each day while there are some of us who consider prayer to be the last or least of our priorities of the day. It is not that we do not want to pray, but depending on our time and mood, we pray accordingly. We talk to God based on our need and urgency. If it is something critical for us, we ensure that we set apart time, humble ourselves and pray with much seriousness. And when things seem to be going ok, we might merely pray for the sake of praying to check it off the list or just pray casually.

Prayer is our privilege and it has been given to us as the strongest weapon for a Christian. When we pray, we directly pull strength, wisdom and encouragement from God. He is like the power supply and prayer is the chord. We must connect the wire to the plug, in order to energize. Similarly, we must pray and connect to God for ourselves to gain energy from Him. it is not enough to talk about, read books about prayer or keep giving our prayer requests to others; our personal prayer time is essential for our walk and growth in Christ. And if prayer is our weapon to fight against our battles of life, shouldn't prayer be of most importance to us than things or people?

When we stop praying or make God wait, we often miss out on the blessings He has in store for us so no matter how busy we may be, let us give prayer a priority. It is the best thing we can do in our day!

Dear Lord, thank you for giving me the honor to come to in Your presence through prayer. Help me to take my time with You seriously and never take You for granted. Teach me to prioritize my relationships and activities so that I give You our best of time and attention. In Jesus' name, Amen!

Coming to sense - March 10

When he finally came to his senses, he said to himself, 'At home even the hired servants have food enough to spare, and here I am dying of hunger! Luke 15:17

In the prodigal son's story in the Bible, the young man went off on his own, away from his Dad's home. He was under his own belief that he knew what he was doing and could make it on his own. Although the dad tried to convince the young man, he was not ready to listen. He did his own thing until he finally came to his senses and returned to his dad who had been eagerly waiting for him.

Often, we too run off on our own and do our own thing. When we are under our own convictions, we become self-righteous and no matter how much others try to tell us right or wrong, we continue to justify our actions and do what we think is right. We develop a stubbornness that leads us away from the truth and into spiritual darkness. It is only when we come to our own senses, we realize our error and have a willingness to change. It requires logic and until it makes sense to us personally, things will not change.

The prodigal returned when he came to his sense, and so in the same way, if we desire to see a change of our own or in someone else, we need to pray for God to open our eyes, think logically according to God's truth and bring us to our senses.

Dear Lord, thank you for waiting for me with arms wide open. Please help me to come to my sense to understand the things I am doing wrong. Help me not to walk blindly in my own wisdom and righteousness but see Your truth and return to you. In Jesus' name, Amen!

The ball is in my court - March 11

If it is possible, as far as it depends on you, live at peace with everyone.
Romans 12:18

The sport of tennis is where the ball is hit by one opponent with a racket into the court of the opposite opponent who strikes back. The goal is to not have the ball drop in the player's side of the court and should strike it back in such a way that the opponent is not able to return it. The game continues till one player is unable to hit the ball back and loses points, which eventually leads to winning or losing the game.

A fight or argument is like tennis. It requires two opponents who talk or hit each other back and forth. When one yells, the other usually retaliates back with a response. None of us like to lose so we try to get in the final word or throw the last blow to knock our opponent out. But unlike tennis, the true winner of the argument is the one who does not strike the ball back. When the ball is in our court, it is up to us to decide whether we will throw it back which can make or break the argument further. If we throw it, the fight continues but if we do not strike back and remain silent, the heated moment dissolves and ends the game eventually.

It depends on us to start, continue or end the battle with our opponent. So as much as possible, when the ball is in our court, we need to choose not to strike back in order to live peaceably with ourselves and others.

Dear Lord, teach me not to retaliate when spoken against or mistreated. Please help me to walk away in heated moments and leave it up to you to handle it. May the peace of Jehovah Shalom be upon me in all circumstances. In Jesus' name, Amen!

Let us go to the other side - March 12

For we walk by faith, not by sight. 2 Corinthians 5:7

A mountain has two sides to it. The side we stand in front of and face is the one that we must go through in order to get to the other, unseen side. By looking at the elevation and steepness we may feel discouraged that we will not be able to climb it. But when we are at the foot of the mountain, we have no other choice but to make our way through it. As difficult as it may be, we strive upwards and finally cross over it to see the beautiful other side of the mountain which was not visible before.

In our journey through life, we come across mountains of difficulties that we face. The hardship may seem unsurmountable and we fear that we cannot cross it. We may get discouraged as we do not see any other way out and are ready to give up hope. But these mountains are not meant to stop us, rather placed in front of us to make us stronger, build our faith and endurance as we go through them. God never brings us to a mountain and leaves us alone to figure it out our own. But He stays right beside us, encouraging and carrying us through it. He gives us the strength as we climb up one step at a time. It may take a long time and require tremendous patience but if God said, "let us go to the other side", we need to trust that He will get us there despite the storms and dangers that come in our path.

There is always an unseen, other side of the mountain awaiting us, but we must first climb through what is seen in front of us. What we perceive may seem impossible to accomplish, regardless we must continue to walk in faith towards what is not in sight yet.

Dear LORD, as I go through difficult paths in my life, please help me to not feel disheartened by my current view but continue to walk by faith and strive forward to the other side, keeping my eyes on You. I know there is a beautiful testimony awaiting on the other side so help me to endure as You bring me there. In Jesus' name, Amen!

So if the Son sets you free, you will be free indeed. John 8:36

The Israelites came to a dead-end situation after they left Egypt. They faced the Red Sea in front of them and the Egyptian army behind them. What seemed to be an impossible way out of the situation, God made a way for them and parted the sea so that the Israelites could pass through. When the enemy saw this way of deliverance that God had made for the Israelites, they assumed they could also go through the same passage and pursue God's people. They failed to realize God had not made the way for them, it was meant only for the Israelites.

Often, the enemy tries to invade into our path of deliverance and come after us. Even while God has declared us free, the enemy still pursues us in attempt to destroy us. He comes behind us thinking that he will overpower us and bring us out of the path and back into his bondage. But we need to remember that if God has called us to freedom, then we truly are free and nothing or no one can take that away from us. The enemy can pursue us all he wants, but he cannot succeed if we continue to walk on the way of deliverance that God has made for us. Many of us have the tendency to still be fearful as we walk on the impossible way that God has set for us. We say we trust God and thank Him for deliverance, yet we keep looking back in fear of the enemy pursuing us. We need to understand that if God did not want us to be rescued, why would He make a way to begin with? He would not allow the enemy to prevail over what has been declared free. As mighty as the Egyptian army was, they could not prevail over what was not meant for them, therefore, we must keep our eyes on the path which God has made for us and follow our course of victory without worrying about the pursuit of the enemy behind us.

Dear LORD, thank you for making a way for me where there seems to be no way. You are a God of impossibilities so as You lead me through the path which is impossible in my sight, please help me to trust You and keep my eyes focused on You alone, not the enemy behind me. Once You have declared me victorious, help me to claim the victory! In Jesus' name, Amen!

Ultimate Helper - March 14

I lift up my eyes to the hills. From where does my help come? My help comes from the LORD, the Maker of heaven and earth. Psalm 121: 1-2

In times of distress, we naturally look up to someone or something to help us. If it is a sickness, we consult and seek the best medical treatment. If there is financial shortage, we look for ways to get more money. When there is trouble of any sort, we usually run to friends or family for help. The things that we look up to for help are described in this bible verse as "hills". Because the "hills" may seem bigger and stronger than us, capable of more than what we can, we tend to seek and rely on people and things to rescue and deliver us.

But we need to realize that there is a higher source of help than what we find in people, places and things. Our real help comes from God. He is above all and the basis through whom our needs are met. God is the one who sends us help through people, directs us to the right places and aligns things in order to get us through whatever we face.

Therefore, instead of going through different channels and means to find aid, why not look directly first towards the LORD, our ultimate helper! Our primary thought and action ought to be to look to God through prayer no matter how big or small or issue might be. Thereafter as He guides us, we take the next steps for our need. God has given us the privilege to approach Him and is pleased when we turn to Him instead of trusting in other "hills". We need to trust God with all our heart as He knows what He is doing and will not fail us.

Dear LORD, thank you for being my ultimate Helper who is higher and above anything or anyone else. Help me to rely on You foremost and trust You with in my struggles. Teach me to look to You first and allow You to help me before I try to find help in myself and others. In Jesus' name, Amen!

"Sir, we wish to see Jesus." John 12:21

Saul was an anti-Christian who went places to persecute and punish those who called themselves Christians. The Christ whom Saul persecuted, met him on the way to Damascus where a persecutor turned prophet. A blinding flashlight changed Saul to Paul and changed his life forever. When Paul had an encounter with Jesus, he no longer was the same old person, but his life took a turn for better forever. Instead of going against the word of God, he embraced it and led others to Christ also.

Many of us are walking on the road of Damascus. It may not be that we are on the way to persecute other Christians but are believers ourselves who persecute the name of Jesus in our own personal way of living. We may be known as Christians but everything about us goes against Christ. Christians are Christ-followers, which means that we believe in Jesus, His word and abide by God's truth. But if the way we live our lives daily proves otherwise, we cannot truly be Christians.

In order to have a true conversion, we need to have an encounter with Jesus. We need to have the "Damascus Road experience" like Paul that turns our life upside down for Christ. We need to meet God personally to be saved. Only when we see Jesus, we can have a true change, so we need to pray for God to shine His light upon us which makes us realize our errors and lead us into truth.

Dear LORD, as I walk on my Damascus road, having my own agenda, doing whatever seems right to me, please come and meet me on the road. Help me to have an encounter with You that changes my life forever. Instead of walking against You in my daily sinful choices, help me to walk blameless with You, a changed person in Christ. In Jesus' name, Amen!

Withdrawal symptoms - March 16

No temptation has overtaken you except what is common to mankind. And God is faithful; he will not let you be tempted beyond what you can bear. But when you are tempted, he will also provide a way out so that you can endure it. 1 Corinthians 10:13

The unpleasant physical, emotional and mental feeling that we experience when we stop doing something is called withdrawal. These withdrawal symptoms are mostly associated with the stopping of drugs or alcohol, but withdrawal also affects us when we try to stop a habit or change our lifestyle from those things or people that are spiritually harmful for us. When we surrender our lives to Jesus, He points out areas that are not pleasing to Him and the Holy Spirit convicts us to get rid of them. And when we decide to live by God's standard and give up those things that hinder our relationship with Him, we feel a tremendous opposition against it.

The devil plays a vital role in withdrawal. He takes full advantage of our weak moments and cause us to fall into sin again. While we are already feeling down and missing our old habit, the devil attacks us by putting thoughts in our mind that try to justify our actions. He comes up with excuses that make us believe that we are not doing anything wrong. He keeps bringing that which we want to give up to us over and over and make it nearly impossible for us to resist. And if we let our guard down and cave into his temptation, we fail.

Therefore, we need to have a strong will and a determination if we are ready to give up something. We need to give our best to be disciplined, self-controlled and resist the withdrawal symptoms that come against us. God will not deliver us out of something which we are not fully prepared to give up. Only when we are ready and determined, God will move and deliver. If we are serious about our decision, God will help us overcome any temptation and withdrawal we may feel. When He sees our faithfulness and willingness, God makes us able.

Dear LORD, the more I come closer to you, the more opposition I feel from the devil. You know my heart and willingness to change so please help me to resist temptations and be self-controlled in my weak moments. Help me to keep my eyes on You as I strive to live holy and righteously. Thank you for giving me Your strength through which I can do anything. In Jesus' name, Amen!

Overflow of blessings - March 17

Give, and it will be given to you. A good measure, pressed down, shaken together and running over, will be poured into your lap. For with the measure you use, it will be measured to you. Luke 6:38

We use wheat flour for cooking almost daily, so we purchase it in big quantities and empty it out in large container for storage. While transferring the flour from the bag into the container, we need to shake down and tap the container around the sides to press the flour down in order to fit the entire batch. The container is then filled tightly to the rim with flour, often even overflows when we try to close the lid.

When God is pleased and blesses us with something, He is not stingy in giving nor does He just partially bless. When He gives, God gives abundantly, shaking us down and filling us to the rim that we cannot contain it. God sees and knows every little thing we do and does not pass us by. He is aware of our little acts of kindness, our good heart and things that we do for others. Often, we may think that nobody notices our sacrifice, or the unfair things said or done to us privately, but nothing is overlooked by God. In due time, He repays each one according to our deeds. His blessings come pouring down from heaven, not as showers but storms when we bless others in disguise.

Therefore, let us continue to bless others wherever we are capable. And while we do good, let us not do with a stingy heart or give partially, but completely empty ourselves out so that God can fill us with His blessings to the overflow.

Dear LORD, thank you for being so generous to me with Your blessings. Teach me to be like You and give as You do. Please help me not to worry about receiving rewards back from people but look unto You for the outpouring of your Holy Spirit and heavenly blessings. In Jesus' name, Amen!

God is not a man, so he does not lie. He is not human, so he does not change his mind. Has he ever spoken and failed to act? Has he ever promised and not carried it through? Numbers 23:19

Our response towards others mostly depends on our emotion. When we are in a good mood, it is easy to like people and get along with them. We are ready to forgive and let go of things when we are feeling happy and all is well. But when we are upset or mad about something, we tend to change our attitude and outlook quickly. We are not willing to let go easily, and things seem to bother us much more.

So based on our emotional status, our relationships, attitude and outlook fluctuate towards people and most often towards God also. We seem to be more optimistic when we are in a good mood but more pessimistic when our mood is down. On our good days, it is convenient to love God, sing praises and pray to Him. It is easier to take Him at His word and trust God when we are not being tested. But when we are hit with hard times and our emotions are all over the place, our feelings about God also tend to bounce around. We may pray but our prayers are filled with negative emotions and we doubt and question our faith. It is hard to take God's word to heart when His promises seem to be going in the opposite direction of what we are going through.

But our faith and relationship with God must not fluctuate according to our mood. Regardless of what our emotional state maybe, our feelings and attachment to God must be in a steady state. God does not change His mind, and His love for us does not depend on how He feels about us at a particular time. And in the same manner, our love and hope in God too needs to remain the same regardless of our emotional condition.

Dear LORD, thank you for Your constant love towards me. Would You please teach me to love You and others in a steady manner and not based on my circumstances and mood of the day? I give you control over my thoughts and emotions that they would align with Yours. In Jesus' name, Amen!

Don't postpone till later - March 19

"Show me, LORD, my life's end and the number of my days; let me know how fleeting my life is. Psalm 39:4

I cannot stop thinking of the sudden death of the famous basketball player, Kobe Bryant who got killed alongside his daughter in a helicopter crash. I wonder what his morning was like. Was his family busy like ours and they went out of the house thinking they will return home like any other day in the past?

For most of us, the first hour or two of the beginning of our day might be the busiest. We may not get out of the bed until we absolutely must and then we rush around to get ourselves or kids ready to go where we need to. These first minutes of our day are probably the tensest moments where anger flares all around and anticipation of fulfilling the agenda of the day already has us emotionally stressed. We get all worked up before it even begins, and we run out of the house in a hurry without even taking a second to look at each other or saying a proper bye. We just assume we will see each other back after a few hours when we return home and catch up then. We live life as if it is in our control and we determine what we do with it.

How we live our life is ours to choose but how long we will live is at God's discretion. None of us are guaranteed a certain life span and we do not know when or how it will end for us. We may think we will come back home and make up for our morning busyness in the evening or will make up for our mean words or actions later. But what if we do not get a chance to return? What if our last words and actions were truly our last ones which we do not get another opportunity to make up?

We will leave this world and no longer have any pain or emotions to deal with for our self, but our memory of good and bad lasts with those whom we have an attachment with. It is the left-behind loved ones who must deal with regrets and sorrow for the rest of their lives.

So as busy as we may be or think we still have time and chance, let us not take life for granted and plan to say I love you, sorry, or thank you for later. The next minute to live is not in our hands, so let us seize every moment we do have as if it's our last one and leave a good memory for others just in case we don't get another opportunity.

Dear LORD, please help me not be too busy, be selfish or arrogant to hurt others and postpone my appreciation or apology for later. Thank you for the gift of life and I ask You to teach me to value time so that I make the best of every moment. In Jesus' name, Amen!

Love by choice - March 20

In fact, this is love for God: to keep his commands. 1 John 5:3

A robot is a machine, designed by a programmer who can control its functions. It can only do what it has been programmed to do and nothing more or nothing less. The absolute control of the robot is in the programmer's hand.

God is our creator, but He has not programmed us as robots. He could have wired us in such a way that we would obey and submit to Him automatically, but God's purpose in creating us humans is for us to love, worship and to follow Him with our own free will. He has given us the freedom of choice and left it up to us individually to make our decisions. God has given us direction and showed us His way, but it is up to us to choose which way we will go.

We often do things in our own wisdom and strength and then blame God for the bad things that happen in and around us. But it is our own human disobedience towards God that causes us to sin and hurt each other. It is our own decision about following the patterns of the world, all influenced by the devil who brings disaster on to us and blocks our way to eternity with God. It is not God's will that any of us should perish and therefore has provided a way, but the decision is in our own hands whether we want to be saved.

God's love for us is automatic because that is just who He is. God is love and therefore He just loves regardless of who we are or what we do. Nothing can change about that. But our love and submission to Him is not wired to be automatic, it must come from our own heart and by our own choice. And if we say that we love God, the decision to love and obey Him would just come willfully, not forcefully!

Dear LORD, I want to love and submit to You willingly because You are the way, the truth, and the life. You love me unconditionally and I too choose to do the same with You so would You please help me to love You with all my heart, mind and soul. In Jesus' name, Amen!

He replied, "Blessed rather are those who hear the word of God and obey it. Luke 11:28

Often when I tell my kids to clean their rooms, they say yes right away. They will go over their plans about when and what they will clean, even watch a YouTube video some time about getting tips on how to clean. Often, I even hear them on the phone telling their friends about their plan of the day which includes cleaning up their rooms. Yet, after all the talks and planning, at the end of the day I will still find their room as it is; uncleaned and postponed till later for whatever their excuses are. They may feel good about themselves for their thought processes, but I feel disappointed as my expectations were not met.

We often do the same in our Christian walk. We plan on getting our act together, we pray about it, read Bible and books, discuss with our friends, attend Bible studies and take notes but at the end of the day, we remain the same old person.

Anything that needs attention, needs execution. It takes effort, discipline and a determination to get things done which we want to accomplish. But if all we do is talk and plan, and if are room remains uncleaned, all else is in vain. The entire room may not instantaneously get cleaned altogether but it takes one drawer after the other, one corner at a time. Similarly, we grow in Christ one step at time, one sin after the other and that is all is required to please God.

Therefore, if we are serious about our faith and walk with God, we must do much more than just talk. We need to implement and put into practice what is expected from us through the word of God.

Dear LORD, please help me to be the doer of the word and not just a hearer. Give me wisdom to know what and how to do and say things which are right in your eyes. May I not just be a talker and give someone false hope only to let them down later but help me to put into practice what You expect from me. In Jesus' name, Amen!

Pray even if you don't feel like it - March 22

...The crowd rebuked them and told them to be quiet, but they shouted all the louder, "Lord, Son of David, have mercy on us!" Jesus stopped and called them. "What do you want me to do for you?" Matthew 20: 30-32

My husband and I were talking about how hard it is to pray on some days. It could be our busy schedules, tiredness or other distractions that come in our way of praying and spending time with God. Just when I begin to pray, someone knocks on the door, the phone rings or I hear a text message notification which I "must" respond to. Then some days my heart is heavy with so many burdens and my mind filled with countless thoughts that being still in God's presence seems nearly impossible. There are times when I am sitting down to pray but feel as if someone is shutting my mouth and words cannot come out. Truthfully, sometimes when I am so discouraged or in despair, I just do not feel like praying but rather crawl in bed and just cry about it.

But the more we do not feel like praying, the more we need to force ourselves to pray. The devil knows very well that there is power in prayer and it can change things, so he tells us to be quiet and does anything to stop us from praying. He comes as "crowd" in the form of excuses and distractions to stop us from praying. But we must cry out above the noises and come to Jesus. The more opposition we face, the more we need to cry out to God. We are better off praying amidst our circumstances or even when we do not feel like it because the deliverance or breakthrough that we have been waiting for could be just a prayer away. But the devil tries to hinder us from receiving the answer and ruin our peace and faith in God.

Therefore, we must overcome the obstacles thrown in our way and pray even more fervently and louder than the noises of the crowd around us. When we pray with all our heart and might, our prayer reaches to God's throne and makes even Jesus stop and ask us "What do you want me to do for you?"

Dear LORD, thank you for the privilege of prayer. Through prayer, I can meet and bring my requests to You who is mighty to save from anything that I am dealing with. So please help me to resist the forces of the devil and still pray even when I am too busy or just do not feel like it. In Jesus' name, Amen!

Sin to let it sin - March 23

Remember, it is sin to know what you ought to do and then not do it. James 4:17

As an ice breaker for his sermon, the Pastor asked the congregation which football team they were rooting for in the Superbowl game. Majority of the congregation cheered for one team while only three of us stood up for the other team. It was kind of embarrassing as we got booed and sneered at. It did feel a little awkward even though the jokes were meant to be funny and to be taken lightly. Before I stood up, I was contemplating in my mind whether I should or should not as I know I was going against the "norm", but I did it anyway because that was the truth for me.

Throughout the course of our day, we are indirectly presented with the question of our faith. In every choice that we make, in everything we say or do, we represent whose side we are on. We often go with the flow and "norm" of the world to fit in. We may not want to be the only weird one standing up, so we decide to be on the same side as others and do what everyone else is doing. Even if we believe otherwise, we feel afraid and remain quiet to avoid opposition or draw attention to ourselves.

Being a Christian often requires us to go against the crowd. It takes courage to stand up for what we believe in without the fear of what others think of us. It takes self-control to not do or say things which are normal in the world's eyes. It may feel awkward and we may gain enemies over it, but if we know the truth about God, we cannot remain silent. And after knowing the truth, if we still decide to be quiet about our faith and walk in the worldly patterns, it is considered as a sin in God eyes. Therefore, if we know the truth, we must do what is right!

Dear LORD, give me courage to stand up for You through my words, actions and deeds. Help me not to worry about what others will think of me but only consider whether it pleases You. Please teach me Your truth and help me to do what is right in your sight. In Jesus' name, Amen!

The best book to read is the Bible - March 24

For the word of God is alive and active. Sharper than any double-edged sword, it penetrates even to dividing soul and spirit, joints and marrow; it judges the thoughts and attitudes of the heart. Hebrews 4:12

While doing my work, I usually have my earphones on and listen to sermons or Christian worship songs. I learn a lot through these messages and songs. When I am not clear on a subject, I refer to different websites, study guides or ask other preachers to explain. I often get clarification and answers to my questions but many times I receive differing explanations which leave me even more confused.

I am learning that the best teacher to refer to is God himself and the best book to learn from is the Bible. The Bible is not biased nor is it based on any culture or ideology. It comes directly from God and He tells us the truth straight up regardless of our biases, preconceptions or doubts. We could twist or interpret His word differently in our righteousness or wickedness, but God tells us as it is – the good, bad, and the ugly. Nothing is hidden from God's sight and He does not cover up anything from us either just to make us feel good. He shows us our faults and He guide us into the truth.

God's word is referred to as a sword, not just a regular sword but a sword with sharpness on both sides that when we hear His word, it penetrates completely and cuts us to the core from every side. His word deeply divides the truth from error, and it blesses and condemns where needed. And even more, God's word is timely. He speaks to us through His word at the right time. We could have read a certain Bible passage over and over previously but when we are in a circumstance, that Bible passage speaks to us in a different way which we never thought of before or paid attention to. That is God's word becoming alive and working in us at the due time.

Dear LORD, thank you for speaking to me through Your word which is true and timely. Please give me a sound mind and clarity to recognize and obey Your word. Help me to rely on Your Holy Spirit to teach and guide my path through life. In Jesus' name, Amen!

Don't rush God - March 25

For the revelation awaits an appointed time; it speaks of the end and will not prove false. Though it linger, wait for it; it will certainly come and will not delay.
Habakkuk 2:3

It took 25 years for Abraham and Sarah to have the child God had promised to give them. I can imagine what each day of those 25 years must have been like for them. During the waiting period, Abraham and Sarah must have felt lost, become self-conscious, endured sneers of people and doubted God. And while waiting, they made their own decisions in the meantime thinking these might be how God wants to fulfill His promise, only to find out later that God had better plans, but they did not wait on Him.

Any kind of waiting is hard, even more so if it is long as 25 years. If we do not see immediate results of a promise given to us, we assume that either God forgot about it or that we misunderstood what He meant. We look at our current circumstance which may be the total opposite of what God has promised and find it difficult to continue to trust Him. We then take it upon ourselves and try to help God fulfill His promise by our own intellect and force it on us.

Not all of God's promises are meant to be fulfilled according to our timeline. God's timing is perfect and makes it happen when the time is right according to His plan. He has a purpose for our waiting. And while we may think God is just sitting idly and not doing anything about it, He is at work in us and for us behind the scenes. Sometimes He makes us wait until it is impossible for us, and then He does the impossible so that we cannot take the credit for ourselves.

So, if we are in a waiting period, let us not rush God or make our own implications in the meantime. God is faithful in keeping His promise and it will be clear when it happens so just wait for it!

Dear LORD, help me to wait for Your promise to be fulfilled in my life, according to Your timeline and not mine. Allow me to see beyond my circumstances and hold on to Your word you have given me. I know it will happen so let my faith increase when my time seems to be running out. In Jesus' name, Amen!

Idle mind is devil's workshop - March 26

For those who live according to the flesh set their minds on the things of the flesh, but those who live according to the Spirit set their minds on the things of the Spirit. Romans 8:5

I normally do not take naps or "rest" during the day. I am always on the go, running around and getting things done. Sometimes though, God causes me to slow down and gives me a forceful rest by allowing me to be under the weather and get sick. While I got sick recently, I had no choice but to put everything aside and just lay in bed. Also, because I was not feeling good, I really didn't have the same energy to read my Bible and pray as normal, so I literally just lay on the bed, watching TV off and on and sleeping. But while I was doing nothing, my mind was still busy in idleness.

It is said, "An idle mind is the devil's workshop" which I can attest to. In my idleness, I could literally sense the devil at work in my mind. He brought thoughts which I would normally never dare to think of and put ideas and temptations in my head that were hard to resist. I could not understand why I was feeling a certain way but soon came to my senses and realized that these were the works of the devil taking advantage of my free mind. So as soon as I acknowledged this, I had to force myself out of bed, get into my prayer closet on my weak knees, and overcome it by reading God's word and praying it out.

It is pertinent that we do not allow ourselves to get into an idle state of mind and leave it open as the devil's playground. Our mind is the first gate that he looks to enter through and if we entertain even a small thought, he penetrates deeper and starts destruction from within.

Therefore, we must remain vigilant in all situations and fill our minds with God's word alone. The devil cannot get in if we do not allow him to, so let us ensure that we do not give him permission to roam around in our heads!

Dear LORD, as soon as I find myself in a mind-state where I should not be, please help me to shut off the thought immediately and convert it into praise and prayer. Help me to be mindful of my thoughts and not allow them to grow deeper. Always teach me to keep my keep my mind on You. In Jesus' name, Amen!

And this is what He says to all mankind: 'Look, to fear the Lord is true wisdom; to forsake evil is real understanding.' Job 28:28

When we think of fear, we refer to someone or something that is scary and frightening. A person who has or can inflict harm on us could make us terrified to be in their presence. A horror movie could be scary as the images that we see make us afraid.

When we refer to God though, it is not the same kind of fear that we relate to scary objects or people. The fear of the LORD is that of reverence. To have reverence is to have admiration and respect for someone. It is to praise and honor them for who they are and to bestow our love on them. When we love somebody, we treat them with respect and do not do anything that could hurt them. When they are in our midst or anything related to them, we ensure that we handle all with care. We learn of their likes and dislikes so that we do not upset them by our behavior or intent. Because we value our relationship, we that we could hurt or disrespect our loved one by our words or action and therefore we take every measure to treat them with highest regards.

In the same manner, our fear of God is that of love. We love Him not due to the fear of losing our blessings or being punished for our sins, but because of who He is. We fear God out of reverence for His majesty, love and power; not because He is awful or scary.

Dear LORD, even though You are the most powerful God, the King of the Universe, You are the most loving, humble, and approachable God. I thank you for the privilege of being called Your child. Please help me to love You and follow You because of who You are and not out of fear of punishment or penalty. In Jesus' name, Amen!

Hosanna or crucify? - March 28

They took palm branches and went out to meet him, shouting, "Hosanna!" "Blessed is he who comes in the name of the Lord!" "Blessed is the king of Israel!" John 12:13

When Jesus fed, healed and did other miracles, the Jews were quick in accepting Him as their king and blessed His name with shouts of Hosanna (Hurray for saving). But the very next day, they forgot all his favors and were quick to shout "Crucify him" when they saw that Jesus was in trouble and possibly would not do any more miracles or feed them. They came under the influence of their leaders and denied Him rather than accepting Jesus for who He was and what He meant to them. It just showed that the people never really accepted Jesus as their king from their hearts but used Him for their selfish purposes.

How often do we shout Hosanna to Jesus when He does something good for us and how quickly we crucify Him in our hearts when we feel disappointed?

Most of the time we accept Jesus because He answers our prayers and provides for us. We say we love and trust Him when all is well but when times of trials come our way, we forget that He is the one who can mend our hurt, make provision for us and save us. God always comes through for us but in His time and way as He is much more knowledgeable and powerful than we are. He works in mysterious way which may not make sense to us in the moment, so we doubt His faithfulness. But we need to be assured that God remains faithful to us regardless of our unfaithfulness to Him. We should not accept or deny Jesus according to our needs and emotions. We need to decide whether He is the LORD of our life or not. Either we sing "Hosanna" or "Crucify", but not both!

Dear LORD, please help me not to change my opinion about You based on how You deliver. You are God and that does not change so I sing, Hosanna to the King of Kings! I invite You to come and be the King of my heart. In Jesus' name, Amen!

Shake it off - March 29

No weapon formed against you shall prosper, And every tongue which rises against you in judgment You shall condemn. This is the heritage of the servants of the Lord, And their righteousness is from Me," Says the Lord. Isaiah 54:17

The Apostle Paul and his friends tried to build a fire on the island they were shipwrecked on. Paul collected wood and apparently there was a venomous snake hidden in the sticks. When he dropped the wood in the flames, the snake jumped out of the fire on to Paul's hand, releasing its poisonous venom on him. People around him watched for his reaction to run, scream and waited for Paul to die as they knew how deadly the snake was. But to everyone's surprise, Paul's reaction was not what people were expecting. He just shook the snake off his hand as if no big deal and carried on with what he was doing. Paul knew that God had promised to be with him and if He did not forsake him during all the previous hardships he faced, Paul was certain that God would not let him down this time either. So being confident in God, Paul did not allow this to pull him down in fear and defeat.

We too get attacked in life by all sorts of "snakes" such as sickness, financial issues, marital problems, family trouble, temptations and desperation. The devil jumps up out of nowhere and charges against us with these things to destroy us. But it depends on us how we handle it. We can get scared and run to others for help or we can be like Paul and just shake it off. We all have experienced God's faithfulness throughout our lives, and we need to have that faith that He will do it again. And while we face these difficulties, people around us watch for our reaction. They lie in wait for us to be overcome by our circumstances and give up, but we need to prove them otherwise. We need to trust our God and shake off the "snake" that comes against us.

Dear LORD, please help me to remember that You are with me and not cave into fear or worry about anything. You are our God who is mighty to save so I shake off all those things that try to come against me and my family. I claim this in Jesus' name, Amen!

Up close and personal - March 30

Draw near to God, and He will draw near to you. James 4:8

I am mesmerized by airplanes. I could sit at an airport all day and watch planes take off and land, unload tons of baggage and hundreds of passengers at a time. If we have never been inside of an airplane or seen it up close, we cannot fathom how massive and powerful this entity is. From watching it fly above in the sky, we may not think of it much as it just appears like a tiny bird but only when we come in close proximity to it, we can see what a giant it is and how powerful is its sound, energy and capacity.

Similarly, for those of us who have only heard of God could never comprehend who He is or what He is capable of. From a distance God may just seem vague, tiny being who we may not give much attention to but in order to truly know our God, we need to come close to Him. Only when we come near to God, we start to recognize His magnitude and majesty. We need to spend time at the "airport", in God's word to understand what He has done and observe Him closely to see what how much He is capable to handle. We need to put our trust in Him, sit back and watch God at work as He carries us through our journey.

Therefore, let us remember, in order to know God intimately, we must come close to Him. We cannot just look up in the sky, have an imagination or idea about God and assume that is all He is. We need to invite Him in our hearts, spend time in His word, pray and ask for our spiritual eyes to be opened to see His splendor and goodness. When we ourselves get close to God, the nearer He comes to us also and reveals his glory and power.

Dear LORD, I thank you for opening my spiritual eyes to see You up close and personal. Please help me to remain in You and allow You to shine your light on me to understand who you truly are and who I am in You. May I never limit You by my thoughts and imagination, but I pray for a pure heart to see Jesus. In Jesus' name, Amen!

Levels of foolishness - March 31

Give instruction to a wise man and he will be still wiser, Teach a righteous man and he will increase his learning. The fear of the LORD is the beginning of wisdom, and the knowledge of the Holy One is understanding. Proverbs 9: 9-10

There are three levels of foolishness which we all fit into at some point in our lives – The Simple, Fool, and Scoffer.

The Simple are the least foolish as they are naïve and gullible. They can be easily led astray because they believe everything and fall for it without giving much thought. They are however open to learning from their mistakes and can make a change. The Fools are a step ahead (or backwards?) who are grounded in their own opinion and regardless of how many times corrected, they still make the same mistakes repeatedly without learning a lesson. The Scoffers are the worst type who can be looked as the "wise fools" who know what they are doing and choose to do the wrong despite being told the truth. They are wise in their own sight and are determined to lead others as well into their foolishness.

We do not like to call ourselves a fool, but it is the reality which we all have experienced in our lives. We must examine ourselves and see where we land on the chart of foolishness. In some manner, we behave and do things which make us fit one of this category at least once in lifetime. But in order to not be a true fool, we must heed instructions and live by the word of God. It must begin with the fear of the Lord which is the beginning of wisdom.

Dear LORD, because I love You also, I do not want to hurt You and am fearful that I will do something to cause You pain by my foolish behavior. So, help me God, to be wise and virtuous. Help me to learn from my foolish mistakes from the past and may they cause me to be wiser and a better person in Christ. In Jesus' name, Amen!

April

Servanthood - April 1

"A new commandment I give to you, that you love one another: just as I have loved you, you also are to love one another". John 13:34

The day before Good Friday is known as Maundy Thursday in remembrance of Jesus taking his final Passover meal with His disciples. It is when Jesus also conducted the first communion and washed His disciples' feet. Maundy is a Latin word which means "command" which He gave to love one another, the way He did by humbling Himself and serving them instead of asking to be served.

We all love others, but often only when it is convenient and when we are reciprocated in the same manner. We believe in equality and so we also express our love and return it with the same measurement as it was given to us. But Jesus Himself demonstrated what true love is by lowering Himself and washing the feet of His disciples, teaching us that it doesn't matter what our status or position may be, we must have an attitude of servanthood and treat others better than ourselves. When we lower ourselves and lift others up, we demonstrate humbleness and that is what God wants us to.

Also, as we participate in communion and do what Jesus did that night, we must not neglect the rest of the events of that evening either. It is not only about eating a piece of bread and drinking grape juice to remember Jesus' love and sacrifice but also for us to love others genuinely and selflessly.

True Christianity is not only about believing in Jesus but also about following His example and living and loving like God does, considering others better than we, and serving instead of being served!

Dear LORD, please help me to serve others with an attitude of servanthood. May I never be filled with pride and lord it over to others, instead help me to lower myself and humbly love like You do. In Jesus' name, Amen!

Attached to the cross - April 2

And he said to all, "If anyone would come after me, let him deny himself and take up his cross daily and follow me. Luke 9:23

We have heard of many recent events where individuals have lost their lives for refusal to deny their faith in Jesus. Many of us would say that we too would be willing to die for Christ if we were put in this position. I am confident that we would, and hopefully none of us are placed in such extreme positions.

However, we do face the pressure of accepting or denying Christ in our day to day lives. In everything we do, the big and small decisions that we make, we are given a choice to either deny ourselves or deny Christ. Satan pressures us to get involved in those things which Jesus would be against. And when we choose to follow him, we clearly deny Christ and accept Satan. If we call ourselves Christians, then we need to refuse to live by the standards of the world and choose Jesus in all matters. It may be the less popular thing to do, we may lose some relationships over it, or even be hated for standing up for what we believe in but if we say we love our God, then we should be willing to die to our pleasures and live for Him.

Knowing that we may not face life-threatening persecution and are safe, we can easily say that we would be willing to lose our lives for Christ. But how many of us pick up the cross that we've been given to carry and die spiritually for Jesus in our daily living by choosing to do what is biblically right, walk away from temptations, remain quiet when spoken against, shut off impure thoughts, do good for evil and love for hatred?

It is easier said than done. So, if we serious about our relationship with Jesus, let us prove our loyalty to Him through our daily living and not just by our empty promises.

Dear LORD, please help me to keep my focus on You as I choose to pick up my cross and follow You. In everything that I do and say, help me to think how You would respond and do the same. May I be detached from the pleasures of the world and be attached to the cross and live my life by how you exemplified it on the cross for me. In Jesus' name, Amen!

Do it again - April 3

"No eye has seen, no ear has heard, and no mind has imagined what God has prepared for those who love him." 1 Corinthians 2:9

O ur son's first on-campus class was in the same room of the University where I had attended my last class before I graduated many, many years ago. I was nostalgic to see our child reach the same age and be in the same place where I had been at that age. Now I can clearly comprehend the meaning of this Bible verse and see the fulfillment of God's promise over me. When I had been at that age and uncertain of my future career and plans, God had given me the assurance that He knows the plans He has for me and they are to prosper me and not harm me. Through the years I have seen God fulfill His plans in my life as I gracefully witness the promised years according to His will and purpose. Things that I had never imagined or thought of are coming to pass before my very eyes.

God's faithfulness never changes nor does He change as we change and go through different phases of our lives. We may become doubtful and question God but He is confident about His promise and once He has promised it to us, He will bring it to pass somehow through ways which we can never think or dream of. God never retracts His promise over us regardless of how unfaithful we are to Him.

In these days of uncertainty, just seeing our son in my place, assured me of one more promise of God. God told Joshua as he was about to take Moses' place as the leader of the Israelites that "As I was with Moses, so I will be with you".

What a reminder to us, as God was with us in our times, He will be with our children! He will raise up "Joshua" as leaders for the next generation to lead them towards God.

Dear LORD, thank you for Your promise over my life that I see being fulfilled according to Your will and timing. Thank you for allowing me to see the unimaginable, unfathomable things which I had never thought of before. Help me to trust You even more and no matter what I face in life, may I continue to rest in Your promise for my future and that of our next generations. In Jesus' name, Amen!

Death could not hold Him down - April 4

Jesus said to her, "I am the resurrection and the life. The one who believes in me will live, even though they die; and whoever lives by believing in me will never die. Do you believe this?" John 11: 25-26

Many people were probably upset that we were not be able to celebrate Easter during the Covid-19 lockdown. True, that we may not have been able to celebrate Easter in the traditional and business form with Easter bunnies, Egg hunts and Easter brunches and all, like we are used to, but for the first time we had the opportunity to celebrate Easter for what it really is. God shut down all other ways of celebration so that we could focus on what Easter is truly about.

Easter is not about man-made traditions like we think. Easter bunnies, baskets and egg hunts have nothing to do with Easter. Easter is just another name for the beginning of Spring, new life. And since we see more bunnies and lilies come around this time, we have used these as a symbol of Easter and have started to put our focus on such instead of the true reason for this special day.

The real reason for celebration of this day is because it is the Resurrection Day of Jesus Christ who rose back to life after He was crucified on Good Friday. If it were not for this day, Christianity would be worthless. Christianity is the faith and worship of the living God who is not an imagination or some dead person or object. Death had no power over Jesus and could not hold Him down. Even if we killed Jesus in His human body, He rose back up again, He is Alive and living. And He has promised to return to take us back to live with Him eternally.

We need to understand that Easter can never be cancelled. All powers of hell could not cancel the resurrection of Jesus Christ. Therefore, we must celebrate the resurrection of our Lord Jesus Christ from our hearts and truly reflect on what it means for each one of us individually.

Dear LORD, thank you for Your victory over death and being our God who is alive and real. Please help me to believe that Jesus' resurrection is not only for one day of the year to be remembered. Jesus is alive and I too must resurrect from my old, sinful ways and live each day for You, not just on Resurrection Sunday. In Jesus' name, Amen!

In a twinkling of an eye - April 5

Then, together with them, we who are still alive and remain on the earth will be caught up in the clouds to meet the Lord in the air. Then we will be with the Lord forever. 1 Thessalonians 4:17

For many as soon as Easter is over, we think that God's story is also over. Some believe that Jesus' story only extends from His birth to resurrection. They think that once He rose back from the dead, Jesus is back up in heaven and from there He watches over us and takes care of our needs until we die. But the story is not finished yet and the next chapter is about to begin! According to the prophetic timetable of the Bible, the next major event is about to take place. And it might be like what we are experienced during the shutdown due to the Covid-19 pandemic. We noticed that people are missing from everywhere. There was hardly any human sound around and we could clearly hear the birds chirping. Our streets, roads, malls, schools, churches, and offices were mostly empty. There were only a hand-full of essential folks to be seen.

But when the next biblical event takes place, the essential people in God's eyes will be the ones missing, and the non-essential folks will be around. This event is referred to as the Rapture. It is when in a matter of the twinkling of the eye, God will snatch away those people who are alive and have believed in Jesus. They will be caught up in clouds with God in a snap and be completely gone from earth. Streets, roads, malls, schools, churches and offices will only be partially full of only those folks who have chosen not to accept Jesus. For those who are remaining, there will be chaos and confusion as people will not understand what happened and how to bring it back in order. Life for those left behind will not be the same any longer and will have to endure more hardships that are yet to come. To spare His people from the awaiting tribulation to take place, God will remove His children first before all these takes place. Only those who have not believed in Jesus and still deny Him, will be left on earth to deal with it.

The Rapture is surely to take place soon, but we just do not know the exact time or date. God has given us warning signs to watch out for which have already started showing and know that time is at hand. It will occur like a thief in the night so we must be ready at any moment.

Dear LORD, may I be prepared for You when You return. Help me to live righteously so that whenever that moment arrives, I will be found in You. I pray for those who do not know You yet that they will not waste any more time in ignorance but take this opportunity while they still have it to accept You. In Jesus' name, Amen!

Blind faith - April 6

"Watch out for false prophets. They come to you in sheep's clothing, but inwardly they are ferocious wolves." Matthew 7:15

A ministry scam was unfolded recently where a church named "His Name is Flowing Oil" distributed and "healed" people using Bibles which the ministers claimed had holy oil flowing through these Bibles. Upon investigation, the leader admitted to buying gallons of mineral oil from a local Tractor Supply Co. The Bibles were basically dipped in this oil and given out to people who believed that the oil that was dripping was holy and supernatural.

We all have a spiritual need and look for someone or something to meet it. Particularly, when we are vulnerable to sickness or an issue which we are facing, we become prone to accepting whatever is presented to us as spiritual truth. Especially when it comes to Christianity, because we know that there is power in the name of Jesus, many of us fall for anything that comes in the name of Jesus. And that is how many false preachers and prophets scam people using the name of Jesus. Even certain videos and text messages that are sent to us telling us to pray and forward them to a certain amount of people in order to be blessed or healed, are nonsense and have no truth in them. God does not need the approval of certain amount of people in order to do something. Nor do we need to subscribe or order any healing oils, blankets or material that claims to have some spiritual power in it. There is only one source of truth and power, and that is Jesus Christ himself. There is no other medium to get to Jesus, He is directly available to us through prayer and faith.

The Bible clearly warns us to beware of those "wolves" who come in sheep's clothing to deceive people. We cannot have blind faith and just believe and do something because someone claims it in the name of Jesus. We need to test everything and see if it is from God before we believe it. If it truly is from God, it will most definitely be proven as truth. We need know the word of God intimately, be wise to discern between truth or false and not just blindly follow unfaithful rituals and leaders.

Dear LORD, please open my spiritual eyes to see Your truth in every matter. Help me not to be deceived by false teachings, have counterfeit faith in materials or go through other channels to come to You. Thank you for making Yourself directly available to me and giving me hope in You to meet my needs. In Jesus' name, Amen!

No room for negativity - April 7

For by your words you will be justified, and by your words you will be condemned. Matthew 12:37

The Battle of Jericho was the first battle fought by the Israelites in the conquest of Canaan. The walls of Jericho fell after the Israelites marched every day once for six days around the city and seven times on the seventh day then blew their trumpets. During the six days of marching, the Israelites were ordered to march in silence, without raising their voices or saying a word.

From pervious experiences since the times of Moses, Joshua had witnessed the complaining and grumbling done by the Israelites so he knew what kind of things they would say. So, he commanded them to be silent until the right time. Their negative words uttered could be heard by their enemies which would give them an opportunity to take advantage of their weakness and come against the Israelites. Therefore, they were told to be silent and not ruin the good that was coming up shortly.

Our words have power to make or break. If we have believed and uttered something by faith once, yet start doubting and speaking negative afterwards, we cancel out our faith. We give devil an invitation to destroy our faith and courage when we show him any signs of weakness or fear. He is always listening to our words and the moment we utter something negative; he adds fuel to the fire by adding doubtful thoughts in our head and cause us to be fearful and give up.

Therefore, it is critical to watch what we say. We need to turn our doubtful words into faith-filled words and turn our negativity into thankfulness. Instead of saying "if", let's replace it with "when" and thank God in advance for what He will surely do.

Dear LORD, set a watch over my mouth that I only speak words of faith and those that build up. Please help me to not allow my circumstances to utter negative, doubtful words. Teach me to turn my worry into worship and claim the promises that You have made to me. In Jesus' name, Amen!

"Anyone who listens to my teaching and follows it is wise, like a person who builds a house on solid rock". Matthew 7:24

Every morning my phone is bombarded with text messages and forwards, flooded with Bible verses and encouraging words of the day. It is a good reminder about God's word and sometimes just what we need to hear. But often these messages are just passed around without much meaning to the sender or receiver. In many cases, the sender does not even bother reading the message but just forwards it along to others who they think the message may pertain to. They just forward it because it looks interesting and the receiver too may read it just for the sake of reading it. It is just passing around of information that we have gotten from somewhere else. Due to technology, we are overloaded with all sort of information, but our brain does not know what to do with it.

This includes information about the Bible that we are overloaded with each day. We educate ourselves with tons of information about God's word. We may know everything we need to know about the Bible and its truths, but just knowing about it does not serve any purpose if do not abide by it. What good is to just send and receive these biblical messages if we do not take them to heart? The purpose of reading God's word and any messages related to it is to learn from it so that we can walk in it. They are meant to encourage us about God's love, promises and to build us up in Christ. But if we just toss these messages back and forth to each other without giving it much thought to it ourselves, we devalue God's word and make it quite common. Like a precious jewel that we would not handle lightly and pass it along so easily, so is any information about God's word which we must treat as priceless when it is in our possession in any form.

Dear LORD, thank you for giving us technology to share Your word around. Please help me to not take it lightly though and pass it around like any other forwarded messages that I receive but teach me to meditate and abide by what has been shared to me. Open my heart to learn first before I share it with others. In Jesus' name, Amen!

Criteria for heaven - April 9

If you confess with your mouth that Jesus is Lord and believe in your heart that God raised him from the dead, you will be saved. Romans 10:9

Filling out applications for acceptance into college is such a tedious process. It requires so much information and has many eligibility criteria such as GPA, attendance, SAT scores, essays, and extra-curricular activities. Everything is scrutinized in detail before an institution considers the student for acceptance.

Thank God that our acceptance into heaven does not have such tight measures. Unlike colleges, God is not impressed with our list of church-related activities, perfect attendance in church, amount of donations that we give, or how we score in knowledge of the bible. It does not matter to God whether we are an executive of a company, leader in church or what our prestige is amongst others. All our money, titles, and good works may gain us acceptance to worldly institutions, but these are worthless at the gates of heaven.

The only criteria to be saved and get into heaven is to acknowledge Jesus Christ as our only God, believe in His death and resurrection, and confess our sins. God will not hold us accountable for our confessed sins nor will He keep track of how many times we have failed him and stumbled. If we come clean in front of Him and accept Jesus as our savior, He accepts us just as we are with no fear of rejection. Everyone is eligible to gain acceptance into heaven, but it is a matter for us to decide if that is where we want to go.

Dear LORD, thank you for not being a demanding God and setting up high standards to be accepted into Your heavenly home. It cost You Your life to get us admission into Your kingdom, so please help me not to take it lightly but be grateful for Your undeserved mercy upon me. In Jesus' name, Amen!

No one should seek their own good, but the good of others. 1 Corinthians 10: 24

William Booth, the founder of the Salvation Army, when asked to give a speech about the Salvation Army, summarized it in one word "Others". He basically covered his whole message through this word to describe the works of the Salvation Army and challenged us to think of Others. The mission of the Salvation Army is to serve others by first providing necessities of the physical body such as food, clothing and shelter. And while these needs are being met, we demonstrate God's love through our act of service and lead them to Spiritual Salvation.

The world that we live in today is a "Me" world. We are taught and trained to think of ourselves first and do whatever it takes to please ourselves and accommodate our needs before we reach out help others. But it is a biblical commandment that we ought to also help those in need and not just help ourselves. Many of us hesitate to help others because we have experienced abuse of our helpful nature in the past and have been taken advantage of, but this should not stop us from being generous. God gives us wisdom to recognize a true need and we cannot remain ignorant when someone can use some of what we already have plenty of.

The purpose of being blessed is not to hoard the blessings for ourselves but to share our abundance with those in need. It is a blessing to be able to be able to give, and the more we give the more we receive of God's blessings. Through our giving of our finances, service and time to others, we proclaim God's love.

Therefore, let us not be selfish but think of others also and demonstrate God's love to them through our generosity.

Dear LORD, I am grateful for the abundance of blessings that You have given me. Help me not take it for granted or think that I have earned these. It is only due to Your grace and favor, that I have been blessed. So please help me to bless others by sharing what I have. Help me to love and serve sacrificially like You do. May I reflect You by my selfless giving. In Jesus' name, Amen!

Giving my best - April 11

But I, the Lord, search all hearts and examine secret motives. I give all people their due rewards, according to what their actions deserve. Jeremiah 17:10

Our son had an important basketball game yesterday and so I prayed for God to give him the skills, strength and wisdom to play well. I hesitated to pray for him to win as I was not sure if it was right of me to ask for my son's team to win over the other team who may have worked equally hard and also desired it. So, I left the outcome of the game in God's hand and said, "Let my child give his best and may the team who deserves it, win".

We often ask God to give us something, win in games, get highest scores on tests or be recognized as best at work. We ask for His help in receiving the highest level of success, but many times it is not accompanied with our own hard work. In order to win or achieve something, we need to work at it. God takes note of our desire, motive, diligence and labor in what we do and rewards us accordingly. God is delighted when He sees His children work hard and are faithful, and He often blesses us with more than what we ask or deserve because of His favor that rests on us. He aids us along the way and pushes us to do our best by giving us the ability and courage to accomplish it. And when God sees us leaning on Him and doing our best, He gives us His best in return. But if we are in it to win it for selfish purpose or pride, God does not support it.

We can ask God to win or give us something big, but we must take into consideration our own diligence and purpose in it also. It is not that God does not want to give us the victory, but He does not reward selfishness, laziness and half-hearted jobs. He wants us to give our best in everything that we do and enjoy the fruit of our labor.

Dear LORD, please help me to understand that it is not about winning or losing but it is about giving my best to You. Teach me to work hard and be diligent in all my duties. In all that I do, may I represent You by my actions and words. Whether I win or lose, I give You the glory. In Jesus' name, Amen!

Fear and faith cannot coexist - April 12

For God has not given us a spirit of fear, but of power and of love and of a sound mind. 2 Timothy 1:7

We all fear something. There are physical things that make us afraid then there are those emotional and spiritual factors that make us fearful. Depending on what situation we are in, we often dread something negative to happen to us, so we pray about it out of fear. Out of anticipation of something bad happening to us, we draw ourselves to pray. Like Job in the Bible, many of us are fearful for our children so could that be the primary reason that we pray more fervently for them? Is it fear that makes us pray more than our faith? When Job's family was attacked, he said, "What I always feared has happened to me" (Job 3:25). If we dread it, we will most likely have to deal with it but if we do not even expect it by trusting God right from the beginning, we do not give any chance to the enemy.

When we pray out of the anticipation of what we fear will come true, our prayers become ineffective. Our prayers become powerless and they open the door for the thing that we fear to come upon us. As soon as we show a sign of fear in any area, the enemy targets that area and tries to mess us up, mostly succeeding in it as we are already vulnerable about it. The devil pays attention when we pray and what we talk about to others, and he takes note of those things which we fear and plead for. We abort our prayers when they are full of worry and fear. Therefore, our prayers and choice of words ought always to be full of faith, not showing any signs of fear or vulnerability. Instead of expressing fear, we need to express our confidence in God. God has not given us a spirit to fear but to face the devil with boldness and trust in God.

Dear LORD, please help me to not allow fear to rule over me. Teach me to overcome fear with faith. Instead of doubting You and Your mighty power, help me to doubt Satan and his ability. May my prayers not be cancelled out due to my doubt and fear, but may they be effective as I claim victory in Your name. In Jesus' name, Amen!

Don't go to bed mad - April 13

In your anger do not sin. Do not let the sun go down while you are still angry, and do not give the devil a foothold. Ephesians 4: 26-27

One of the best beauty regimes that women normally follow is to take off their make up at nighttime before going to bed. The dirt, oil and make up left on the skin clogs the pores and prevents the skin to renew itself at night. As a result, the skin becomes dull and worsens as it does not have room to cleanse and restore itself.

In the same way, when we go to sleep with anger and hatred built up our hearts, we prevent our mind and soul from renewing new thoughts and feelings. Getting good sleep is not only necessary for our physical bodies but it also calms our mind and makes room for fresh outlook. And when we go to bed with negativity, the devil clogs up our mind with even more bitterness and hatred that we wake up worse than before. In our anger, we end up sinning with hurtful words and actions and if left undone, it continues to grow internally and eventually shows up on the outside in an unpleasant way.

It does not necessarily mean that we must resolve all fights right away no matter what before we go to bed. But we do need to have a heart to want to forgive and be forgiven and to be peaceful about it while we sleep so that when we do wake up, we are no longer angry but have a new, positive attitude to resolve the issue at its earliest.

Dear LORD, help me to ensure that I not only follow outward beauty regimes but also daily cleanse myself internally so that my true beauty radiates from inside out. Remove any negativity from my mind which clogs up Your word from coming through. Make my heart clean so that it can be a dwelling place for You. In all my being, let the beauty of Jesus be seen in me. In Jesus' name, Amen!

Living up to God's standards - April 14

If we are unfaithful, He remains faithful, for He cannot deny who He is. 2 Timothy 2:13

I f it were up to me, things would be different in my life. But thank God they are not! I am not confident in myself as I base daily decisions on my emotions, circumstances and need. I never succeed when I go off on my own and do not involve God. In my own understanding and self-righteousness, I make choices which are not necessarily aligned with God's. I fail all the time on my own, but I am so thankful that God does not fail me. I may not live up to His standards, but I praise His name that He does not expect me to.

God knows our weaknesses and He is aware of all that is going on in our lives. He knows that we fall short every time, but His Hand is not too short to save us out of our mess. We may feel that we let God down but when we feel low, He lifts us up. God does not hold anything against, instead He takes our mess and works with it to turn it into something beautiful.

As unfaithful we may be towards God, He remains faithful. This is who God is! His faithfulness does not vary or depend on how good and faithful we are to Him. We could be swayed by our emotions or situations, but it does not change God. God's faithfulness to us remains the same yesterday, today, and forever. Therefore, we need to remember, that although we are not confident in our faithfulness, our confidence is in God. He is faithful till the end!

Dear LORD, I thank you that I have You to rely on when I cannot rely on myself. Thank you for being my confidence and giving me hope that no matter who I am or what comes my way, You will remain faithful to me. Please help me to stand on Your promise of faithfulness, not on mine. In Jesus' name, Amen!

Unloading at the feet of Jesus - April 15

Give your burdens to the Lord, and He will take care of you. Psalm 55:22

It is a proven fact that when we talk to someone about whatever is bothering us, we feel better afterwards. We may bottle things up in our head and it keeps building up until we cannot contain it, and eventually burst out our feelings.

We often use prayer also as a means of unloading our thoughts. We may get into the posture of prayer and believe that we are talking to God but often our prayers are just us talking to ourselves. We speak out everything that is in our minds, but we may not necessarily talk to God. We could feel better afterwards as if we have said a good prayer, but truthfully, it is just words, a monologue of us pouring out our emotions, thoughts and ideas which do not really have any impact. But for our prayers to make God move, they need to be accompanied with a burden. If our prayer consists only of words but our heart is not heavy while praying, our prayer is not as effective. I am often asked to pray for others but if I just pray without feeling the burden or pain myself, my prayers just come out as words without much impact. But when I pray with full attention towards God, speak every word with faith and with a heavy burden for whomever I pray for, I know then it has drawn God's attention.

Therefore, when we pray, let us not bow down just to empty our emotions but rather carry a burden up to the cross and let God deal with it forward.

Dear LORD, thank you for the privilege to pray and talk to You. Please help me not to take this privilege lightly but understand that I am bringing my requests to You, the one who is powerful and able to answer my prayers. As I pour out my prayer, may it not only be filled with empty words and emotions but with a true burden which causes You to move. In Jesus' name, Amen!

Safe beneath His wings - April 16

He will cover you with His feathers; under His wings you will find refuge. Psalm 91:4

A few years ago, while commuting to college in the train, it stopped at a station longer than usual and there were few police officers going in and out of different carts as if searching for someone. They made their way into my cart, walked over up to me and grabbed the guy who was sitting right next to me. I and all the other passengers sat there speechless in awe. The guy could have hurt me or others to get away or fight back. I was in harm's way, but I did not even know it. I was oblivious to the danger I was surrounded by and sat there comfortably.

This situation reminds me of a little baby chick who is snuggled underneath its Mama chicken. To the chick, it does not matter what is going on outside, it knows very well that it is safe under the wings of its mom and rests peacefully. It is the chicken who looks out for danger and protects its chicks beneath its feathers. The little chick may sometimes try to step out on its own, but its mama would not let it go, knowing the danger that is out there, so it holds the chick tightly until the danger has passed.

We may not be aware of the danger that is lurking out there, but our Heavenly Father does. He puts a hedge of protection over us which we cannot escape from nor no evil that tries to come against, prospers in any way. He watches out for us and will not allow His children to be harmed by the evil one. We just need to trust God and rest assured in His promise and protection.

Dear LORD, I declare the hedge of your protection over my family and loved ones. Give charge to Your angels to watch over us and keep us away from all harm and danger. May we rest underneath the safety of your wings as we go about our daily lives. In Jesus' name, Amen!

Two-way promise - April 17

..."I will never leave you nor forsake you". Hebrews 13:5

We often say this Bible verse as reminder of Jesus' promise towards us when we feel alone, afraid or tensed about a matter. It is a promise of God's faithfulness to be with us regardless of our circumstances or unfaithfulness towards Him. He vows to stand by us and never turn away from us, even for a moment. We take rest in this and claim it with confidence because we know that God is a promise keeper and fulfills what He says.

As faithful God is to us in keeping His promise, we too should be faithful in return with our promise back to Him. It is not be considered a one-way deal but should apply to us as well. We should not expect Jesus to keep His promise while we turn away from ours. If we take Him up on His promise, shouldn't we reciprocate the same? Just as God promises to never leave us or forsake us, we also need to hold on to Jesus no matter what comes our way or whatever happens.

To leave something still has hope for its return. It could be temporary and depending on the circumstances, it may come back. While to forsake means to abandon and give up completely permanently. Often when fear and worry grip us, we may doubt if God has left us and wonder if He will ever come to our rescue. We may also feel that we have abandoned Him, and sin has separated us from each other. But the more our sin and situations try to separate us from God, the more we need to pull closer and cling on to Him.

Dear LORD, thank you for the promise to be with me in all times. I make a promise to You in return that no matter what comes my way, I too will never leave You or forsake You. Please give me Your grace to hold on to You as You always hold on to me. In Jesus' name, Amen!

Surrender to God, not to the enemy - April 18

Do not be afraid of those who kill the body but cannot kill the soul. Rather, be afraid of the One who can destroy both soul and body in hell. Matthew 10:28

When Pharaoh ordered for all baby boys of the Israelites to be killed, Moses' mom hid him for three months but when she no longer could do this, she put him in a basket and let it afloat on the river, leaving the child at God's mercy to do with baby Moses as He pleased. I cannot imagine the pain and sadness in the mother's heart while she had to let go off her precious baby under such adverse circumstances. As difficult as it must have been for her, Moses' mother was unwilling to succumb to the fate that Pharaoh had ordered, instead she was hopeful in God that He was mighty to save the child somehow and let him go.

Satan is like Pharaoh who is after us to kill and destroy our children, marriage, family, finances, health and peace. He is afraid of God's children to do exploits for Him and so the devil, our enemy prowls around to snatch us away. If we submit to his authority in fear, we allow ourselves to be under Satan's dominion. But if we surrender it to God, He works it for us in ways we cannot comprehend. God asks us to put our concerns in a "basket" and send them afloat towards Jesus. It may seem painful to not have control over our situation, not being able to do anything about it ourselves and the fear of the unknown may ache our hearts, but it's better to trust in God and let it go then to surrender it to the enemy.

Just as how God worked it out perfectly for Moses, not only to be saved but provided a way for his mom to be his care taker right under Pharaoh, God can do wonders for us also and turn our situations around perfectly in ways we cannot fathom.

So, whatever the enemy might be after us to destroy, instead of giving up and submitting under him, let's surrender it into God's hand and then watch and wait as He miraculously works it out beyond our ability and imagination.

Dear LORD, as the enemy is out there to destroy me, give me the strength to not succumb under his fear. Instead, increase my faith and help me to submit my worries to You. As You work it out on my behalf, help me to watch and wait with full hope and assurance of Your power which can do the impossible. In Jesus' name, Amen!

Business as usual – April 19

But understand this, that in the last days there will come times of difficulty. 2 Timothy 3:1

With the rapid spreading of the Corona Virus, government officials and businesses were assessing the safety and needs of the public. We had received a message from our boss that although our county was on shut-down, we were considered essential employees and needed to report to work for "business as usual".

Most of us are carrying on as "business as usual" with our spiritual lives also despite what is going on around us. God is giving us clear warning signs of the things and events that would take place such as what is happening currently – plagues (diseases which are unheard of), fires, earthquakes, wars, famine, lawlessness (no morals), cold-hearted (no love or respect for anyone and doing whatever makes "me" happy) and increase of human knowledge, but decrease in belief of God.

Just as a thief does not announce when he comes in to steal, so will God come at a moment which we do not know. But He did provide us with these "signals" to watch out for and be prepared for His coming. The difficulties we are experiencing right now warn us that God's coming is near, and we must not take it lightly and continue as usual as if it is no big deal. We do not have much longer to wait for repentance or ignore it and assume it will go away. The earth and we all will pass away at some point, now or a little later, as our mortal bodies and this physical world are temporary, but we still have our eternal life to live. And there are only two choices for eternity – heaven or hell. The decision is in our hands and must be made in this life-time where we will spend our eternal life.

Therefore, while amid the busyness, we ought to use some time to reflect on our spiritual standing with God. Before it is too late and we miss our window of opportunity of this decision, let us take care of this serious business first with Jesus.

Dear LORD, with all that is happening in and around us, thank you for giving us an opportunity still to turn to You before it too late. Please help me to take this matter seriously and ensure that I am secured in You now and for eternity. Thank you for Your protection over us while we endure the warnings that are blasting around us. I trust You and give You control of my life both now and forevermore. In Jesus' name, Amen!

But he knows where I am going. And when he tests me, I will come out as pure as gold. Job 23:10

The Egyptians were well known for developing the process for purifying gold and creating beautiful gold jewelry. The process involves the steps of mining it from the ground, washing off the dirt and deposits collected on it, and then putting it in intense heat for a few days to burn off any impurities that are wedged in it. After it is removed from the heat though, gold as pure as it can be is obtained.

Many Bible verses refer to us as gold and how God refines us in order to make us the best that we can be. He first plucks us out of the dirt, cleanses us with His holy blood and makes us go through intense heat of trials and temptations in order to purify us from all the impurities that are lodged in us. The process of being heated in the fire may be very painful, hotter than we can imagine, we even feel like jumping out and give up. But if God has chosen us, we are not meant to live a cool, comfortable lives. He tests our faith and places us inside the scorching heat when He sees any debris or impurity in us in order to make us pure as He wants. When we pass through the test and hang in there, the gold that He produces in us is like none other; we come out better and stronger than before.

Gold is gold and it can never lose its value once it is purified through the refiner's fire. Are you ready to be refined?

Dear LORD, when I cannot comprehend the purpose of the storms and trials that come my way, please help me to trust You as You lead me through the fire. Let me be still and know that You are God and know what You are doing with my life. May I be grateful for the refining process as You remove the impurities out of me which keep me away from You. It is my heart's desire to be holy so refine as needed to be fit for Your kingdom. In Jesus' name, Amen!

Standing in the gap - April 21

"I looked for someone among them who would build up the wall and stand before me in the gap on behalf of the land so I would not have to destroy it, but I found no one". Ezekiel 22:30

When the plague came on the Israelites due to their complaining against Moses and God, God's wrath had come upon the nation and He sent a plague which spread like a wildfire, killing people in its way. Moses ordered Aaron, his brother the priest, to take his censer (vessel which holds burning coals from the altar) and add incense (fragrance) in it and stand quickly in the pathway of the plague, between the dead and the living. The incense that would be offered up to God as an atonement for the sin of the people was meant to appease the wrath. When Aaron went and stood in between the gap and offered the incense whose fragrance reached up to the skies, the plague stopped!

Incense, in the Bible, represents our prayers. We as believers in Christ have the priestly duty to offer our incense of prayer and stand in the gap of the storms that rage against us. The only and foremost effective way to stop the enemy is by our prayers. We've taken prayer lightly and removed it out of our homes, schools and offices but it's about time we realize that there is tremendous power in prayer and need to bring it back as it is a requirement from God. While things of the world seem to be out of control from our hands, it is time to open our eyes and see who truly is in control. Collectively as followers of Jesus, we need to intercede on behalf of the rest of the world and seek God's help.

But we must first humble ourselves and turn from our wicked ways and seek God with all our hearts, then we will find God, and He will listen to our cry!

Dear LORD, thank you for the privilege of prayer. Help me to understand the power of prayer and use it as a tool to reach out to You for help. Help me to pray whole-heartedly and seek You by humbling myself before You. Thank you in advance that You have heard my cry as I stand in between the gap and offer You my incense of prayer on behalf of myself, my loved ones and nation. In Jesus' name, Amen!

God Positioning System - April 22

Show me your ways, LORD, teach me your paths. Guide me in your truth and teach me, for you are God my Savior, and my hope is in you all day long.
Psalm 25: 4-5

We use GPS for directions which starts guiding us right from our house. To get to a certain highway, it often takes us through a longer, different route than the inside roads which we are familiar with. Although we know the way, we usually follow the direction given by our GPS, ending up in wasting more time and fuel.

Similarly, we find ourselves wandering in circles spiritually to find our way or find an answer, even if we know it already. We consult with all sorts of other "GPS" such as media, internet, books, and friends who all have varying answers and suggestions to our problems, causing us wander and be lost.

Even though we know very well that there is only one guide, the Bible, which points us in the right direction, we usually refer to it last. We know the direct way to our answer, but we choose to follow the advice and inputs of others rather than turning to God's word right away. And even when we eventually turn to it, we often interpret it in different ways to make it suitable to our needs. We rely on our own wisdom or the wisdom of others to interpret the meaning of the Bible and tell us what to do. These only leads us to being more confused and lost.

But instead of wandering around through different avenues and following the directions of everyone else, we need to refer to and only listen to the God-Positioning-System of our life that points us in the direct direction, the Bible.

Dear LORD, may Your word be my handbook of life which I refer to first for all answers. Help me not to misunderstand it and take on a different meaning than what it truly means. Please be my teacher and instruct me into all truth and holy living. In Jesus' name, Amen!

Order of priorities - April 23

But be sure that everything is done properly and in order. 1 Corinthians 14:40

When the pandemic of the Coronavirus hit our planet and affected all people across the globe, we felt like the world turned upside down. Though, I believe that it has caused us to turn back the right side up again in many ways.

We humans have forced the world in reverse order by going against God. We have gone in the opposite direction of every principle that God taught us in His Word. What God calls good, we call it bad, what God says is right, we say it is false; totally disregarding His commandments and doing everything which God has told us not to. Majority of the world population has completely removed God out of their lives, living in unbelief and without any morals. It has become a "Me" world, doing whatever seems right to each. We have completely changed the order of God's system, His values, ethics, principles and priorities, and now while He is bringing us back into order, we call the world as turning upside down.

The primary order of our priorities should be God, family, and others which God is putting back into perspective for us yet again. He brought to halt the "others" such as hanging out, parties, sports, dining out, spending money on unnecessary stuff and leisurely activities and forced us to be with our family so that we can rebuild those relationships which had ignored due to our busyness. God freed up our schedules and shut out the "noises" around us so that we could have quiet time and restore our relationship which we cut off with Him. We were placed in this position so that we could realize our human limitations and need for God's intervention. As much as we have made ourselves to be self-sufficient, self-pleasing, God-free society, it's about time that we open our eyes and understand that we are nothing without God and our lives must revolve around Him first.

When God brings us back into the right order, let us truly accept it as the truth and keep it that way!

Dear LORD, thank you for putting us back into the right order of Your value system. Please help me to be convicted of this truth and make every effort to keep my priorities straight by keeping You foremost in my life and then my spouse, children and afterwards extend out towards others as needed. Please give me the heart and wisdom to abide by Your wonderful design of significance which you have created for us. In Jesus' name, Amen!

Royal family member - April 24

And He said, "Unto you it is given to know the mysteries of the kingdom of God". Luke 8:10

Many years ago, in the news I heard about an Indian nurse who committed suicide because she gave away details about Princess Kate's pregnancy to a Radio Station unknowingly. An Australian radio station had made a prank phone call to the hospital where Princess Kate was admitted for treating her acute morning sickness due to pregnancy. The hosts of the radio stations pretended to be Prince Charles and Queen Elizabeth and were able to get through to the ward and get details which were broadcasted throughout Europe. Upon hearing of the hoax call, the nurse was so embarrassed and so fearful of the consequences about leaking details about the Duchess, that she committed suicide the next day.

I am so fascinated with the Royal family, Buckingham Palace and its royalty that it made me really think about how powerful the Royal family truly is that someone actually took their own life in fear of the Queen due to sharing of their personal information. Thank God our King is not like that. Even though Jesus Christ is the king of kings and Lord of lords, He is the gentlest of all. He is available for us to meet Him whenever we want and approach His throne without fear. God is full of grace and mercy, and we can run to Him and find peace rather than fear. Our king does not hide any details from us about His kingdom, rather He came Himself in the humblest way to tell us about it and to show us the way to His majestic palace, which is far beyond comparison to any earthly palaces. Everyone is welcomed into His kingdom regardless of who we are and what we have done. He gives us the right to be called His children and become a part of His Royal family. There are no consequences of our sins if we ask God for forgiveness. All He asks is that we truly accept Him as our Savior and allow Him reign in our hearts.

Dear LORD, thank you that I have the freedom to approach You whenever I want and confess my sins without the fear of retribution. Thank you for giving me the right to be called Your child. I am honored to be a part of Your Royal family. Please help me to live up to our family name and bring You glory by my life. In Jesus' name, Amen!

Blame game - April 25

"For I know that I'm to blame for this violent storm that is against you." Jonah 1:12

Lately we received certain videos which suggested that due to the sins of idol worshipping of some Christian nations, certain disasters have come upon us. The hardships that we face have often been attributed to some specific sins and disobedience of a group of people.

When Jonah fled from God's presence and took a ship going in the opposite direction, God caused a storm to come on the sea which affected not only Jonah but also the other sailors with him in the ship, and whoever else might have been in the sea at that time. It was due to the disobedience of Jonah as an individual though that brought this storm on them all together.

In the same manner, we should consider our own sins as an individual that could have attributed to the hardships that we face as family, church, community or a nation. We all play a significant role in disobedience towards God and must not blame each other. We may not be the ones who worship a man-made statue, but we all worship other forms of idols such as people, food, phone, sports, addiction, etc. Anything that we replace God with, is an idol and we all are guilty of idol-worshipping.

So, let us reflect on our own sins before we point at someone else. None of us are better or holier than anyone else when it comes to sin as the Bible says, "All have sinned and fallen short of the glory of God" (Romans 3:23). Instead of wasting our time and energy playing the blame game, we should focus on repenting of our own sin and ensure that we are right with God as individuals first and then collectively.

Dear LORD, please help me to focus on my own disobedience towards You rather than pointing fingers at others. Help me not be a judge and be ready to throw a stone at anyone else when I myself am guilty of many unmentionable sins which only You and I know. Please remove idols from my life which I have replaced You with and lead me to personal repentance. In Jesus' name, Amen!

The invisible enemy - April 26

For we do not wrestle against flesh and blood, but against the rulers, against the authorities, against the cosmic powers over this present darkness, against the spiritual forces of evil in the heavenly places. Ephesians 6:12

The Coronavirus is also called the invisible enemy. We cannot predict who has it and whom it is going to next. We can only detect it after the damage is done. A nurse explained that "In a combat, you know where the shots are coming from but in this war, we fight against an invisible enemy and cannot tell from which direction it attacks". If the virus came with some obvious signs on a person, we could stay away but how could we hide or stay away from someone or something that we cannot even tell has been affected? The best we could do is stay indoors, try not touch anything that has come from outside and wash our hands frequently.

This virus is a good example of how an invisible enemy works. Satan operates just like this and we are in a spiritual warfare with him. He attacks us with spiritual viruses such as anger, gossip, lust, pride, lying, stealing and cheating. These viruses are unseen to the physical eye as they stem from within and hard to detect. The devil infects us with these and penetrates our mind and body causing us to fall into sin. We then infect others by pulling them into our sinful mess and cause them to fall also.

If we fail to recognize the symptoms and guard ourselves against his attacks, we become Satan's target. Therefore, we should protect ourselves by keeping ourselves isolated from worldly desires. We must focus on God's word so that we do not give the devil any room to enter in our minds and corrupt us. We need to continually refresh and cleanse ourselves by prayer and repentance. These viruses are as deadly to our spiritual body as the coronavirus is to our physical body. Therefore, let us take every measure to protect and guard our body, mind and soul against these enemies.

Dear LORD, thank you for always being there for me and helping me with my physical and spiritual battles. I do recognize that I too must engage in this war and do my part so please help to be vigilant and increase my strength and faith to fight against these foes. I claim that no weapon formed against me will prosper by Your help and power working in me. In Jesus' name, Amen!

Leave room for God's plans - April 27

"For my thoughts are not your thoughts, neither are your ways my ways," declares the LORD. As the heavens are higher than the earth, so are my ways higher than your ways and my thoughts than your thoughts". Isaiah 55:8-9

For our son's 18th Birthday, we had made some plans of celebration. We had decided that we would do such and such and had everything figured out. Lo and behold, none of it happened as we had planned due to the pandemic situation that forced mostly all plans of weddings, parties, sports, conferences and other functions to be cancelled or postponed to an indefinite date. A few months prior to the onset of the plaque, none of us would have imagined ourselves to be in the situation we dealt with.

We just expect life to go on as usual each day by our plans and desires. We design our course in life and often fail to factor God's plan in it. We live and plan according to our limited understanding about everything. But God plans with the overall picture in mind. Many times, we override His purpose and end up failing because our will does not align to God's. Therefore, while making any plans and deciding to do something, we must seek God's will in it and allow Him to be a part of our agenda. It is not that God does not want us to think for ourselves and make plans, but we must leave room for God to modify them. If we trust in God then we must acknowledge that His ways are always better than ours and everything that happens to us, happens for a reason. God's plans are for our own good so whether we agree or not, we ought to surrender to God and allow His will to prevail ours.

Dear LORD, please help me to trust in Your plans as You unfold them for me day to day. You are the God of the past, present and future and know what is good or harmful for us so I invite You to take over my agenda and align it according to Your master plan. Help me to be open to Your will and come in agreement with You however you lead me. In Jesus' name, Amen!

Social distancing - April 28

After leaving them, he went up on a mountainside to pray. Mark 6:46

We were given orders by authorities to practice social distancing during the Covid-19 pandemic. According to the guidelines, we were to keep a physical distance between two bodies, at least six feet apart in order to minimize contact.

God also used this situation to distance us from the worldly things. He removed us from all activities that kept us busy and away from Him. But when physical distance was enforced, we came closer to each other by engulfing ourselves in social media using our technological means. We all spent more time on our phones and tv, checking people's social status, and even "spent time with God", by participating in multiple online prayer services. Truthfully though, for some of us, these are only excuses and indirect way to socialize with each other while still being in the confines of our isolated homes.

God has given us the time of quietness purposely so that we can withdraw ourselves away from the rest of the world and spend some one on one time with Him. Jesus himself practiced social distancing often by pulling Himself away from everyone else and spend quiet time in prayer and meditation.

If Jesus thought it necessary to withdraw from people and be by Himself with His Heavenly Father, then shouldn't we have a much more need for it?

It is good to socialize, check up on and pray with others, but we must not consume all our time fully to these. We must continue to practice social distancing literally, away from everyone and everything else, and isolate ourselves alone with God to be refreshed and rejuvenated in our walk with God.

Dear LORD, as You give me the opportunity to pull myself away from my busy schedule, please help me to use that precious time to come closer to You. Give me a heart to understand the value and need for social distancing. And help me to isolate myself from others to be in Your presence and give You my undivided time and attention. In Jesus' name, Amen!

Den of robbers - April 29

Search me, O God, and know my heart; test me and know my anxious thoughts. Point out anything in me that offends you and lead me along the path of everlasting life. Psalm 139: 23-24

After His triumphal entry into Jerusalem, Jesus entered the Temple and saw how it had turned into a marketplace (buying and selling of sacrificial things) and a place of worship of people (honoring the priests and pharisees) instead of a true place of worship of God. Jesus was overcome with righteous anger and drove out the people who were misusing this Holy place. He was mostly angry with the pharisees, the teachers of the law, who encouraged it and themselves did not follow what they preached. As a physical building is a place of worship of God, so are our bodies whom Jesus has called as His Holy Temple because God's Holy Spirit lives in us. We as individuals and collectively make up the church of God. So, we each have a responsibility as individuals and the church body put together to keep God's Temple holy.

These days, the church has become a house of worship of people, materials and unrighteousness rather than a house of worship of God. There are many who misuse their power and talents to blatantly do what is wrong in God's sight, and still justify themselves righteous. We as individuals also abuse our Holy Temple and misuse our bodies. We are God's children and are called to keep our temples holy which means we need to take care of our physical and spiritual body by watching what we do with it. Things that we eat, drink, see, hear, say, think and do affect our body, mind and soul. Therefore, it is necessary that we live a holy life and make our body a dwelling place for God.

If Jesus came into our churches today and into our individual temples, I am confident that He would find many unrighteous things and events taking place that would cause God to get angry with us. Jesus' anger is righteous, and He is a just God who cannot tolerate unrighteousness to exist in His temple. So, if want to God's spirit to live within us and be a part of our church, we must allow God to sweep us and drive out everything that is a reason for Him to exit from us.

Dear LORD, please cleanse my body, mind and soul from anything that causes You to be unpleased with me. Please show me those areas in my life which need cleansing, and may I allow You to wash me with Your blood so that my body truly becomes Your holy temple. Please remove impurities and all unrighteousness from our churches also so that they genuinely become Your dwelling place and not a den of robbers. In Jesus' name, Amen!

Vaccine for sin - April 30

For God made Christ, who never sinned, to be the offering for our sin, so that we could be made right with God through Christ. 2 Corinthians 5:21

When disease germs enter our body, they start to reproduce. Our immune system recognizes these germs as foreign invaders and responds by making proteins called antibodies. These antibodies' job is to help destroy the germs that make us sick and then to protect us from future infections. This is called immunity, the preparedness of our body to fight future attacks. And vaccines help us develop this immunity. Vaccines are made from the same germs (or parts of them) that cause disease. But the germs in vaccines are either killed or weakened so they will not make us sick. Our immune system reacts to the vaccine in a similar way that it would if it were being invaded by the disease — by making antibodies. The antibodies destroy the vaccine germs just as they would the disease germs. Then they stay in our body, giving us immunity. So, if we are ever exposed to the real disease, the antibodies are there to protect us.

Similarly, Jesus' death behaved like a vaccine to fight against sin. Since we are born with a sin nature, Jesus came into this world to fight against sin by becoming a sin himself so that we could be cleared from the punishment of sin. Sin invades our body by starting off as a desire for something that is against God's law. And when we turn that desire into action, it becomes a sin which results in our eventual spiritual death.

Therefore, it is necessary that we prepare ourselves ahead of time against the invasion of sin by getting vaccinated through Jesus' precious blood which fights against it. When we allow Jesus to penetrate our hearts, the more immune we become to sin, and it does not destroy us.

Dear LORD, thank you for being my defense system against the sin in my life. If it were not for Your blood that was shed on the cross for me, I would be dead to sin. But because of Your grace and love only, I am considered righteous in God's sight. Please help me to use Your word and prayer as my antibodies to fight against the sin which continuously tries to invade my spiritual body. In Jesus' name, Amen!

May

Faith building - May 1

...If you have faith the size of a mustard seed, you will say to this mountain, 'Move from here to there,' and it will move; and nothing will be impossible to you.
Matthew 17:20

The land of Israel was under severe famine and Elijah was praying to God to let it rain. Elijah sent his servant seven times to go outside and look towards the sea to check if rain was in sight. Six times the servant came back saying there was nothing in sight. But every time the servant gave a negative answer, Elijah continued to pray and did not give up until finally the seventh time, the servant saw a small cloud as big a man's hand rising in the sea. Elijah's faith and prayer finally paid off and the little cloud grew bigger and by the time it came to land, there was a heavy downpour.

Mostly when we pray, we pray as if to receive an answer right away. We feel as if we have prayed with all our heart and are confident in an answered prayer immediately. And when we do not get what we asked for, we get discouraged, start doubting God, give up on Him, and start finding our own solution to the problem. But we need to learn from Elijah that even when he did not see his prayer answered right away, Elijah did not give up and stopped praying. Instead he prayed even more and continued until his prayer was finally answered. In the same manner, when our prayer is not answered quickly, we must not get discouraged but rather pray even more and with more urgency. We must not give up thinking that God is not listening, or that His answer is no.

Every time that Elijah prayed, he had to build his faith, starting from none to as small as a mustard seed. And when God saw Elijah's faith and fervency, He answered him back with a cloud as small as a man's hand. Faith as small as a mustard seed can grow and move mountains, and a cloud as small as a hand can build up and cause flooding. God often waits for our faith to build up and then responds us with downpour of blessings which we could not have imagined before. Therefore, when we feel our prayer is not getting an answer, God is waiting for our faith to be built up. And when our faith grows, the more the closer we are to an answered prayer. The reply is already on its way, we just need to see it coming by faith.

Dear LORD, please help me to not get discouraged and give up when I do not receive an answer from you right away. Instead increase my faith and help me to continue in prayer without worrying about how long or how many times I need to pray. May my faith-filled prayer reach your ears and cause you to move on my behalf. In Jesus' name, Amen!

Blind spot - May 2

And if your eye causes you to sin, tear it out and throw it away. It is better for you to enter life with one eye than with two eyes to be thrown into the hell of fire. Matthew 18:9

In driving, a blind spot is any area immediately surrounding our vehicle that cannot directly be observed by the driver within the normal field of vision. It is that awkward view where another vehicle is close on the side but is not in our view since it is not directly in front of us or behind us. In order to notice it we must physically turn our head to see it and evaluate its closeness to our vehicle before proceeding. If we fail to recognize the vehicle in the blind spot, we end up in a disastrous situation.

In life, there exists people in our life who are in our blind spot. These are folks who we are close to and they walk side by side in our circle of family, friends, peers, church and community. We have a closeness to them and build our trust and comfort zone around these folks. There are genuine family and friends who care for us and truly come along side us in our journey of life through thick and thin, but not everyone that is near us are for our good. There are those who block our vision of the truth, disrupt our focus from God, cut us off on the road and provoke us to fall into sin by swerving us off the path that God has planned for us.

Often, some of the closest people to us are in our blind spot and the most dangerous. Therefore, we must turn our heart through prayer and ask God to give us vision to recognize the folks who may be a danger to us spiritually, emotionally and off course physically. We as Christians often force ourselves to love, bear and live peacefully with everyone knowing it's a command from God but we need to know that the Bible says, that "as much as it depends on you" which implies that after we've done our best to resolve and restore, if there still remains animosity and any other sinful act between us, we must remove ourselves from those specific people and situation. It is time for us to evaluate people who are in our life and check if they are pulling us down or building us up in Christ. We may not necessarily be able to detach ourselves physically from certain folk, but we can remove ourselves from harm's way by detaching spiritually and emotionally.

Dear LORD, give me wisdom to recognize people who are close beside me in my blind spot. May I be alert for spiritual danger and by Your help, remove myself away from those areas that seek to make me fall. I give you permission to search my life and remove anyone who is a threat in my righteous walk with You. In Jesus' name, Amen!

Recall God's miracles - May 3

When you have eaten and are satisfied, praise the LORD your God for the good land he has given you. Deuteronomy 8:10

After Jesus miraculously fed the crowd of over 5,000 people with only 5 loaves of bread and 2 fish, He had the disciples pick up 12 baskets full of leftovers of broken pieces. I'm pretty certain that if Jesus had the ability to multiply the loaves and the fish, He was also capable of knowing exactly how many people were there and would've multiplied it just enough for everyone to eat satisfactorily without having any left overs. But Jesus purposely had the leftovers and made the disciples collect the broken pieces to remember this miracle and God's power. Which of course, the disciples forgot as soon as they were hit with the next storm and trouble came on them once again.

After having witnessed God's miracles in our lives, we too quickly forget them as soon as we come across another issue. Jesus continues to deliver us over and over and we continue to doubt Him over and over. As soon as the winds and waves of difficulties hit us and shake up our life, we tend to forget God's goodness and become fearful once again not only of our circumstances but also fear if God will come to our aid this time around.

The disciples had collected the baskets to remind them of how mighty our God is and nothing is impossible for Him to do yet they succumbed to fear and doubt. In the same way, God has given us our memory of broken pieces to carry with us, not to haunt us but as a reminder of how God delivered us the last time and give us hope that He can do it again.

Therefore, the next time when we find ourselves in a storm, we must look at our broken pieces of the past and recall God's miracles and call on Him to deliver us again. If He made a way before, He would surely come through again, but we must keep our eyes on Jesus and basketful of blessings that He has given to carry with us.

Dear LORD, thank you that You have given me numerous examples in my life to remember Your goodness. Please help me not to forget those hardships which You delivered us out of when we come across our next adversity but continue to trust You to come through again. Increase my faith to be confident that if You did it then, You will do it again. In Jesus' name, Amen!

The domino effects - May 4

If God is for us, who can be against us? Romans 8:31

We all must have experienced at one point in our lives that when something goes wrong, everything goes wrong. When one thing starts to fall apart, like a domino effect, everything else too seems to go down also. There is a spiritual reason behind this. There is a constant battle over us between God and the devil. The devil is always on a look out to destroy us and does everything in his power to pull us down. His goal is to disrupt our faith and loyalty to God. When Satan sees our closeness to God, he continues to add more chaos, confusion, afflictions and temptations to our lives till we cannot sustain any longer. He throws every obstacle in our way as we keep holding on to God and sifts us around so that we would fall out and eventually give up. But God, on the other hand, counter measures every attempt of the devil by making us stronger. The more opposition that we face, God increases our strength. The more the devil tries to shake us up, the more God stabilizes us. He will not allow His children to fail if we continue to remain in the battle from God's side.

Therefore, it is necessary from our part that we do not give up but remain close to God, particularly during times of adversity. If we ourselves become fearful and allow the devil to take away our joy and hope, then God unwillingly remains silent until we are ready for His help. God does not wish for His children to suffer or be snatched away by the devil, but He will not deliver us out of something that we ourselves do not want to be delivered of. In order for God to move on our behalf, we too must be willing to accept God's help. We must make the first move away from the devil and towards God. When God sees our effort and eagerness, He takes over and fights for us. And if God is with us, the domino effect of adversity can reverse and make us stand upright again!

Dear LORD, please help me not to succumb into the devil when hardships come my way. Although the devil may try to shake up my faith, I thank You for building me up even more. Please help me to remain true to You just as You always remain faithful to me. In Jesus' name, Amen!

Fight like there is no tomorrow - May 5

Be alert and of sober mind. Your enemy the devil prowls around like a roaring lion looking for someone to devour. Resist him, standing firm in the faith... 1 Peter 5:8-9

Our 14-pound puppy, Teddy was attacked by two approximately 60 pounds dogs when were on our walk recently. The two dogs charged at Teddy out of nowhere, grabbed by him by the tail, tried to drag him, and then pulled him by the stomach and neck, ready to bite and hurt him. My husband and I had to fight off the dogs to save our dog. It was a scary couple of minutes, but we did all that we could to help our poor little helpless dog. We never imagined ourselves in a situation like this, particularly fighting big dogs since we both fear dogs to begin with. But in that moment, it did not matter how big or scary our opponent was, the love-instinct just kicked in and we did what we needed to do and fought with all our might.

Talking about it afterwards, we both agreed that our lives are like these kind of attacks by the devil. This invisible enemy charges at us suddenly and attacks us and our loved ones. He pounds at us from all direction, ready to devour us. But we too must learn to be vigilant and ready to fight back. If we get scared and run away, we can be sure that he would snatch us and our children away. So, we must not allow him to do that. We need to understand that we are in a spiritual warfare and be prepared to stand up against our foe. It does not matter how big or scary our opponent may be, as long as we have our weapon with us, we can face him. David only had a sling and 5 stones with him but his confident was not in these; David's confidence was in the name of the LORD. In the same way, we may not have any physical abilities to fight against our enemy, but we do have that one powerful weapon which can move mountains and kill giants. This weapon is Prayer and we must be equipped with it.

While we are in a spiritual warfare and under the attack of the devil, we must not retrieve in fear and give up so easily. Just the way we fought the dogs regardless of our ability, we must rely on the power of prayer and fight back with all our might in the name of Jesus.

Dear LORD, give me the courage to fight the enemy as he attacks me and my family. May I use my weapon, my prayer, to stand up against the foe. Please help me to fight this battle on my knees and not allow the devil to snatch me or my loved ones away from you. I trust in You and claim victory in Your mighty name. In Jesus' name, Amen!

Standard of beauty - May 6

But the LORD said to Samuel, "Don't judge by his appearance or height, for I have rejected him. The LORD doesn't see things the way you see them. People judge by outward appearance, but the LORD looks at the heart." 1 Samuel 16:7

The first thing that most of us get attracted is through a person's appearance. The way we look exteriorly, present ourselves, and treat others is what makes us likeable or dislikeable as a person in general. Some are genuine in displaying their true self while some put on a façade such as dressing just to impress, sweet talking, and doing beyond necessary just to be liked by others. We judge by what we see and how appealing the outward is to us. That is the reason why businesses spend so much money on their commercials to attract us by sight to purchase their product. If it looks good on the outside, we go buy it and later we may find out that it is not all that as it was portrayed to be. We waste our time and money on things chasing after things that do not turn out to be good for us after all.

God knows this very well and so He does not waste time looking at our outward appearance. We cannot impress Him by our looks as He himself has made us in His image and everything that God makes is beautiful already. In God's sight, beauty is not about having a pretty face, being dressed up in fancy clothes and adorned with expensive accessories. These are the measurements that the world uses to describe beauty, but God measures our beauty by who we are as a person from inside and what we spend our time on. We also cannot try to impress Him with our words or deeds as He knows our intention behind it; and so, if it is not genuine, it does not mean anything to God. The only thing that matters to God is the condition of our heart towards Him and others. It is the integrity of our heart and the purity of our mind is what God judges us by.

Therefore, let us be more concerned with our inner self than our outer appearance. He sees what our heart is like, what our mind and body are occupied with and how we behave in the confines of our private lives.

Dear LORD, the world's standard of beauty is looks, physique, fame and fortune which is the total opposite of Your standard of beauty which is holiness and purity. I want the beauty of Jesus to radiate in me, so I pray for a clean and pure heart. May I not run around to acquire the beauty that the world expects but only be concerned about the beauty from within which You expect. In Jesus' name, Amen!

Tell it to the mountain - May 7

"Have faith in God," Jesus answered. "Truly I tell you, if anyone says to this mountain, 'Go, throw yourself into the sea,' and does not doubt in their heart but believes that what they say will happen, it will be done for them. Mark 11: 22-23

Many of us say that we pray to God throughout the day, not necessarily in prayer posture with eyes closed and sitting or kneeling but having conversations with God in our mind while going about our business. Speaking for myself, I am constantly in conversation with God during the day, but my conversations are mostly I talking to God and reminding Him of all the issues that I am facing. I find myself reiterating the problem in my mind and telling God about how big and difficult it is and continually asking Him for help.

When we do this, we magnify the problem to God instead of magnifying God to our problems. We all have "mountains" of problems that we deal with individually. And the bigger the mountain, the bigger our tension seems to be. We find ourselves occupied with thoughts and worries during the day and lose sleep over it many nights. We keep bugging God about it also by constantly bringing it up and nagging Him. It is good that God does not feel bothered about it, but it just shows our distrust and doubt in God's abilities.

Therefore, we need to learn to do the opposite. Rather than continuously telling God about how big our mountain is, we need to continually tell the mountain how big our God is. Whenever thoughts of worry and fear enter our mind, we need to remember and claim Bible verses that speak against these negative circumstances. We must counteract our worry with God's promises and speak them out boldly so that we hear it ourselves, as well as the mountain and it throws itself into the sea by our faith-filled proclamation.

Dear LORD, help me not to idolize my problems by giving them too much attention. You are bigger than my problems so please teach me to trust and claim Your promises over my life that You are always with me and have everything under control. Give me eyes to walk by faith and not by sight of what is going around me. In Jesus' name, Amen!

Stubborn child - May 8

I will give you a new heart and put a new spirit in you; I will remove from you your heart of stone and give you a heart of flesh. Ezekiel 36:26

After I fed my little dog, Teddy, some real chicken, he refused to eat anything else. No matter what else I would put in front of him, he did not touch it. He just looked at me as if I made a mistake and waited for me to give him chicken. Teddy would moan and groan, walk around feeling weak, but he would rather do that than eat anything else. His food was right at his disposal but because of his stubbornness, he chose to suffer than to change his mind to eat and be happy.

Some of us are stubborn just like Teddy. Since we have tasted the worldly pleasures, we do not want the heavenly manna. We would rather go through life spiritually hungry than to eat the eternal bread God has to offer. We insist on doing things our own way than to trust God to give us His best. We would rather be deprived of His blessings than to admit our need for Him.

God keeps knocking at the door of our heart and continues to offer us the spiritual food, but we refuse to eat it. We do not think much of stubbornness, but it has to do with pride which is a sin. Pride makes our heart harden and rebel against God even more. It is the root of all evil, and humbleness is the root of all good.

Therefore, if we struggle with stubbornness, especially in our relationship with Christ, we must ask God for help to let go our pride and give us humble heart.

Dear LORD, please soften my heart towards You so that I do not become set in my own ways. Remove from me any stubbornness and arrogance which block my blessings. Fill me with gratefulness to humbly accept Your love and presence in my life. In Jesus' name, Amen!

Spiritually Mature – May 9

Older women, likewise, are to be reverent in their behavior, not slanderers or addicted to much wine, but teachers of good. Titus 2:3

A popular Bible passage on Mother's Day is Proverbs 31. Most of this passage is about what a virtuous woman is and how she takes care of the home and her family. But being a virtuous woman does not just end with the matters of physical provisions but also is being spiritually mature and maintaining a godly character amongst her family, friends, church and the next generation of women as an elder. The characteristics of this kind of a woman are described in the book of Titus in the Bible.

The first and foremost feature is that of being a godly woman, dedicated to God in all that she does. As a reverent woman, she takes her relationship with God seriously and it shows in her everyday behavior. She represents God by holy living and conducts herself as "priestly" in all matters. Being a godly woman, she restrains herself from slandering others. She keeps control of her tongue and does not engage in gossip, harmful talk and backbiting, but rather only allows true and wholesome talk come out of her mouth which builds others up, not tear down. If not addicted to alcohol, a godly woman is not mastered over by any other habits either such as TV, phone, food, fashion, money, fame, bitterness, lying, stealing or cheating. Instead a Titus 2 woman is self-controlled and disciplines her body to not be under the control of anything or anyone else but the Holy Spirit living inside of her.

The spiritually mature woman is also a teacher who herself has learnt the word of God and imparts her biblical knowledge to those around her. Being known as a virtuous and godly woman, she is observed and looked upon as a role model therefore she ensures that she sets a godly example to her husband, children, grandchildren, in-laws, friends and everyone around her. She demonstrates the teachings of the Bible by her own way of living. And lastly, the godly woman not only teaches and tells others what to do, but she trains by coming alongside and helping others in their walk with God. Instead of judging or pointing fingers, she understands and assists in their struggle by witnessing, teaching and giving a helping hand through the process.

Dear LORD, please help me not only be a virtuous woman for my family but become a Titus 2 woman by setting a godly example to others who are watching me. Help me to be pure and holy so that when others look at me, they see Jesus Christ radiating through me inside out. Teach me to be a Christ-centered role model from which others can learn godly and righteous living. In Jesus' name, Amen!

Infinitely forgiven - May 10

As far as the east is from the west, so far has he removed our transgressions from us. Psalm 103:12

God is very particular with His words when He describes something. Did we ever wonder why God chose to say east and west rather than north or south? If travelling in the north direction, one can only go so far geographically (up to north pole) and must travel back in the south. And it is the same when travelling in the south. There is a limit to north and south, but east and west do not meet and have no limits. No matter how far we travel east, we can never reach a point where we must return westward. Therefore, God used east and west to describe how far He has removed our sins from us. Once God forgives, He really forgives and never returns to it.

However, it is us who often treat our forgiven sins as north and south. Although God has forgiven us, we do not forgive ourselves and keep returning to it. This is the work of the devil who constantly reminds us of our sins and makes us doubt God's forgiveness. The devil likes for us to remain in a miserable state and so he keeps bringing up our sins to make us believe that we are not good enough for God. But we need to comprehend that if we have truly repented of our sins, God has genuinely forgiven us and will never hold us accountable for it. We will never have to answer for our forgiven sins because Jesus has already paid the price for it and cleared us. He is faithful at His word and once He has said it, its Yes and Amen; forgiven and forgotten.

We too must not test God and keep doubting His promise. We only need to ensure that we have truly repented of our sin, ask for God's forgiveness and move in the direction of east and west, not north or south and return to it.

Dear LORD, thank you for forgiving me of my sin and shame and giving me a promise to never bring it back up against me. Please help me to accept Your forgiveness and not allow the devil to devalue Your sacrifice by making me doubt You. By Your help, may I remove myself from my sin as far as east is from the west. In Jesus' name, Amen!

Undergoing training - May 11

Praise be to the LORD my Rock, who trains my hands for war, my fingers for battle.
Psalm 144:1

When David stood in front of Goliath, he did not just step out randomly to fight the giant. He had previously been under "training" as a Shepard boy which God chose for him as an occupation to prepare him for this giant task. During the years while David watched over his flock, he even fought a lion and a bear and tackled many other dangerous situations. These he faced so that when the right time came, David was not afraid to fight Goliath either.

We may not realize the significance of our daily routine tasks, nor understand the purpose for the difficulties that we go through in the present. We may also become impatient and want to see immediate results, but these tasks and obstacles are "training material" which God uses to shape us for a bigger purpose. The work that we do, the time that we spend, people whom we meet, and challenges that we face all prepare us for a bigger state that God has planned for us to deal with. We may get tired of doing our routine duties, not think much of our talents or feel discouraged when we are faced with adversities, but we must remember that these small details build us up for a higher calling. Only when we remain faithful in our little tasks and give our best, God puts us in front of bigger things to fight against and win.

During his years of shepherding, David had learnt to fight and experienced God's mighty power to save. So, at the right time when He and the giant collided, David fought and defeated his giant with confidence in the name of the LORD and with the skills which he had acquired through the years.

In the same manner, our daily efforts may seem insignificant to us in the present, but God's intent is to build us up so that at the right time when He places us in the battlefield, we are equipped to fight and win. Therefore, let us not despise our small beginnings but continue to remain faithful in little things for bigger things yet to come.

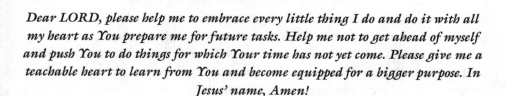

Dear LORD, please help me to embrace every little thing I do and do it with all my heart as You prepare me for future tasks. Help me not to get ahead of myself and push You to do things for which Your time has not yet come. Please give me a teachable heart to learn from You and become equipped for a bigger purpose. In Jesus' name, Amen!

Faultless before God - May 12

Plead my cause, O LORD, with them that strive with me: fight against them that fight against me. Psalm 35:1

A s a part of the human nature, it is difficult to overlook an insult. We take it to heart when someone says something negative to us or about us. We feel hurt when we do not get the respect that we know is due us. The reason why we feel such emotional stress is because we look for people's acknowledgement. Our mind revolves around what others think of us; therefore, we are in a constant need for such attention and approval.

Opinion of others should not affect us, particularly if we know who we are in Christ. If we are certain of our faithfulness and can stand faultless in front of God, then we do not need to worry about someone else's thoughts towards us. To justify their own negativity, people often look to others to blame and point fingers, but it does not mean they are correct, and we are at fault. View of others does not alter how God views us. People may have untrue ideas about us based on their own understanding, circumstances or bitterness but if we also engage ourselves in their war, we leave an open invitation for the devil to infiltrate us with anger and resentment. Then we are no better than others if we behave likewise and return evil for evil.

Therefore, it is necessary to guard ourselves against such evil attacks by constantly reminding ourselves of who we are in Christ and how he has taught us to handle such adversities. As hard as it may be to remain quiet, we must display God in us by returning love for hatred. God knows us inside out and so we should allow Him to plead our innocence and fight the battle. He has said that "Vengeance is mine" so let us allow God to be our strength for our weakness and handle it in His timing. We just need to remain true to God and to ourselves.

Dear LORD, please help me to not accept the negative opinion of others about me and make it true for myself. I know who I am in Jesus Christ, so I ask You to help me remain faithful to You regardless of my circumstances and emotions. I pray for change of stubborn hearts and restoration of relationships who are stuck in such state. In Jesus' name, Amen!

What is your name? - May 13

But Jacob said, "I will not let you go unless you bless me." And he said to him, "What is your name?" And he said, "Jacob." Genesis 32: 26-27

J acob cheated his dad by pretending to be his elder brother Esau and robbed the blessings that were stored by Isaac for Esau. In order to escape his brother's, avenge, Jacob had to flee from home. After many years when Jacob was on his way back home, God met Jacob and wrestled with him throughout the night. Jacob would not let God go and fought with Him until God truly blessed him. I believe that all through the years while Jacob was away from home and prospered with a big family and possessions, he felt guilty about what he had done. So now that he was going back, Jacob wanted to ensure that God still loved him and will bless him for who he really was. Jacob knew that all the blessings he had received thus far were from deception and was afraid that they were about to be taken away from him. Therefore, God brought Jacob down to a point of confession about who he truly was and asked for Jacob's name. It was this moment that Jacob confessed and accepted his true identity in front of God. For Jacob to be right with God and continue to be blessed, Jacob had to be sure that he knew who he was in God's sight–humbled and forgiven.

We too often pretend to be someone who we are not and deceive people. In order to receive praises and blessings from people, we often hide our true self and only show the "good" side. We do not show or confess the secret sins such as a cussing, gossip, lying, selfishness, bitterness, envy, pride and lustful eyes. We rob people of their trust and respect for us by pretending to be who we are not. We may even try to fool God and justify the reasons for our sins. But God knows who we really are inside out and wants to bless the true us, as He does not support or bless any sin. We might gain the riches of the world and reach a certain status but if it is gained through any deceptive means, sooner or later it falls apart unless we humble ourselves and acknowledge our sinful self to God.

God wants us to bring the real "me" to Him, with all of our sin and shame and confess it all so that when He asks, "What is your name?", we can truthfully tell Him without hiding or pretending.

Dear LORD, please help me not to deceive You, others or myself by pretending to be someone who I am not. I humbly bring myself to You with all my sin and unrighteousness and ask for Your forgiveness. Help me to move forward in life forgiven and clear, knowing my identity and being confident of who I am in You. In Jesus' name, Amen!

It's not surprising - May 14

Even though I walk through the valley of the shadow of death, I will fear no evil, for you are with me. Psalm 23:4

When we are hurt, sick or undergoing an adverse circumstance, we are often encouraged by others who say to us "Don't worry, you'll be fine" or "Nothing will happen to you". Although we mean well by saying it to each other, how can we be sure of it? Many Christians are under the impression that because we are Christians and believe in a God who is almighty and powerful, nothing bad can happen to us, and that God keeps us away from all harm and danger. But this is an untrue statement if taken literally. Illness and hardships are a part of life, both for the godly and ungodly. It rains both on the just and unjust alike. Which means that while we live on this earth, all of us are susceptible for facing trials and temptations in life. But the big difference between the two is how we, as believers in Jesus, handle our circumstance and our faith.

Although we face various trials and troubles, the godly have complete faith in Jesus to be by our side and give us strength to endure whatever comes our way. God never told us that we would never experience pain nor face storms in life, but He did say that He would be with us no matter what we face. He did not promise to keep us away from it, He promised to be with us through it. The outcome of our storm might not be what we expect but regardless of the result, we still trust God that He only does what is best for us as His thoughts and plans towards us are so much bigger than what we think or plan.

We must not find it surprising when we as Christians undergo trials and sufferings. Nor should we question God as to why He allowed it because the purpose behind it is for us to build our faith, be stronger in God and be used as a vessel to bring others to Christ. So, unless we've received a confirmation from God through much praying and are confident of our faith in it, we shouldn't generally just recite these statements but rather accept our situation, hand it over to God and trust Him to see us through it according to His will and timing.

Dear LORD, please help me trust You with all my heart regardless of what situations I face in life. May I not to be ignorant about my faith but truly be faithful, fearless and confident that even though I face any hardship or evil, You are always with me. Please help me to accept Your will and be prepared to face the foe with You by my side. In Jesus' name, Amen!

Be prepared - May 15

Preach the word; be prepared in season and out of season. 2 Timothy 4:2

The day I committed my life to Jesus Christ is my spiritual birthday. On that day, God had revealed to me the talent He has given me and shown me the purpose of my life. I have surely seen His promise fulfilled in my life through the years. And God has confirmed it for me many times such as on the anniversary of this special day.

As soon as I woke up and came down for breakfast, my phone rang and was asked to join a zoom church service and give a sermon instantaneously because of an issue they had encountered. It was an emergency request and was given just about 5 minutes to get on and start talking. So, I ran back up and told my husband who started running around to get the camera and everything ready, while I started changing my clothes and fixing myself up a bit while figuring out what on topic to speak. Lo and behold, the cameras turned on and I was able to deliver an instant message off my memory which I had shared previously a few months ago. As soon as it was over, I found myself sweating and feeling God laughing at me (in a funny way), telling me that I passed His surprise test!

My husband reminded me of this Bible verse and now we clearly understand what it means. We as Christians, are called to always be ready to share God's word with whomever God puts in front of us, whether it is a one on one talk or a group. God wants to use us as His mouthpiece to reach someone for His kingdom, so it is our responsibility to seize the opportunity when God gives us. In that moment, we do not need to worry about what or how we will say it; if we are ready and available, God puts His words in our mouth to reach someone's heart.

Every excuse or a denied chance to share God's love and opportunity for eternal life, is one soul lost. So,

we need to ensure that we do not become the reason for someone's eternal damnation. Therefore, we must be ready whether we are prepared or not for God to call us on duty at moment's notice.

Dear LORD, thank you for counting me worthy and using me as a vessel for Your kingdom. Please help me to not come up with excuses and reasons when You call out to me. Just the way I expect You to come to my aid instantaneously, may always I also be available for You, regardless of time or circumstance. In Jesus' name, Amen!

*And pray in the Spirit on all occasions with all kinds of prayers and requests.
With this in mind, be alert and always keep on praying for all the Lord's people.
Ephesians 6:18*

While having a minor argument with my son, he told me "just go away in your closet". He meant it to get rid of me and end the conversation, but he gave me the answer to what I needed about our argument. I took his notion as a compliment also and told him that is exactly what I will do. It is a compliment because my children know that when I am in the house, I spend most of my time in the closet, my prayer room, and pray for them and about everything.

Similar to the Situation Room in the White House where combats and missions are planned and carried out from, my closet is my little War room where I meet with God, and together we discuss how we will tackle the enemy who tries to come against me. God is my General who directs and equips me for battle. When I sit at His feet and listen to His instructions, God strengthens and gears me up to go fight the battle that I am facing.

Prayer is that one powerful weapon that nothing can stand against. There is tremendous power in prayers that are said and claimed in Jesus' name.

We may not be strong enough physically or any other way to tackle life's problems on our own, but if we can get on our knees and surrender our struggles to God by faith, the victory is ours.

The enemy fears our prayer so whenever we have the opportunity, let us go in the closet to fight him on our knees and do not let him get away with it

---

Dear LORD, thank you for the blessing of prayer. Please help me not to take it lightly and ignore the opportunities You give me to come and talk to You. Teach me to prioritize my time and activities so that I keep prayer as the most important part of my day. In Jesus' name, Amen!

Born Again - May 17

So, if the Son sets you free, you will be free indeed. John 8:36

May 17, 2007 is a special day for me. It is the day when I came to truly know Jesus Christ and surrendered my life to Him as my Lord and Savior. Born and raised in a Christian family with all biblical values instilled in me, I did my best to live a Christian lifestyle. However, it was not until this day that I clearly understood who Jesus Christ is and what it means to be a Christian. I personally experienced His forgiveness and moving forward, gave Jesus Christ full control of my life to lead me where He pleased and committed myself to follow Jesus.

Commitment is easy to make but keeping it is difficult though, as I experience it daily while trying to grow in Christ. The more we understand Jesus and His word, the more we realize how sinful we are. And the more we try to turn away from our sin, the more pressure we feel to go back to it. That is just how the devil works! He will not leave us alone so easily but tries everything in his power to bring us back under his bondage of sin. But if God has declared us free, we are free in Christ, and no matter how many times we may stumble, fall and succumb to the pressure of sin, God will not hold that against us. He knows we are sinful by nature and to go against it is not easy for us, so He remains patient and faithful to us even when we become unfaithful to God. He encourages us to keep trying and not give up as He promises to never give up on us.

We probably will never reach the state of perfection throughout our lifetime, but we can learn from our mistakes and continue to remain a "work in progress" as we allow God to work in us and shape us into His character day by day.

Dear LORD, thank you for saving me! I acknowledge that I am a sinner and I let You down over and over but thank you, LORD for not giving up on me. Help me not to give up on myself either but learn from my mistakes and keep trying. By Your Spirit helping me, may I continue to rise higher and higher in You. I commit my life into Your hands, please help me to live for You wholly. In Jesus' name, Amen!

Message must go on - May 18

He must increase, but I must decrease. John 3:30

At Pastor Billy Graham's funeral, Pastor Ravi Zacharias said, "A great voice is gone but the message still goes on". Often, we aim at accomplishing certain things in life so that people could remember our work and what we did. We try to leave a legacy of our own remembrance rather than the cause. We want our name to be carried on. Many politicians contribute and participate to gain popularity for themselves, some preachers preach for acknowledgement as a great speaker and many folks do things to get accolades from others, all hoping that people will continue to remember them rather than the purpose they carried.

When we become the focal point ourselves, the message that we try to assert gets lost. We as Christians are called to proclaim the good news of Jesus, but when we start to proclaim our own name or works, the good news loses its significance. We may say we are lifting God's name higher by doing such and such, but we indirectly self-glorify ourselves in the name of Jesus. But if we are serious about spreading God's word to the world, then we must hide behind the cross, not stand in front of it. At any time when we are presented with an opportunity to share the name of Jesus, then only Jesus should be the topic of our conversation. People must only hear from our mouths what God has done for us and not what we have done for God. We must live the footprint of God for people to follow and not imprint our own names.

Great preachers such as DL Moody, Charles Spurgeon, Billy Graham and Ravi Zacharias have left the earth, but their message of Jesus will continue to resonate for the coming generations. And such should be our goal also – whether we are remembered or not, our message of Christ should be remembered and continue to have an impact.

Dear LORD, at every given opportunity, may You be the one I proclaim. Teach me to work behind the scene and keep You in the spotlight. Please help me to live my life in such a way that people can see Christ in me and remember me for who I am in You and not what I have done for you. In Jesus' name, Amen!

Berlin Wall - May 19

Do not take revenge, my dear friends, but leave room for God's wrath, for it is written: "It is mine to avenge; I will repay," says the Lord." Romans 12: 19

In 1945 when Germany was divided, a huge wall separated East and West Berlin. One day, some people in East Berlin took a truck load of garbage and dumped it on the West Berlin side. The people of West Berlin could have done the same thing, but they did not. Instead they took a truck load of canned goods, bread, milk and other provisions, and neatly stacked it on the East Berlin side. On top of this stack they placed the sign: "EACH GIVES WHAT HE HAS".

We often give and expect like for like. It is not easy to sit quietly, turn the other cheek or simply walk away when someone does us wrong. Our human tendency is to take revenge, talk back and throw the same garbage that was thrown at us, if not more or worse. But before we retaliate, we need to remind ourselves who we are as a person in Christ. God has taught us to love, be tolerant, sympathetic, and forgiving. And this can only happen if we have Christ in us. And if Christ is in us, we should only know how to love, not hate!

How can we radiate Jesus through us if we are not filled with Him or His love? How are we any better if we do the same to others? Everyone is right in their own eyes and pride does not allow us to accept our fault. And this world also teaches us that when we let something go and not get even, it makes us a coward or a weakling. But to walk away and not strike back takes more courage than it does to do so. God knows when we are wronged, and He does not let the enemy get away with it. He fights for us and gives us justice, but in His own way and timing. So, we must not rush God or act on His behalf. We must allow God to handle our mistreatment.

Revenge is for God so let Him deal with it. Our duty is to remain who we are, continue to do good and give our best because that is what we have. We must not return the trash or worry about how mistreated we are. Instead we simply need to love, not hate and give food instead of garbage.

Dear LORD, I pray for peace in hearts and minds of those who are hurt and angry. As humans, we feel offended and insulted when treated unfairly and injustice is done unto us but please help us to follow your example and remember how you handled it – with love and peace, not hate and revenge. You know all matters of my heart so help me to allow You to fight my cause and not take it upon myself and make it worse. In Jesus' name, Amen!

Do not disturb - May 20

And He withdrew Himself into the wilderness and prayed. Luke 5:16

While I was in my prayer time, my phone rang, and I saw that it was my husband who was calling. Because he called unusually at that time, I picked up his phone thinking if something was wrong or if he needed me urgently. It turned out to be no big deal and had called casually. After talking to him, I felt the conviction of God right away that I put God aside to pick up a phone call and that too with the worry of something being wrong. Two things I learnt from this incident.

One, when we are in God's presence in prayer or Bible reading, our focus should solely be on Him and must not allow any disruptions to take away our attention off God. Any person or thing which we place before God becomes our idol, even if it is momentarily. My phone became my idol at that time. Therefore, we need to be careful to choose who we worship and not give precedence to any other over God at any time.

Secondly, I just proved that I did not trust God as I picked up the phone in fear of something being wrong. While I was in the midst of reading and praying God's promises, shouldn't I have faith that even if something was wrong, God is there, and He can handle it? By answering the phone, I relied on my own wisdom to find out what was going on and trusted in my own ability to figure it out if something did happen.

When we are in prayer, the best thing to do is to put away the phone on silent and not touch it. If we anticipate a phone call, it is better to address that first and then go into prayer, rather than have our mind wandering about it and praying with partial attention. The devil does not like us to pray as he knows our prayers can mess up his plans, and so he tries to distract and stop our conversation with God. From our part, we too must not allow ourselves to get distracted but focus on God by isolating ourselves and away from all disturbances.

Dear LORD, please forgive me for putting You aside for other things in my day. Teach me to prioritize my activities and put You first in all that I do. Please help me to not allow distractions to take away my focus from You as speak to me during prayer and throughout the day. In Jesus' name, Amen!

Do what you need to do today - May 21

"You set the time!" Moses replied. "Tell me when you want me to pray for you, your officials, and your people. Then you and your houses will be rid of the frogs. They will remain only in the Nile River." "Tomorrow," Pharaoh said. Exodus 8: 9,10

During spring and beginning of summer, our home gets invaded by some type of little bugs that we find crawling around our property and in the house. This year, it seemed to be the year of the black ants. They are so tiny and look harmless, but it was so irritating to find them all over the place. No matter how much bug spray or baits we used, we found these little pests everywhere. I just wanted the "ant season" to be over so that we could have an ant-free house.

I cannot imagine what it must have been like for the Egyptians to deal with the plague of frogs. The entire land was infested with frogs all over. Frogs were in the kitchen, food, bed, closets, bathroom, fields, barn, etc. It must have been so difficult and disgusting to be surrounded by frogs all over. Yet when Moses asked Pharaoh the time, he should pray for God to get rid of these frogs, Pharaoh replied "Tomorrow". If I were in Pharaoh's place, I would say, "do it right now and get rid of these frogs immediately!" But Pharaoh decided to wait and still deal with these frogs one more day.

Often, we have "frogs" in our life which need immediate attention but for some reason or the other, we put them off to a later time. It could be an addiction, bad habit or a sin which we know is not right in God's eyes, yet we like to indulge in it and are not in a rush to get rid of. There could be projects or duties that are lingering around but we come up with excuses and continue to live with the mess rather than fix what is broken. There also could be relational issues which cause us heartache, but we ignore them and allow them to bother us in our mind and take away our peace rather than deal with them right away.

None of us are given a promise for tomorrow, all we have is today so we must not leave things for tomorrow what can be done today. If we come up with excuses and choose to remain with the "frogs" that cause us to sin and make us miserable, we may not have an opportunity later to repent, fix, or turn away. We must seize the occasion and pray to God for deliverance at the first sign of the "frog".

Dear LORD, please help me identify the "frogs" in my life that make me miserable and take me away from You. While I have the promise of today, would You please help me repent of my sin, turn away from things that make me fall and fix my broken relations. Teach me to value today and live life to the fullest in You! In Jesus' name, Amen!

Already answered - May 22

Before they call, I will answer; while they are still speaking I will hear.
Isaiah 65:24

While we had to make a quick visit to a friend's home to drop something off, we did not call them in advance to let them know we were coming as were hoping that they would not be home. We just planned to drop it off at the doorstep and leave. Due to the pandemic situation, we wanted to follow the social distancing rules; but out of courtesy, our friends would adamantly invite us in, so to avoid an uncomfortable situation, we just prayed casually that they wouldn't be home. Because the LORD knew that we had plans to go there and also would pray for such a little request as this, He was already at work on it and created our friends' schedule in such a way and timing that they truly were not at home when we went to their house. They had left just a while ago before we got there.

Before even Abraham's servant prayed for a sign to recognize the right girl for Isaac, knowing what he would ask for, God had already planned out the day for Rebekah who was on her way to the well to fetch water. By the divine plan of God, she met the servant at the right time and said the exact words that the servant had asked God to hear from the chosen bride for his master's son.

You see, God knows our every need and desire. He is aware of those minute little details of our life and is always willing to help. When our way pleases Him, God is ever ready to hear our prayer and answer us. He does not wait to hear from us first and then begin to decide how and what He will do to answer our plea. God is omniscient and knows what we will ask for, so before we even call out to Him, God is at work ahead of time. He starts aligning the right people, places, things and circumstances in order so that they work out as we prayed for. If our prayers are sincere, within God's will and are prayed with faith in God, He is willing to grant our heart's desire and begins His work before we even think of it.

Dear LORD, thank you for going ahead of me and working things out on my behalf before I even become aware of it. As I bring You my prayer request, I look forward to seeing how You will unfold the plan which You have been working on. Give me faith to see You at work prior to me asking You. In Jesus' name, Amen!

Keep it full - May 23

Fix your thoughts on what is true, and honorable, and right, and pure, and lovely, and admirable. Think about things that are excellent and worthy of praise. Philippians 4:8

Our car needs gasoline in order to run and take us places. If we do not fill the tank with gas, we cannot get anywhere. Also, if it remains empty and is not filled, the tank itself will start to rust and be damaged. Our spirituality is like the tank. It continuously needs to be filled with God's word, prayer and fellowship in order to run. If we do not pay attention to the gage of our spiritual tank and allow ourselves to get to a state of emptiness, we put ourselves in danger of spiritual attacks. The devil is always on a look out for an empty mind to fill it with his sinful ideas. We live in a sinful world and if we are devoid of God's presence in our life, we end up doing sinful things which we ought not to. If our mind is empty, the devil is ever ready to fill it up with his sinful ideas as the saying "An idle mind is the devil's workshop". Many a times, he leads us to that emptiness by distracting us with busyness of other things or idleness so that we do not fill our spiritual tank by spending time in God's word or prayer. He does whatever it takes to keep us away from God so that we become empty and cannot operate much further.

Therefore, it is always necessary to occupy our minds with godly thoughts and be prayerful. Instead of having wandering thoughts, we need to read God's word and ponder on His goodness. Instead of having unhealthy chats with others, it is better to have meaningful conversation with God through prayer. We must not allow idleness to take away our focus of who we are in Jesus and what He expects from us as His child. Let us fill the emptiness with the presence of Jesus and the Holy Spirit so that there is no room for Satan to enter in!

Dear LORD, please always help me to be occupied with You. Remove the idleness that take me away from You. Fill my emptiness with Your anointing and let my cup overflow with Your presence in my life so that I do not have room for anything else but You. In Jesus' name, Amen!

Test and see - May 24

Dear friends, do not believe every spirit, but test the spirits to see whether they are from God, because many false prophets have gone out into the world. 1 John 4:1

Residents of the city of Berea located in Macedonia were known as Bereans. The people of this town had high morals and nobility. When Paul the apostle visited them and talked about Jesus, they did receive his word with all gladness but at the same time, they examined Paul's word and matched it to the scriptures. They did not just blindly believe Paul but ensured that what he taught agreed to what was written in God's word.

Most often when we go to church or listen to a sermon on any media such as Livestreams, YouTube, Radio, Podcasts, Telecasts, Telephones, etc., most of us do not sit with our Bibles opened to follow the preachers' teaching. Because we are under the impression that the preachers know best and must be well trained, we do not doubt or question their teaching. We simply take them for their word and believe whatever they say.

But the Bible itself teaches us that we must not believe every person who speaks in the name of the LORD. The devil too knows the Bible very well but that does not mean that he teaches us the truth. He twists God's word and makes it believable so that if we are not careful or know the truth about God's word, we fall for his lies and into sin.

Therefore, we must be like the Bereans, be eager to hear God's word but also be vigilant to test every spirit that speaks it and see if what was spoken is according to the word of God or not. If there is a contradiction, we must raise the question and not be afraid to ask for clarification. If it is not valid, we must not believe it and be led astray.

Dear LORD, please help me to spend more time studying the Bible and understand it well. Give me discernment to recognize Your word against anything else and not fall for the lies of the devil who speaks through many so-called "preachers" in Your name. Help me test every spirit and only believe the one that speaks the truth by Your anointing of the Holy Spirit. In Jesus' name, Amen!

Return indeed - May 25

Come back to your senses as you ought and stop sinning. 1 Corinthians 15:34

In the story of the Prodigal son in the Bible, the son left his home and squandered all his dad's money on worldly pleasures. He made a foolish decision to not only leave his home but also demanded his portion of the inheritance while his father was still alive. The young son's behavior was mostly influenced by his friends whom he listened to and headed towards destruction of his own life.

When we hear this story, we mostly think of it in negative terms of an individual who went astray. But the good news of this story is that the son Returned Home! It took him a while but sure enough, the prodigal child came back. Sometimes when we have a prodigal in our life who either literally ran away from home or is far away from God, we start to expect negativity of the situation to carry all the way through. We assume that it will end like the way it started, if not worse. It took some time and was not until the young son in the Bible story hit rock bottom of his lavish living that he came to his senses and decided to return home. In the same way while our prodigals are on their own, God continues to work in them and from their own experiences and poor choices, He makes them realize their need for forgiveness and turn around.

We all are prodigals in some way when we walk on the wrong path of a sin, addiction or any other track where we remove ourselves away from God. While we may think we do not need God or may feel that we have gone too far, God does not give up on us but continues to make a way for us to return to Him. He uses the same sin which led us away from Him to make us realize that we need to get rid of it. After we have indulged in it for a while, we come to our senses and began to hate our sin. And that is the moment where God brings us to so that we willingly want to get away from it.

So, if we have a prodigal or feel like one, we have the great hope that when we hit rock bottom, God is there to catch us and bring us back home!

Dear LORD, please forgive me for thinking that I can survive without You. Help the prodigal in me to come to my sense and realize a need for a turn around. Give me a hatred for my sin and sinful lifestyle so that I willingly become ready to give up on it. Thank you for never giving up on me even when I ignore You and push You out of my life. In Jesus' name, Amen!

Endless tunnel – May 26

When you pass through the waters, I will be with you; and when you pass through the rivers, they will not sweep over you. When you walk through the fire, you will not be burned; the flames will not set you ablaze. Isaiah 43:2

"Through" means to move from one side and out the other side of an opening, channel or location. I love to go through a tunnel under a big mountain or waters. We can see it approaching as we get closer to it, then we enter from the small opening and drive through a long, winding road which seems endless sometimes. The entrance of the tunnel goes out of sight and the exit is nowhere to be found as we just drive along. If it were not for the lights and signs to guide us through it, we could not drive even an inch forward. But eventually after driving inside of the tunnel for a while, we can see the light at the end of the tunnel and finally come out on the other side to a beautiful, new scenery.

The circumstances that we face in life are like a car passing through a tunnel. Once we are in it, it may feel like there is no way out and seems like an endless journey. We may start to lose patience, become hopeless and wonder if we will ever come out of it. But just as how tunnels are meant to transport us from one side to another, our circumstances are meant to take us from strength to strength. They serve as a means for us to grow spiritually and deepen our faith in God. Our adverse situations that we go through in life deepen our need and trust in God.

A car is not meant to remain inside the tunnel but pass through it, in the same manner our circumstances are not meant to be stationary or be stuck with us forever. They are meant to be mobile and bring us out to a beautiful other side. Furthermore, when we approach the mountain of trouble, God does not drop us off at the entrance to the tunnel and leave us there to navigate our own way out, He comes along with us all the way. He gives us His strength and patience as we slowly but surely move from darkness into the light. And along the way, His word serves as a light to our feet and guides our path.

Dear LORD, when my circumstances seem to be an endless tunnel, please increase my trust in You as I move along it. I thank you that my troubles and trials are not meant to be stuck with me forever but are there temporarily and to bring me closer to You. Thank you for being by my side and giving me the strength to endure as I pass through it. In Jesus' name, Amen!

Sinner and the Saint - May 27

Little children, let us not love in word or talk but in deed and in truth. 1 John 3:18

When we think of Prodigals, we generally think of children who have run away from home and are living in their own way. But there are also "silent" Prodigals who live at home yet are rebellious. In the story of the Prodigal Son in the Bible, the elder brother was such that he lived close with his Father but was bitter and fulfilled his service merely as a duty and not out of love or respect. One son was physically away while the other was distant from the heart.

Many of us can relate to the elder prodigal son. We may call ourselves Christians and perform all our religious duties, but our hearts are not truly connected to God. We do serve God, but our service might be out of fear that God would punish or not bless us if we do not participate in church activities, give donations, read bible or say our prayer. We consider it as an obligation rather than our honor. In the same manner, we do our godly duty to bring others to Christ, but our effort could be to just please God. In fact, sometimes we feel angry and bitter when we see good things happening to "bad" people or when we see someone repent and turn their lives around. We feel that since we are ones to who do all the work for the LORD, we should be the ones to reap all the blessings and forgiveness, not others.

But we need to know that God is a God for both the sinner and the saint. He does not look at our years of service or how much we have done for the LORD, nor does He care how far we have run away from Him. All God wants from us is a repentant heart and humbleness of attitude in all that we do for Him. We all are prodigals in God's eyes, whether away or within but our good Father is waiting with open arms to welcome us back. Will you come home?

Dear LORD, please forgive me for being bitter towards someone when I see them blessed by Your forgiveness. Help me to serve You without being selfish or having any ill motives towards anyone. Let my heart break for what breaks Yours and my heart rejoice for what makes You glad. In Jesus' name, Amen!

Tell the truth - May 28

You shall not bear false witness against your neighbor. Exodus 20:16

When we think of being a witness for someone, we usually picture standing in a court room and giving our testimony of what we saw or heard in an instance. Most of us are under the belief that the commandment to not bear false witness pertains only in legal matters and we take it as probably the easiest to keep as we feel that we may never encounter a situation where we would need to go to court and be a witness. But this commandment also applies to our daily, personal matters and what we say about others casually. We all tend to overthink and make assumptions about what someone else must have said and or done. Based on our assumption or "educated guess", we create a false image or story in our head and often convey an untrue message without knowing the full truth.

The key to being a witness is to only say and testify that which we have seen with our own eyes or heard with our own ears. When we make a statement about somebody without knowing the entire truth or by adding a probable reason which we have not observed ourselves, it is called bearing a false witness. It is also a root of gossip which continues to spread beyond the reality of a matter and accuses the innocent.

As the Jewish proverb says, "Let not your mouth speak what your eyes have not seen", we must be mindful of what we say about others. We may be never be called into the courtroom to give our witness, but we are constantly in the presence of the omniscient God, the Highest Authority, therefore we must only tell the truth and nothing but the truth!

Dear LORD, please set a watch over my mouth and teach me to be careful about what I say of others. Help me not to lie and blame anyone without knowing the full truth of a matter. Help me to be honest and only say what builds up, not tear down or accuse. In Jesus' name, Amen!

Little things matter - May 29

One who is faithful in very little is also faithful in much, and one who is dishonest in a very little is also dishonest in much. Luke 16:10

We were expected to measure our body temperature before we go into our workplace as a precautionary step of the coronavirus. As I was in a hurry one day, I thought to myself that I do not need to measure it every day since I felt fine and no one would know whether I took it or not. So, I proceeded to walk out and right away heard God's voice in my heart saying, "But I know". I turned right back around and put the thermometer in my mouth to measure my temperature.

It does not sound like a big deal for a minor act like this, but the minor things are what show how faithful we are. We often do the right things in front of others because we know that people are watching and have a reputation to maintain, but being a person of integrity is doing the right thing in all matters even when no one is looking or will ever find out. It is about having reverence for God and always striving to do right for His name's sake. Although we could escape the eye of people how can we deceive God? Can God be stopped from coming inside the closed doors? Can we keep God on the other side of our TV, computer or phone screens when we are watching or texting things that we should not be? Can we close God's ears when we gossip and say negative things?

As insignificant it may be, once we are convicted about our unfaithfulness, it is our responsibility to do what is right. We may inadvertently fall into sin and not realize it till later but once we are aware and continue to do it, it is an intentional sin. Had I gone to work without measuring my temperature even after I was convicted, it is a sin for me, against my company who may never know, and against God who always knows.

Dear LORD, thank you for Your Holy Spirit who convicts me when I am being unfaithful. Please teach me to be faithful even in little things because these little things lead You to trusting me more with bigger things. May I be a person of integrity and never do anything to hurt You or others. In Jesus' name, Amen!

Rottenness - May 30

Search me, O God, and know my heart! Try me and know my thoughts! See if there is any offensive way in me and lead me in the way everlasting. Psalm 139: 23-24

While picking out some blueberries from the container, I noticed some rotten ones which were sticking to the good ones. So, I threw out the bad ones in order to preserve the good ones as the rottenness can spread and spoil the entire batch of the blueberries.

In the same way, it is essential that we recognize and remove the rotten things from our life that can cause damage to our full being. Whether it's a physical addiction that hurts our body, an ungodly thought that corrupts our mind, or a sin which separates us from God, if not stopped immediately can continue to grow and spread until it devours our entire physical, emotional or spiritual self.

We often do not take things seriously until they become big and then we cry for help afterwards. We become over-confident in our self and think that we have full control and can stop whenever we find ourselves going over the limit. But we must understand that the limit of evil is right at the start. If we let our guard down and give the devil even a little head space, that is all he needs to sip in and penetrate his way throughout and cause full ruin. It is easier to overcome and be freed before a habit becomes an addiction, a thought becomes a mindset, or a sin becomes our lifestyle. It is better to live without one such thing than to be destroyed completely. Therefore, we must recognize and cast it away at the first sign of rotting so that one bad thing does not lead to the destruction of our whole being.

Dear LORD, please search out my life and point out the things and people in my life that are a cause of my physical, emotional or spiritual rottenness. Help me to not entertain any thought or action which leads me into sin. May I be vigilant for every foul thing that enters my mind or heart and with Your help, may I cast it out immediately. In Jesus' name, Amen!

"Because he loves Me, I will deliver him; because he knows My name, I will protect him". Psalm 91:14

"Nepotism" had been surfacing on every Bollywood headlines as one actor was a victim of such. Nepotism is the practice among those with power or influence of favoring relatives or friends, especially by giving them jobs. Due to nepotism and favoritism by other famous actors and directors, the newly emerging hero was not able to get any further roles and was cast out of the film industry. Not being able to sustain himself any longer, the actor committed suicide at a young age.

In this cruel world of fame, business and religion, in order to be successful and go higher, one must know a somebody of a higher influence as a reference to raise them up. Even within the church, nepotism plays a big role where instead of utilizing anointed members to carry out God's work, only selected members who are backed up by family names or higher authority are favored, whether anointed or not. Due to these types of monopoly, we see flopped movies, businesses and churches as it becomes about people trying to please the authoritative figures and leaders seeking glory from people.

Thank God that we all are a part of God's family and He does not favor one over the other. He does not discriminate or is partial towards anyone. Favoritism is a sin which the Bible clearly speaks against (James 2:9). And if God does not show favoritism then why should He be ok with us doing that to each other? We all are His children and He deals with each one according to our availability, not ability. To be a part of God's family and to be used for His kingdom is only dependent on whether we know His name and are willing to work with Him, not the other way around.

To succeed in this physical and spiritual world, the only name we need as our reference is the name of Jesus Christ. Do you know His name?

Dear LORD, thank you for knowing me intimately and giving me the right to be called by Your name. Thank you for choosing me for who I am and not whose reference I bring to You. Please help me to honor Your name in all that I am as I belong to You. In Jesus' name, Amen!

June

Straight to God - June 1

..."Bring the boy to me". Mark 9:19

The father brought his demon-possessed son to Jesus' disciples to heal him. Since the boy was in this condition since childhood, we can be certain that the parents must have done everything they could to treat their child. But nothing seemed to have worked and when they heard about Jesus, the father brought his son there. The disciples tried to help and heal the boy, but they could not. The difference between them and Jesus was that the disciples' focus was not on the authority of God but on themselves. They were too concerned about the healing than the healer himself.

Jesus has said it multiple times that the power to tackle any problems lies in prayer. There is power in the name of Jesus and when we sincerely pray in His name, we can see results. But often we put our focus on other means first. Yes, we may pray about it, but it is also coupled with doubt, fear and reliability on other things or people also. Amid these things that swarm our mind and divert our attention, we lose focus off Jesus. We become busybodies trying to figure it out every other way instead of bringing it straight to Jesus. When all else fails, we eventually go to Jesus as the last resort. But our first resort should be to bring it to Jesus. Even if we think of it as insignificant to pray about, pray for it any way. If it concerns us, it also concerns God. We may not be able to pray with faith in the moment, but God can help us overcome our unbelief also. So, instead of making our way up to God slowly by stepping on other things one step at a time, just bring the "boy" directly to God.

Dear LORD, please forgive me when I wait and seek the help of others instead of coming to You right away. Please help me to understand how powerful You are, and nothing is impossible for You. Help me to overcome my unbelief and believe in the name of Jesus. Thank you for giving me the privilege to bring to You directly whatever concerns me. In Jesus' name, Amen!

Ruled by emotions - June 2

Know this, my beloved brothers: let every person be quick to hear, slow to speak, slow to anger. James 1:19

Most often we are ruled by our emotions. We allow our circumstances to dictate who we are and how we behave at a given moment. When we are happy and everything seems good, we behave well and treat others well also. But when we are upset or angry, our attitude changes and we become a whole new person. In the heated moments, our Christianity goes out the door and we say and do things which we regret later. When emotions take over, we let the evil side of us come out which we have been working so hard on to get rid of from our lives.

Therefore, to have self-control is always crucial. If we strive to be Christ-like, we must discipline our body, mouth and mind to behave like Jesus in all situations. As difficult as it is at the time, we must quiet ourselves down and remember who we are in Christ. We need to put ourselves in His feet and think about what would Jesus do (WWJD) and do likewise. It takes a lot of effort on our part to remain silent when we are falsely accused or to walk away when we are treated unfairly but by doing so, we have already been victorious. We are transparent with God and if He knows our innocence, then we have no need to prove ourselves to anyone else. We just need to be still and allow God to fight on our behalf. Other people's opinion or treatment towards us does not alter who we are, therefore, we must not submit to the negative emotions of anyone else and determine ours also.

We do not represent Jesus when we act based on our emotions so we must not compromise our character for our circumstances.

Dear LORD, would You please help me to submit to Your authority and not to be ruled by my emotions. Always help me to be spiritually minded and train myself for godliness to represent You regardless of my circumstances. Thank you for giving me Your peace and patience to hold me down beyond how I feel. In Jesus' name, Amen!

It's not always about me - June 3

Everyone looks out for their own interests, not those of Jesus Christ.
Philippians 2:21

The three most common questions of a typical teenager are "Can I have money?", "What's there to eat?" and "Can I go there?" I often wonder why they are so selfish and always about them wanting something? As I found myself thinking about these questions, it clicked me that is not this what we do to God? All we do is continuously ask God for this and that. Our prayers are mostly full of such demands about wanting more money, better provisions of food, clothing, housing, health and places to go. We go to God with a laundry list of things and majority of our time spent in prayer is about what we want. Just like a good parent, God does provide for our needs and gives us the desire of our hearts, but He also longs for us to just want Him and nothing else. He desires for us to spend time with Him because we love Him, not because we need something from Him. God yearns for our love in return for His, although we can never compare ours to His. He just wants us to give Him our best of time, attention and faithfulness.

So, instead of being selfish and making it all about what we want, sometimes we need to ask God what He wants from us. Instead of giving a list of things to do for us, we should give God a list of what we have to offer and ask Him what He desires. And our prayers do not necessarily have to be about us talking only, we must learn to sit quietly in His presence and allow God to speak so that we can hear His voice and listen to what He wants from us.

Dear LORD, thank you for always meeting my needs and blessing me with more than I deserve. Please help me not to be selfish and only think about my interests but be mindful of what I can do for You in return. I know I can never repay You back for everything that You do for me but help me to offer You my best in whatever I can give. In Jesus' name, Amen!

Flawless - June 4

The LORD will perfect that which concerns me; Psalm 138:8

To be perfect is to be without any flaws, blemishes or defects. It is exact and accurate. When we think we are confident about something though, it is never perfect. It is filled with doubts, worry, anxiety and dependent on our circumstances. We wish our life were perfect, but we all have people and concerns in life which tests our faith and confidence. But all these come in our life to make us stronger and grow our confidence in God. The adversities lead us to draw close to God and see a need for His help. It is hard to see God at work or understand what He is up to in the present, but when we see in hindsight, we can see how beautifully God worked everything out.

Our God is a perfect God and everything He does is precise and accurate. God does not make mistakes nor is He ever unsure of anything He does. He knows the things that bother us, He knows about the people who are out there to harm us, and He knows the loved ones whom we care about and their needs. God knows it all and will take care of it just perfectly in due time.

Therefore, if we feel lost and have a hard time to grasp what and why things are happening the way they are, let's be assured that God is not lost and He is at work about everything that matters to us. We may not be confident in ourselves, but God is. We may not see it, but God already has it figured out from start to finish. Our concerns are His concerns and is at work to make it right.

Dear LORD, thank you that You are my good Father and always have my best interest in Your heart. Please help me to remember that You are perfect in all Your ways and nothing You do is there for my harm but for my good. Give me eyes to see by faith Your perfect will for my life. In Jesus name, Amen!

Upright posture – June 5

Blessed is the man who walks not in the counsel of the ungodly, nor stands in the path of sinners, nor sits in the seat of the scornful. Psalm 1:1

Posture is the position in which we hold our body upright. To have good physical posture we must train our body to walk, stand and sit straight. Similarly, we must train our spiritual bodies to be upright in the LORD. According to this Bible verse how, where and with whom we walk, stand and sit determine our spiritual uprightness.

We must be mindful of whom we walk with. Ungodly are those who live independently from God and their perception is only humanly or earthly. They behave and live according to the standards of the world only. When we walk in our journey of life surrounded by such folks, they eventually rub off their ideas onto us and if we follow their guidance, we fall off track from our walk with God. Therefore, we must be careful that we do not walk or take advice from those who do not have the fear or love for God.

We must also be watchful of where we stand. Often, we are confident that we know our limit and would not allow ourselves to fall into sin. We get close to the fire and test ourselves in the heat, expecting to pull ourselves away when it gets too hot. But the devil is out there to destroy us so when we get close, he pushes us right into it without us even realizing how and when we got there. So, to avoid being in danger of falling into the fire of sin, God tells us to not even go anywhere and stand where sin is. We must stay away from any path which leads us to sin.

And lastly, scornful are those people who are hateful, unrespectful, quick at mocking and making taunting remarks. The Bible clearly states to not associate with such people nor even sit in their company as they can drag us into their negativity and we too become like that, giving birth to hatred, bitterness, anxiety and anger within us that is not even our own.

Thus, we must consider our walking, standing and sitting in order to maintain an upright posture in front of God and be blessed by Him.

Dear LORD, please help me to train myself for godliness and choose carefully with whom I walk my life with, where I go and in whose company I sit. Teach me to discern between good and bad according to your standards and help me to remove myself away from any persons or places that seek to make me fall. In Jesus' name, Amen!

More than I need - June 6

Look at the birds of the air; they do not sow or reap or store away in barns, and yet your heavenly Father feeds them. Are you not much more valuable than they? Matthew 6:26

In a country like America where water quality is probably the cleanest and purest compared to many other countries, Americans still spend billions of dollars on bottled water than to drink tap water right from the convenience of their kitchen sinks. According to the Beverage Marketing Corporation, bottled water was an $18.5 billion industry in the U.S. in 2017.

Yes, there are factors such as high lead content which lead people to opt for natural spring water, but the main driving force is nothing more than marketing strategies. The lead content in our water is not as significant but bottled water companies have created such a fear about it that people believe that if they drink regular water from the tap, they will get sick and die sooner. Many of the bottled water that we drink are nothing more than simply filtered-tap water, yet our minds are manipulated in feeling better about it and we end up spending so much money on water than need be. There are places and reasons for which one must need these additional resources but many of us just fall for the advertisements and use it for pleasure rather than need.

The more we have, the more we demand. Satan is the master of maneuvering who twists and turns our blessings into fear, and we end up adding our own human touch to what God has already created and called it good. God knows what we need and provides the best for us yet due to our own intelligence and selfishness, we step on God's toes and reach for better than what He has already provided.

Because we have been blessed with an abundance and so many options to choose from, we take our blessings for granted and start to devalue what has been given to us. We must learn to be content and trust God to meet our needs. If He waters the grass and trees and gives the same water to drink to the birds and animals, are we lesser than these in God's sight that He should not give us good water to drink or food to eat? Are we not more valuable than birds and flowers?

·Dear LORD, You are my Jehovah Jireh, my provider who continues to bless me with abundance so please help me not to demand more than what is needed for my life. Teach me to be grateful and content with what You give me than rather than question and over-ride your provisions. In Jesus' name, Amen!

Key ingredients - June 7

And I am sure of this, that he who began a good work in you will bring it to completion at the day of Jesus Christ. Philippians 1:6

Before I begin to cook, I like to have all necessary vegetables, meats and ingredients cut and lined up in order beforehand. So that when I start to cook, everything I need is ready for me. As I use the ingredients one by one and see them mixing and blending with the rest, I can smell the wonderful aroma and cannot wait for the output of a delicious meal. But if an ingredient is left out by mistake, I can taste the difference and know that the dish is missing something. Every little ingredient contributes its own, special flavor so if it is left out, it can make a flavorless product. However, if it consumed by itself, it does not taste as good. Therefore, all ingredients as good as they may be on their own, make the best meal if they are mixed and used together.

We all are like individual ingredients of a recipe for a specific family, community or a nation. Individually, we all have our own flavor, texture and have been born and raised in different environments and conditions. We may think that our flavor is the finest and we are better than others based on our looks, structure and where we come from. But only until we have been blended and become a part of a combined mixture, the best of our flavor is released.

Also, the good and bad experiences of life are like ingredients. Some may be sweet and soft while some may be bitter and hard. But God has placed each one of them as necessary ingredients to make a wonderful life for us. We may deem some experiences and people as pointless ingredients who only add an unpleasant taste to our life but until it all comes together at the end, do we understand how necessary they all are.

God has designed us and what we face in life as key ingredients which contribute to the final plan or product He has in mind. On an individual basis we have been created to perfection so that our flavor brings out the best in others around us and together we release an aroma which is acceptable to God.

Dear LORD, thank you for creating me in a unique way to add flavor to the delicious future You have prepared for me. Please help me not to count myself better or look down to others but understand that every person and experience are all necessary ingredients to create something beautiful for my life. In Jesus' name, Amen!

Everything - June 8

For I can do everything through Christ, who gives me strength. Philippians 4:13

This bible verse is considered the motivational verse. It is used to encourage someone and build up their confidence, especially when faced with sickness or in accomplishing something positive. I was reminded that this not only pertains for the purpose of acquiring good health and wealth but also for those things in our life that need to be corrected and freed from.

We all are slaves to some secret sins which may be only between God and us. Whether it is an addiction of some sort or a sin of lust, pride, anger, jealousy, lying, cheating or bitterness, we find it hard or nearly impossible to be freed and get rid of by our own. Our spirit may be willing, but our flesh is weak, and we often fall into these sins repeatedly. So, this verse serves as a reminder to us today that no matter what our issue may be, internal or external, physical or spiritual, everything can be done with the help of Jesus Christ who gives us strength! He equips us to endure sickness and struggle, wisdom for decision, patience in hard times, energy in weakness, power to walk away, and resistance towards temptation.

Often, we feel ashamed to bring our sin and shame to God and try to fight the battle ourselves. We feel embarrassed or guilty to bring it to God and we suffer internally. Or we may know it is a sin but since we enjoy it, we ignore it and try to reason it out to God with the help of the devil who gives us every excuse for our every sin. But if we call a ourselves child of God and if He has convicted us of our sin, we must repent and turn away from it.

And this is the meaning of "everything" in this verse that no matter what it is, anything and everything can be accomplished with God's help if we have a willing heart to do so.

Therefore, we do not need to allow the devil to limit our thinking on what God can do and what we can do through God. If we are ready to do it, it is Yes and Amen with God also!

Dear LORD, thank you for giving me encouragement through Your word that no matter what I struggle with, I can face it and be freed in the name of Jesus. Please help me to look to You for help to overcome all that hinders me from becoming who I am in You. You are my everything who can do anything, and so can I! In Jesus' name, Amen!

Be mindful - June 9

Watch yourself and doctrine closely. 1 Timothy 4:16

One of the things that I have started to ask God for myself is to be mindful of my ways. Majority of times we do things routinely and mindlessly to which we do not pay much attention. There is a vast difference between being mindful and mindless which we need to consider.

When we do things mindlessly, we blurt out words without thinking of its impact on others, we do things which we often wish we had not done, and also unnecessary thoughts that drive us crazy contribute to our mindless activities. These things we do because we act on impulse and do not give it much thought. We become hasty to act on temptation, get provoked and are vulnerable to do and feel what others say to us. Because they are done routinely and often do not come with any major consequences, we feel as if it is alright and it becomes our lifestyle. But it is these little things that we count as insignificant is what leads us into trouble. Little things do not stay little but they grow and if we do not take control over it, it takes control over us. I often find myself in a space where I am regretful of what I said and did right after it is done and feel foolish about it. I wish I were smart to have thought about it before I acted a certain way. Once it is said and done, we cannot go back and undo it no matter what.

Therefore, it is important that we take heed to all our ways and think before we say a word or act upon something. Being mindful is about being aware of what we are about to do and weigh its consequences before we do it. It is about making a conscious choice or decision to do something, whether it is minute or major.

And that is why my prayer is, to be mindful so that I have the discernment to know ahead of time what is right and wrong and behave in such a way that is acceptable in God's sight alone and no regrets attached to it.

Dear LORD, please give me clarity and a sound mind so that I am clear about the steps that You have ordered for me. Help me not to be quick on jumping to conclusions, over-react or become over-excited to do anything which I find myself later to be wrong and hurt myself and others. Always help me to keep my mind on You . In Jesus' name, Amen!

I will follow Jesus - June 10

Then Jesus told his disciples, "If anyone would come after me, let him deny himself and take up his cross and follow me. Matthew 16:24

While driving, I was listening to the song "I will follow" by Chris Tomlin. I was enjoying myself singing along to the lyrics "where You go, I'll go; where You stay, I'll stay; where You move, I'll move; I will follow You...". Then I heard Jesus' voice in the background "Prove it!"

I was stopped in my tracks with my head bowed in shame, knowing that I have proved myself wrong all the time. How many places have I gone where Jesus would not go? How many times I have stayed still when Jesus has told me to stay or not move until He moves? I have done the opposite more than I have done what He has asked of me. Then how can I sing, "I will follow You?".

It is easier said than done. We are quick to read our Bibles and recite Bible verses off memory. We can also sing aloud the words of a song and get excited about the music and tune, but if we are not the doers of the words that we speak and sing, our worship is meaningless.

Unless we do what, the Bible says and it becomes a part of our life, we really are not followers of Jesus. We may call ourselves Christians by religion but if our walk and deed does not follow in the footsteps of Jesus, we cannot be considered true disciples of Jesus. Yes, we can certainly fail and let God down but if it is a habit and lifestyle which we cannot let go and still continue to live in it, then we are followers of the world, not Jesus.

In our daily walk we must take into mind where we are going, who we are with and what we do and say. If Jesus would not come along or agree with our thoughts and actions, we must stop and trace ourselves back to Jesus' footsteps and follow Him!

Dear LORD, please open my eyes to look back to see where I have fallen off track from following You. You are the way, the truth and the life so please hold my feet firm to Your path and follow You with all my heart, mind and soul. Help me to go where You go, stay where You stay, move when You move and love whom You love. In Jesus' name, Amen!

In the middle of the night - June 11

But while everyone was sleeping, his enemy came and sowed weeds among the wheat, and went away. Matthew 13:25

Often, I find myself awakened at 3 a.m. in the middle of the night. At that time, I feel a great nudge in my heart to get up and pray. Many a times I have avoided it as my body is so tired and my eyes can barely open. But I have learned to overcome these and get up and pray any way. When I pray at this hour, I sense a deeper connection to God. I feel as if He is speaking more and I am just listening. I have found myself continuously praying beyond the sound of my alarm clock and do not even realize how long I had been praying.

The significance of praying in the middle of the night is to cancel out the plan of the devil which is he is planning for us when we wake up. Satan works best while we are asleep, both physically and spiritually. He plants weeds in our mind which we wake up to and it continues to grow into our day. Thoughts of bitterness, anxiety, lust and all evil are planted in the middle of the night. It is said that it is the fourth night of the watch, between 3 am – 6 am, that satanic agents are returning from these evil duties. And so, it is this time that God wakes us up to reveal these evil plans and cancel them out with prayer before they occur. We may not realize it but there is a great battle raging over us in the spiritual realm and while the devil is forming his attack, God often causes us to wake up and fight it out before it takes root. We must engage ourselves in this spiritual warfare and fight with God to destroy the enemy before he destroys us.

The devil is not limited to any specific time to wage his war against us and is always on the lookout to devour us. However, while our body and mind are resting, he seizes this as the best opportunity to target our minds. Therefore, we must always remain vigilant and be willing to pray it out. It may cause us a little discomfort to get out of bed half asleep, but if we can get ourselves to go pray at an hour when the devil is not expecting us to, there is no hindrance between God and us; it's a clear road to God's throne without any distractions.

Dear LORD, please help me to heed Your voice when You prompt me to pray. Help me not to ignore it and give importance to my sleep or other activities over Your conviction to pray. You have given me the weapon of prayer so teach me to use it, even if it is in the middle of the night. Open my eyes, ears and heart to hear You speak as You instruct me. Thank you for watching over me and giving me the courage to oppose the forces that form against me. In Jesus' name, Amen!

For my own good - June 12

And even when you ask, you don't get it because your motives are all wrong—you want only what will give you pleasure. James 4:3

I love to share my food with our dog, Teddy. He loves to eat what we eat but lately due to some reactions he has been getting which has made him sick, the Vet has advised us not to give him any table food. For Teddy to remain healthy, it is important that we only feed him his own dog food and nothing else. So lately as hard as it is for me, I try not share my food with him. He scratches and barks at me while I eat but I just ignore him or turn my head the other way. He gives me his puppy eyes and looks so disappointed at me when I do this but I know what I'm doing is for his own benefit and so regardless of how much be begs and barks, I do not give into him. As the owner of the dog, we know what is good and bad for Teddy and because we love and care for him, we must do what is best for him whether he likes it or not.

In the same way, we feel disappointed when we ask God for something and He does not give it to us. We may question God as to why He is not listening to us or turning down our requests. It might seem good to us, but God knows in the long run how bad it could be, so He keeps us away from it. It may look pleasing to us in the present and that is all we can think of having, but if its harms outweigh the benefits, God will rather not give it to us then to see us suffer. We can shout and stomp all we want but thank God that He does not give into all our demands because He knows they are for our own pleasure but with eternal consequences.

Therefore, let us understand that if our prayers are not being met the way we want or if God is saying no, it is not because He does not love us or is being harsh towards us. It is because He loves us too much to see us hurt by giving into our every demand. God always has our best interest in His heart and has a reason for why He does what He does. So even if it seems unfair now, we need to learn to trust God when He does not give us what we want each time.

Dear LORD, thank you for loving me too much to not give me everything I desire. It may seem pleasing in my own eyes but because You know how harmful it is for me, You keep me away from it. Please teach me to accept Your No and be thankful for it even if I do not understand why. You know why so let that be enough for me and leave it in Your hands. In Jesus' name, Amen!

Baton of faith - June 13

Rescue those being taken off to death and save those stumbling toward slaughter.
Proverbs 24:11

In ancient days when enemies went to war, if the King was captured and killed, the conqueror also killed all the captured king's sons and grandsons in order to prevent the entire family line from ever coming back on the throne. When King Saul was killed, the caretaker of Mephibosheth, King Saul's grandson, tried to save the young child and fled from the enemy. While running away, she dropped the young boy who ended up being crippled the rest of his life.

The devil is set on destroying us, the King's children! He is threatened by our relationship and victory in Jesus, so he is chasing us down to kill and destroy. We as caretakers of our children have been given the responsibility to save them from Satan's hand. We need to grab, run and rescue them from destroying our youth, the next generation. Many of those under our care may not be strong in the LORD to fight for themselves, so God has placed us in their lives to be the means of protecting and pointing them towards God.

So while we are in the process of saving and running from the enemy, we need to ensure that we don't trip over fear, doubt, worry or discouragement that we end up stumbling, causing our dear ones to fall and become crippled. Rather we ought to hold them tight in our constant prayers and run with endurance, hope and patience towards the safety net of God's arm. Even if any have been crippled due to our mishandling or due to their own fault, Jesus is seeking and waiting to show His favor and mercy on His children. Will you rescue your loved ones from Satan's hand and lead them to Jesus?

Dear LORD, help me to acknowledge that the baton of faith must be passed on to our next generation. The devil is out there to demolish the next generation from knowing You so please help me to do my best and rescue our children from Satan's stronghold. By prayer and faith, help me to carry our children and run so that I can save them and prepare them for the continuation of Your work for the future generations to come. In Jesus' name, Amen!

I got this - June 14

The LORD himself goes before you and will be with you; he will never leave you nor forsake you. Do not be afraid; do not be discouraged." Deuteronomy 31:8

On KLove radio station the hosts were asking the listeners to describe the year 2020 in three words. Many called in with impressive answers and I started to think what my three words would be. "I Got This" was the answer that came to my mind. It was not me saying this about myself, but it was as if it is God's reply to me. What we are going through in this world lately have been unpredictable and something we never imagined ourselves to experience. The coronavirus pandemic, cancers, natural disasters and violence are growing tremendously. And the way of lifestyle and beliefs of people just seem out of this world in these times. Many marriages are on the verge of divorces, families are breaking apart, drug-alcohol addictions, prodigals, identity issues, suicides, corruption, back sliding of many religious leaders, etc. have become a part of our general news these days.

When we hear of such, fear and worry can grip our hearts but through these all, God gives us gentle reminder that "I Got this". He's the got the whole world in His hands. There is no person, place, animal or thing that God cannot control or override. All that is happening around us is undoubtedly scary and we wonder if it will ever end but no matter what or how long it takes, we must put our trust in God and allow Him to handle our situations and circumstances. The storm can rage all around us, but we can rest assured under God's protection and be safe under His wings. He has promised us that He would never leave us nor forsake us so let us put our hope in God and believe that if He's said "I Got this" then He has really got it!

Dear LORD, thank you for Your promise to be with me and carry me through no matter what I face. We may not know or feel capable of controlling what is going on around us by ourselves but whatever it may be, You've Got it so help me to believe it and trust You with all my heart. In Jesus' name, Amen!

...But where sin increased, grace increased all the more. Romans 5:20

consider myself a neat freak. It bothers me when I see things out of place or stains anywhere. Until I clean it up, I feel restless. As I was cleaning the bathroom, I noticed some stains which I attempted to wipe off using an all-purpose cleaner. The stains were stubborn but so was I and would not give up until I removed it. The tougher the stain, the harder my effort in erasing it. I kept scrubbing and trying more harsh and stronger cleaners until finally the stains were off.

This reminded me of how God is towards our sins. There is no sin tough enough for God to ever remove. Sometimes we may feel that our sins are too many and too rough for God to ever forgive us. The devil continues to remind us of these and keeps etching them in our mind, making us feel like a filthy rag that can never be made clean again. But God on the other hand, is Mr. Clean who has the best remedy for cleansing us spotless. His blood can wash all our sins away and make us white as snow again. It does not matter how big or deep our sins are, once we recognize and are repentant of them, God goes to work to purify us. He does not ever give up and leave us soiled. Rather the more our sins, the more His grace pours out on us to forgive and cleanse us of all unrighteousness.

Therefore, we must not be embarrassed or afraid to bring to Jesus the unmentionable stains and sins in our life. He would not look down on us and think anything negative about us. Instead, He awaits eagerly to spray and cleanse us using His one and only required cleaner – the precious blood of Jesus.

Dear LORD, Thank You for the powerful remedy of Your blood which can cleanse all my sins away. Please help me not to hide my sins thinking that You will be mad or cast me away from Your presence, instead give me courage to bring You my sin and shame knowing that the more my sin, the more Your grace abounds. Thank You for scrubbing and cleaning me spotless with Your grace and forgiveness. In Jesus' name, Amen!

Anointed - June 16

For am I now seeking the approval of man, or of God? Or am I trying to please man? If I were still trying to please man, I would not be a servant of Christ.
Galatians 1:10

To endorse is to support, approve or sustain a person or an activity. In many things that we do, we usually do it for the endorsement of people. We work and do things to impress people. Whether we have been called by God to do something or not, we seek opportunities where we can be approved by people. We promote ourselves to gain approval of men over God. And when we do such, many of us have experienced failure in our endeavor as we do it without the blessing of God in it.

When it comes to doing something, particularly for God's kingdom, it is about the anointing and not endorsing! It is God who chooses a person or group for a specific purpose. David was called as the King of Israel by God. He did not go out and endorse himself to be chosen. It was Samuel that came looking for David. In fact, David did not even know that Samuel was in search for him. Until the appointed time, David just minded his own business and continued to do what he was called at that time as shepherd boy. He was considered insignificant compared to his brothers who were endorsed by their father, but that did not stop God from choosing David.

When God endorses, no person can disqualify or disapprove us. At the due time, God sends "Samuel" to come look for us to anoint us to be used for God's higher purpose. We have no need to parade ourselves in front of people to be acknowledged or promoted. We just need to go about doing our business as God has called us for that particular season. And if it is God who has called us for a specific task, He puts His favor on us and equips us in every way to accomplish what He has willed.

Dear LORD, please help me to keep my eyes, heart and mind on You alone as I go about my business. In everything that I do, help me to do it faithfully as if I am doing it for You and no one else. Help me not to worry about impressing or receiving accolades from people but may my heart's only longing be for You to say, "Well done, my good and faithful servant". In Jesus' name, Amen!

Warning Signs - June 17

Therefore, let anyone who thinks that he stands take heed lest he fall. 1 Corinthians 10:12

My daughter and I were driving through the heavy rains recently and came across many flooded streets where we had to take detours. There was one intersection which was pretty flooded, and many cars were struggling to pass by. Some drivers cautiously passed through, but some got stuck in the middle of the road. As we were approaching the intersection, we saw a man standing in the rain, gesturing people to not go through. He warned us also and told us to turn around. Many heeded his instructions, including us and turned around. But some ignored the man's warnings and headed for disaster.

In the same manner, many in this world are headed towards eternal disaster, many knowingly and many unknowingly. Therefore, God has sent messengers who are trying to warn people about it and to turn around from the path of sinful life. The Bible is full of warning signs that cautions us about our sinful ways. Additionally, God sends messengers in various forms like preachers, sermons, devotions, worship songs and music. Even more than ever, God is now sending us loud warning signals through natural sources such as diseases, earthquakes, fires, wars, etc. to get our attention. These messages are being sent our way to show us the truth about the disastrous path that we are walking on, where we are headed and the need for us to repent of our sins as the end times are at hand and we do not have much time left to turn around.

But many choose to ignore these messages and do what they please. They do not take these warning signs seriously but in their arrogance, walk right into eternal damnation. Often, we are too full of ourselves and do not wish to listen or follow the counsel of godly folks who God has sent in our lives. But if we desire to be saved, we must learn to heed the warnings now that God is giving us before it is too late. We need to humble ourselves and be wise in recognizing people, activities and places that cause us to be swept away. If we continue to walk in our sinful path and refuse to repent after we know the truth, it is a sin and our foolishness.

Dear LORD, please help me not to take lightly the warnings that You are giving me about my sinful ways. Teach me how to be mindful of my daily choices and decisions so that I do not continue to walk in the wrong path which leads to separation from you. Thank you for loving me so much to want to save me. I pray that You give me a heart to heed the warnings and turn around. In Jesus' name, Amen!

For many are called, but few are chosen." Matthew 22:14

Indians are known for having lavish weddings where they use up much of their money they have purposely put aside for this special occasion. Generally large number of guests are invited and most of them do attend because who does not like getting dressed up, enjoying great food, partying and socializing with family and friends? Very rarely are those who decline the invitation without any reason and miss out on a such occasion.

Just like an earthly wedding, invitation to the wedding feast in the kingdom of heaven has been sent out to each one of us. The guest list will continue to rise, and more ongoing invitations will be delivered even to the last minute of the occasion, as God does not want anyone to miss out on this once in a lifetime opportunity. He desires that all should come. Many of us have already sent our RSVP and accepted the invitation while there are those who are still thinking about it and cannot make up their mind. They are holding on to the invitation till the deadline, maybe because they are busy with other things or waiting to get a better invite somewhere else. And then there are those who have flatly declined the invitation due to their own pride, prejudice, excuses and reasons. They simply do not want to accept it because they do not believe in Jesus or want any part of Him.

Regardless of who will come or not, God has still sent the invitation to everyone. He does not care whether we know Him, are in close relation, have called Him to our occasions or not, or if we are worthy to be a part of God's kingdom. Everyone is worthy in God's sight and has called each one to come. But only the ones who accept His invitation and actually come to Jesus are considered the chosen ones who get to partake in the heavenly feast.

Let us not be under false presumptions that we are automatically chosen because our family is invited, have connections to a church or know the Bible and about Jesus. It is true that we all have been called to the heavenly wedding feast but each one of us must individually accept the invitation and come to Jesus. It is not enough to be invited; we must show up to be considered the chosen guests.

Dear LORD, thank you for You the invitation to be a part of Your kingdom. Please help me to accept it without any hesitation and consider it a privilege to be chosen. May I come just as I am and not miss it for the world. In Jesus' name, Amen!

Words are not necessary - June 19

Feed the hungry and help those in trouble. Then your light will shine out from the darkness, and the darkness around you will be as bright as noon. Isaiah 58:10

We did food distribution at our church during the Pandemic situation. We handed out hundreds of boxes per week, filled with perishable and non-perishable food items to those families in need. For some of us who participated in the distribution process, the only opportunity we had for conversing with the folks who came in for the boxes was to hand one box after the other and say, "God Bless You and thank you for coming". Handing of the boxes may not have felt like a big deal to us or understood the relationship of meeting a physical need with that of spiritual. The Salvation Army's slogan is "Soup-Soap-Salvation". The way to reach a person is through their stomach first, then provide for the necessities of life, and finally talk about God as it leads. Unless we can satisfy a physical hunger first, our effort to meet a someone's spiritual appetite does not get us far. Giving the box full of food not only provided for their immediate physical nourishment but also spiritual down the road. It was a way for us to share God's love through action.

Many of us back down from sharing the good news of Jesus to others because we feel that we need to talk to them about it which many of us are uncomfortable doing. But words are not necessary to communicate God's love. It can be done in action which is often more effective than words. Therefore, let us not become discouraged in sharing the good news to people on basis of our talk alone. Talk can come later, all we need to do first is be available and hand out the little gestures of love via soup and soap, salvation will follow supernaturally afterwards.

Dear LORD, thank you for choosing us to be Your hands and feet on this earth to demonstrate Your love through the little acts of kindness we do. Please help us not be selfish and think about our needs alone but the needs of others first. Grant us courage to talk about You to others as we not only provide for their physical needs but also spiritual. May Your name and love shine through us in this dark world. In Jesus' name, Amen!

Give God a chance - June 20

For the wages of sin is death, but the free gift of God is eternal life through Christ Jesus our Lord. Romans 6:23

When we gave a Father's Day gift to my husband, just by looking at the bag, he knew there was something quite expensive in it and before even looking at it, he said, "return it". In his head, he was thinking that he is paying for it anyway since I used "our" credit card, so he did not want it. But it was something he needed and had a desire for a while, so we did convince him to keep it.

Many people do the same with Jesus. Before even giving him a chance, they decline him. They assume that it will require some sort of payback to accept Him so before even looking into what He has to offer, they just say no. The gift that God is giving us does not require any payment from our side. Jesus paid it all, so we do not owe Him anything. It is a gift which if we decline, can lead to our own loss. We may think we can get by without Him and may not have the desire for Jesus right now but will realize later that we needed Him after all.

So, let us not deny Jesus straight up without even looking into Him. We must give Him a chance and we will realize that He is the best gift we have ever received.

———————————————

Dear Heavenly Father, thank you that You are my good, good Father who is perfect in all Your ways. In Your perfect plan, You sent Jesus to be the sacrifice who paid for all my sins. Please help me to be grateful and accept this gift without having the fear of paying You back. In Jesus' name, Amen!

———————————————

Memory Pillars - June 21

I remember the days of old; I meditate on all that you have done; I ponder the work of your hands. Psalm 143:5

In ancient Biblical times, people would set up stone pillars as a memory of an event that took place. The purpose of these pillars was to serve as a reminder about the presence and deliverance of God at a specific time and place in a person's life.

We may not use physical pillars these days, but we do set them in our minds as a memory. We use these memory pillars most often to keep reminding ourselves about what we went through, the difficult times, and the hardships that we faced. And whenever we think about it, it brings us down, fill us with sadness and grips us with fear of it happening again. We defeat the purpose of it when we create such us pillars in our head. The true purpose of remembrance of our past events is not to look back and recount the hardships but rather count the blessings of the LORD through them. They are to remind us about the goodness of God and how He delivered us out of it. They should serve as an encouragement, not a discouragement that no matter what we face in life, we have confidence in a faithful God who did it then and will do it again!

It is the devil's way of turning our memory as pillars of weakness rather than strength. Therefore, let us not give him access to turn our joy into fear. Let's ensure that every time we come upon the memory lane of the pillars that we have set from the past, they may serve as a reminder about how mighty our God is instead of how mighty our problem was or will ever be.

Dear LORD, as I think about the past, negative events that took place in my life, please help me to remember Your mighty hand in it which saved and delivered me. Help me not see these as defeat but rather as victory which You won over the attacks of the enemy. May these events take me from strength to strength, victory to victory and to new heights in my faith in You. In Jesus name, Amen!

Remove the junk - June 22

You keep him in perfect peace whose mind is stayed on you. Isaiah 26:3

My husband and I accomplished a big task in the house. We cleaned out the garage which was past overdue for a while. We kept putting it off to some day while in the meantime it kept getting more and more cluttered. Eventually, we impromptu decided to just clean it and so we got to work. As we finally cleared it out, we realized how much we had collected over the years, much of it unnecessary and would probably never need. The garage now looks so organized and has so much extra space which we did not notice before. It was necessary to remove the clutter and get rid of the extra junk as it was not of any benefit but rather taking up space which we could use for better purposes now.

In the same way, it is necessary that we take inventory of our heart and mind and get rid of the junk that we have stored up from the past such as unforgiveness, hatred, bitterness and all sorts of bad habits. Many of us like to hold on to our junk and keep recycling it in our heads. Like my husband who likes to hold on to things for the sake of needing it someday, we too hold on to our unneeded thoughts just in case they come handy and we need to defend ourselves.

Our heart and mind are meant for God to speak into it, but we do not leave any room for Him. We fill it up with things that corrupt our mind and cause it to be clogged up. The clutter in our head just takes away the space which God intends to fill up with His thoughts and purpose. But we become busybodies with sinful and wandering ideas which gets rusted and eventually grows into mold and spreads into our being and causes us to be destroyed.

Therefore, it is necessary that we guard and clean up our body, mind and heart regularly so that it does not become a storage place for the devil. We must take inventory and remove the unholy, impure and sinful things from our life that take us away from God and His word.

Dear LORD, thank you for the reminder that I need to remove the junk from my life that takes my focus from You. Please reveal to me those things which are clogging up my mind and causing me to stray where I should not be. Fill my thoughts with You and may I meditate on Your word day and night. May my life be clean inside out so that it can be a dwelling place for You. In Jesus' name, Amen!

Memorization - June 23

I have hidden Your word in my heart that I might not sin against You.
Psalm 119:11

It takes a little while before I fall asleep when I try to go to sleep at night. As I lay in bed, I find myself replaying the events that occurred during the day and often my mind wanders off into thoughts and imaginations about things that I should've and should not have done. It often leads to worries and sinful activities occurring in my mind until I eventually fall asleep.

Therefore, to avoid being in this state, instead of daydreaming and thinking unthinkable thoughts, I have learned to occupy my mind with meditating on God's word. I start to recite as many Bible verses that I have in my memory and think about them. One after the other, one verse leads to another and I begin to memorize even more each night. The last thought in my head when I fall asleep is about God and it just gives me a peaceful rest. I have also experienced that God often gives me more insight during the night about the meaning of the Bible passages which I had been thinking about before I fell asleep.

A time will come when this book, the Bible, will be taken away from us and we will not have access to God's word easily. Also, we do not have time to open up our Bibles and read God' word every time we are about to fall into sin. But if we have it stored in our heart, it is right there at our disposal and no one can separate us from the living word. If we have God's word handy in our mind, we can use it readily before we sin instead of scrambling for it afterwards. It is our defense system against the devil when he throws temptations and adversity against us.

Therefore, let us make the best use of every available moment to fill it with God's word and memorize as many scriptures. God's word is our sword which He has given to us to fight against the enemy so we must sharpen our sword and be ready to fight our daily spiritual battles.

Dear LORD, thank you for giving us Your word which encourages us in our hardships and gives us hope for the future. Please help me not to take it lightly and read it only when I need to, but may it be my daily bread from which I get my strength. Write Your word on my heart so that I have an easy access to it and may I use it readily under every circumstance. In Jesus' name, Amen!

God is offended - June 24

For the anger of man does not produce the righteousness of God. James 1:20

Oftentimes when we are angry about something or not in a good mood, we end up taking our anger out on everyone who comes in our path. We not only give an attitude to the one person whom it is due, but we lash out on others as well with the same negative attitude. And this does not exclude God! He too becomes the recipient of our anger although He may be the innocent bystander. We may not do it purposefully but when we speak and do things in our anger, we treat God with contempt and indirectly lash out on Him also. Our intent might be to defend ourselves against someone who offended us but while in doing so, we end up sinning and hurting God in the process.

I recall a moment when I had angry thoughts and decided to do something about it which of course would involve saying and doing things that would not be acceptable in God's sight. And as I planned in my head about how I would retaliate, God stopped me in my tracks and asked me "But what did I do? Why are you doing this against Me?"

These words made me pause and think that when we act in an ungodly manner, it is God who we go against primarily. It is God who gets hurt the most when we try to hurt someone else. He always remains faithful to us then why do we play around with our relationship with God and behave according to our mood and circumstance? In our haste and rage, we factor God out of the equation when we say and do things which are unlike Him. But we must consider God foremost and who we are. Other peoples' treatment towards us should not determine how we treat them in return. If we say we belong to God, then we must remain faithful to God and not fall into sin regardless of our temperament or condition. Our relationship with God must not be compromised for our defense or someone else's offense. We must stay true to God; He will handle the rest!

Dear LORD, please help me to always remember who I am in You. Teach me not to act according to my emotions or situation and allow it to interfere in my relationship with You. May my reactions reveal Your righteousness in me instead of the sin. In Jesus' name, Amen!

Three "R" of Prayer - June 25

If you believe, you will receive whatever you ask for in prayer. Matthew 21:22

As I woke up in the middle of the night and was trying to fall back asleep, I saw three words pop up in my head multiple times. I could not make sense of them right away and as soon as I woke up, I wrote these words down and told my husband about them also so that I would not forget. I prayed that God would reveal to me what these words meant, and in the hours and days to follow, God taught me three elements of prayer. These elements are Request, Release and Receive.

When we pray, we need to be aware that we are bringing our needs to the one who can meet them. God knows what we need, and He feels honored when we acknowledge Him as our provider and request it to Him rather than demand and just expect Him to do it. Our prayer requests are a gift that we present to God because through them we show our gratefulness, dependency and recognition of God's authority and power. And once we have offered our gift to God, we must not take it back. We must release it in God's hand to do whatever He pleases. Often, we pray about something and "commit" it in God's hands however, as soon as we say "Amen", we go back to worrying about it and trying to figure things out on our own. We hold a conversation with God about it but in the end, we take our problems back with us rather than surrender them to God to resolve our issues. If we have acknowledged that God is our provider and has the power to meet our requests, we must thank Him and release them to God as if it is His problem and not ours anymore. Lastly, we need to be willing to receive the answer that God has for us. God loves us, knows us and is very aware of our past, present and future. He has a mighty plan and purpose for our lives and only gives us what is best for us. Therefore, we must gladly accept the answer to our requests whether it comes in a form of Yes, No or later.

Therefore, when we pray, we must remember whom we are praying to, give God all authority to work with it and accept what He give us because God always works everything out for our own good.

Dear LORD, You are my Jehovah Jireh, my provider; El Shaddai, the LORD God Almighty who has the power and authority; and Jehovah Shalom who gives me peace over the concerns of life. I offer to You my needs and trust You to meet them according to Your will and way. Please help me to heed these elements of prayer and may I pray to Request, Release and Receive it in Jesus' name, Amen!

Faith over fear - June 26

Do not be anxious about anything, but in every situation, by prayer and petition, with thanksgiving, present your requests to God. Philippians 4:6

It has been studied that eighty percent of our thoughts remain as thoughts and do not come into action. This suggests that we are overthinkers, I myself being guilty of having an anxious mind. I tend to make matters worse in my mind than they really are by thinking all sorts of thoughts, mostly negative ones and driving myself crazy. Most of these thoughts are just ideas and imaginations which I know are not true and mostly likely will never be, yet I get myself all worked up and become worried and fearful.

Being a human being, it is natural for us to be concerned about the things that matter to us. But when we turn the concern into worry, it shows that we do not trust God. When we worry, we doubt God's ability to save and are not confident about His ways, so we take matters into our own hands by trying to figure it out ourselves and end up losing our peace over it.

We do not think of it much, but worry is the devil's way of diverting our attention away from God and towards the things that bother us. He keeps bringing those adverse situations in front of us and keeps reminding us of how much trouble we are in. If we listen to him and give into his tactics, the next thing we know is that a monster of worries has been created in our head and we end up becoming fearful of our own created imaginations.

The bible clearly states that worry is a sin because it causes division between us and God. It takes away our trust and plays with our faith in God. God has not given us a spirit of fear so if we call ourselves the children of God, worry cannot coexist with faith. We must choose one and if we choose faith over fear, then no matter what our circumstances may be or what negative thoughts come in our head, we must learn to shut them off and let God convert our anxious thoughts back into faith and peace.

Dear LORD, please help me to remember that You have not given me a spirit of fear so teach me to trust in You no matter what I face. When negative thoughts come to my mind, please help me to surrender those thoughts of worry and fear to You and allow You to turn them back into faith-filled thoughts. May I be filled with Your peace that surpasses all my understanding. In Jesus' name, Amen!

Wise in my own eyes - June 27

The wisdom of the sensible is to understand his way, but the foolishness of fools is deceit. Proverbs 14:8

When God was pleased with King Solomon, He asked the King what wish God could grant for him. Solomon asked for nothing else but wisdom to rule God's people. So, God granted him his wish and made him the wisest man on earth, in addition to being the richest and the most famous. Solomon's wisdom was so great that other kings and dignitaries from all over came to hear and learn from Solomon.

Solomon was wise for the world, but he ended up as a fool for himself. He did not apply the vast wisdom God had given him to his own life. He gave sound advice and passed fair judgement to others, but he did not follow his own advice nor lived by the principals he taught others.

We are also like Solomon in this way. We are good at telling people what to do, teach others how to live a godly life, pass judgement as if we're better than them but when it comes to our own lives and that of our own, we fail miserably. We lower our own standard while raising the bar for others to live by. The world may consider us wise and look up to us but inwardly our own choices and decisions are foolish. We say and do things which we regret yet fail to learn from them. We prove our foolishness when we continue to make the same mistakes over and over.

Solomon's wisdom may have gained him popularity and pleasures of the world, but he fell short spiritually. He did not apply the same wisdom to make sound decisions that would honor God rather he ended up using that wisdom which displeased God.

So, as we learn from Solomon's foolishness, let us not become wise in our own eyes and that of people, rather let us consider our ways and apply godly wisdom to live a godly life.

Dear LORD, please grant me wisdom to apply it to my life before I tell others. Help me not be wise in my own eyes and do things which may please myself and others but end up being a fool in Your sight. Give me a sound mind to think wisely and live righteously. Help me to set a godly example by my own life. In Jesus' name, Amen!

Reversed priorities - June 28

Seek the Kingdom of God above all else, and live righteously, and he will give you everything you need. Matthew 6:33

There are some of us who have difficulty saying "No" to people. As per my nature, I am not able to say no easily when someone asks me to do something, or if I see that something needs to be done, I'll do it even if it's at my expense, inconvenient, takes a toll on me, and knowing I'm being taken advantage of.

As much as we like to help others and feel that it is our God-given duty to do so, we need to understand that not everything we do is a command from God. We may think so because if it is a benefit to someone else, God expects us to do it. But the truth is, God does not expect us to overwork and get so exhausted making others happy that we burn ourselves out, lose our focus off God, and mix up our priorities that He has established for us.

Our priority is our intimate relationship with God. We need to dedicate a decent amount of time each day to spend in prayer and Bible reading. Our "religious" duty does not measure up too much if we remain so busy doing the works, but do not have much connection with God on a personal level. Our time with God should not be compromised for any other work or person. Our next priority should be our family. All else can wait but we need to ensure that we give our time, energy, affection, and attention to our family first before we branch out to others.

Often, we have our priorities reversed and do other things first and give the rest of the scraps to God, family, and ourselves. But moving forward, let us learn to say no and take an inventory of our daily lives to re-align our priorities and give our best to God first and family.

Dear LORD, teach me how to prioritize my day so that above all else, I keep You on top. Help me not to compromise my walk with You by being busy doing things which You have not called me for. Give me boldness to say no to those things and people who try to take me away from You. In Jesus' name, Amen!

Concerned about others - June 29

Jesus said to him, "If it is my will that he remain until I come, what is that to you? You follow me!" John 21:22

Jesus was talking to Peter about His plans for him and how God would build His church through Peter. And while Peter was listening, his eyes were still on those around him and he seemed to be more concerned about what is going on with others rather than focusing on himself and what God was telling him.

We often do the same by focusing on what is going on with others rather than what God has called us to do. We get caught up in competing, out-doing and being one-up with each other that we miss our purpose for what God wants from us. God knows when we are truly worried about someone, but He also knows when our "concern" may be more with competing or gossiping intent.

This Bible verse teaches us that God deals with each one of us individually His own way. We all have a different purpose and plan for God's kingdom. And while it is good to look out for each other's spiritual needs and be "concerned", it is really none of our business to know or find out what God is up to with others. God will make us available when and where if He wants to but until He does, let us be concerned for ourselves first and follow Him before we try to lead others.

Dear Lord, help me to know what my place is in the work of Your kingdom. Thank you for dealing with us individually and leading us to You in your own way and timing. Please help me to focus on You and ensure I am spiritually equipped first before I speak to others about You. In Jesus name, Amen!

Breathe on me - June 30

The hand of the Lord was upon me, and he brought me out in the Spirit of the Lord and set me down in the middle of the valley; it was full of bones. And he led me around among them, and behold, there were very many on the surface of the valley, and behold, they were very dry. And he said to me, "Son of man, can these bones live?" And I answered, "O Lord God, you know. Ezekiel 37: 1-3

I love watching my puppy chew on a chicken bone. He bites off every chicken piece and sucks off the juice, completely drying out the bone. After he has done, I throw it out as there is nothing else left in it for Teddy to chew on anymore.

Sometimes our life or that of some loved one feels like a dried-up bone. The devil sucked out our happiness, chewed up every ounce of us and ruined our life in sin that we feel dead. We feel hopeless to be ever revived again. But when God asked Elijah the question "Can these bones ever live?", Elijah answered "You know, Lord". As much as it seemed impossible to Him, Elijah knew that God could do it as He is the creator of all beings and nothing is impossible with God. All God had to do was breathe life into those bones as Elijah spoke over them and they came back together, bone to bone, mass to mass.

In the same manner, regardless of how dead our life may seem, God can breathe new life into us. There is nothing we can do that God cannot revive or use again. He can mend our brokenness, cleanse us from our filth and make us anew. It does not matter how long we have been dead and dried up in the valley, God can make us alive again and create a mighty warrior out of us.

God is asking us the same question as He did to Elijah. Do we believe and proclaim that He can, or do we doubt God's ability to make our dry bones live again? The answer is in our faith!

Dear LORD, give me faith to see beyond my dead circumstances and believe that You can revive me again. Breathe new life into me and make me into an army, equipped for Your kingdom. In Jesus' name, Amen!

July

Not by luck - July 1

"Before I formed you in the womb, I knew you... Jeremiah 1:5

We generally wish "Good luck" to someone for their upcoming venture or use phrases like "I'm lucky". But as Christians, we very well know that there is no such thing as luck. Nothing happens randomly or by chance. God is sovereign over all. He knows everything and is in control. His plans are always good, whether they are for us directly or for someone else through us. God is the one who aligns people, places, things and time in order. He does not do things out of coincidence or according to the alignment of stars and palms but has a specific purpose and plan all laid out for us before we were even born. It is not by chance or any luck what we accomplish things in life. It is by God's grace and His perfect will. His purpose is perfect, but it is us who often decide to step out of God's will and go off on our own. We are the ones who take a chance and try our luck to succeed on our own.

Therefore, when we say, "Good luck", we are basically implying good wishes just on a basis of chance; we wish others well but at randomness. But if we truly hope for good, we ought to bless them in the LORD and put our hope in Him to carry out His best plan for them.

So instead of saying "Good luck" we ought to bless by "Best wishes" and "God be with you".

Dear LORD, thank you that You are not a God of randomness or chance. You are a God who created me and fashioned me with a purpose and a plan, way before I was even born. Please help me not to believe and live my life based on luck and accidents but know that it is You who is working for my benefit. Teach me to trust in You and be confident that You are always with me and Your plans for me are simply perfect and precise. In Jesus' name, Amen!

It's not all that - July 2

But I am not surprised! Even Satan disguises himself as an angel of light. 2 Corinthians 11:14

When Abraham gave a choice to his nephew Lot to pick his land, the area of Sodom looked appealing to him from a distant. It was not until he went there and saw the sin of the people, did he realize that what he saw was not what it really was.

We too think that the grass is greener on the other side and look for ways to get there but often when we get there and experience it closely, do we understand that it is not what we thought it would be. We feel deceived by its looks and wish to go back, but it could be too late, and the damage is done.

One of the first characteristics that we feel attracted to someone or something is by the look. If its appealing to the eyes, we are drawn to it. The devil is aware of this and so he disguises himself in the prettiest ways. We often picture the devil with an ugly, scary face but that is not who he is. If he showed his true self, we would be run away from him. But he comes to us in the most beautiful forms that we can imagine such as a person's beauty, physique, money, or food. He lures us into his trap by showing us pleasant things to the eye and make it hard for us to resist. And if we go by the looks only, we often are deceived. Only until we come close to it, we see the flaws and faults in it.

Let us not to judge an article by its title. It may look appealing and interesting by the headlines, but the content could be misleading. It may be attractive and pleasing to the eye, but its end could be deceiving. Therefore, we need to be careful with the choices that we make based on the looks of it alone.

Dear LORD, please help me to be wise in the decisions I make based on its appearance. Looks are deceiving so I pray for discernment to recognize the true from false and not fall for the gimmicks of the devil who tries to entrap me with his attractiveness. In Jesus' name, Amen!

Words and thoughts must agree - July 3

Let the words of my mouth and the meditation of my heart be acceptable in your sight, O LORD, my rock and my redeemer. Psalm 19:14

This Bible verse is often used in prayer when a preacher is about to give a message. It's for asking God to bless the words which they speak from what they have studied and prepared for.

But more importantly, this Bible verse applies to all of us for every thought and word that comes out of our mouth. Some people are good at blurting out whatever is in their hearts and some are good at saying one thing while thinking something else. Their words may be full of sweetness, but their hearts are filled with bitterness.

According to this Bible verse, our words that we speak that others can hear must also match what we think that no one else but God can hear. Mouth only speaks that which has been thought about, even if it is briefly. Like when we say that we "didn't mean what we said", but it did pass through our heart first and therefore we must have thought about it, and that is the reason it came out.

So, let us set a watch our mouth and first ensure that our words align with what we are thinking internally as God knows our every thought, and we cannot fool Him by our words. May both our words and thoughts agree with God!

Dear LORD, give me a sound mind to understand Your word clearly and know how to apply it to my life. Help me to be mindful of what I allow myself to speak and think. Teach me to shut off those thoughts immediately which distract me away from You. May my words be words of wisdom which build up, not tear down. And may my thoughts be clean and holy which bring You honor and glory. In Jesus' name, Amen!

Let freedom ring - July 4

For you were called to freedom, brothers. Only do not use your freedom as an opportunity for the flesh, but through love serve one another. Galatians 5:13

As Americans, we celebrate our freedom on this day and remember those who fought for our country to make us free. Our parents, grandparents, missionaries, and generations past made sacrifices of some form in their lives so that their children and future generations can have better lives. So being free then should not be taken lightly but we need to be grateful for those folks who make a difference in our lives.

As Christians, we celebrate our freedom from sin and death every day. It is Jesus who fought for us to make us free. Our freedom does not cost us anything, but Jesus paid a heavy price for us. He shed His blood and bore the sins of all humankind on the cross to pay the ransom. The devil may keep reminding us of our past sins and make us feel guilty over and over but there is no reason for us to live in the bondage of sin because we are no longer under his submission but a child of God.

Once Jesus said on the cross "it is finished" that means it is done. Once we realize our need for forgiveness and ask Jesus into our heart, it is finished, and now there is no condemnation for us as we have crossed over the border from sin to life.

Therefore, as we celebrate freedom today, let us remember our earthly fathers who fought for our freedom on earth and be thankful to our Heavenly Father who fought for our spiritual freedom and made us free in Christ.

Dear LORD, I am indebted for the liberty to worship You. Please bless those families whose loved ones fought for this freedom. Thank you for delivering me out of the slavery from sin. Help me not to take Your sacrifice for granted but may I ever be so grateful and live my life to honor You. In Jesus' name, Amen!

Don't cross the line - July 5

You say, "I am allowed to do anything"—but not everything is good for you. And even though "I am allowed to do anything," I must not become a slave to anything. 1 Corinthians 6:12

God has set boundaries for us that we should not cross. He knows what is good or harmful for us and thus has set limitations on how far we should go. However, we are like little children who like to do what we are told not to. The moment we are prohibited from doing something, our next impulse is to do it, either out of curiosity or to be rebellious.

The devil is good at pushing us to cross our boundary and get in trouble. He allures us in thinking that the "grass is greener on the other side" and we will miss out on something if we do not try it. He tempts us by showing us the beautiful, superficial aspects of the other side and makes us believe that it is good for us, harmless, there is nothing wrong with pleasing our self, and would be acceptable to God if we expand the boundary a little. And when we come under his seduction and cross that line, we realize it is not as good as it looked from far and we often regret it and wish we had not crossed that boundary. Often, it is hard to go back and undo a damage that has already been done and the guilt of disobeying haunts us to a point of exhaustion and embarrassment.

Therefore, we need to remember that we should not play with fire and expect not to get burned. God has set boundaries for a reason and it is only for our own good. If we are not sure what our boundary line is, we need to ask God to show us and help us to resist temptation and be vigilant against the devil to not cross the line which God has set a limit on.

Dear LORD, please help me to appreciate the boundaries which You have set for me. Your boundaries are meant for me to stay within Your watch and protection so help me not be lured into disobeying You and going off on my own. Help me to understand that I am slave to sin when I choose to be away from You, but I am free when I remain in You. May I embrace my boundaries and be grateful for them. In Jesus' name, Amen!

Admin rights - July 6

Behold, I have given you authority to tread on serpents and scorpions, and over all the power of the enemy, and nothing shall hurt you. Luke 10:19

While transferring data, I inadvertently deleted my devotional list through which I send out my daily devotions. While creating a new group, there was a glitch and somehow it kicked me out of my own group and gave my admin rights to someone else. As an administrator, the individual had all rights to see, add, delete, and modify everything on the group which was supposed to be for my purpose only. I do not recall how or why it happened, but I inadvertently gave control of my group to someone else. To make the long story short, thankfully this access was given to a trustworthy individual who I know well and was able to get my group back from under his authority.

Oftentimes we hand over the authority of our life to Satan without realizing how or why it occurred. If we let our guard down, we end up giving him full access to rule over us according to his will. He takes full charge as the administrator of our life and controls us in how to act and react. His goal is our downfall so when we give devil the authority, we make it easy for him to destroy us. When we allow him to penetrate our lives through people and things, we not only lose control over our own self, but the control goes into the wrong hands who abuses and messes us up.

Therefore, we need to be careful to whom we give access of our life to. The only person who should have full authority over us is Jesus Christ. He is the administrator who watches out for our good. When we surrender and give authority to Jesus, He in turn gives us full access to be called His own children and enables us to withstand the evil schemes of the devil. So, we need to check out our admin rights and see who the administrator of our lives is.

Dear LORD, please help me to examine my life and see who the overseer of my life is. You are my LORD and Savior so please help me to fight and take back what the enemy has stolen from me. I choose to give You the authority over every aspect of my life. Please accept the role of administrator and control my life according to Your will. In Jesus' name, Amen!

No gray area in the Bible - July 7

For I know my transgressions, and my sin is always before me. Psalm 51:3

When we hear about the story of Adam and Eve, many of us say that they if we were in Eve's place, we would never have done what she did but would be smart enough to recognize Satan and not fallen for his trap. But Satan is no different to us today as he was with Eve! And we too are like Eve who fall for his tricks and take a bite of the apple of sin daily which he proposes to us in many forms as innocent and lawful.

The devil entices us with sin and makes it appealing to the eye so that we fall for the temptation. He twists and turns God's word and presents it to us in ways that we too question God. We challenge God's authority and command by doubting, comparing our knowledge to His and do what seems right to us. Satan leads us to disobey God by putting subtle thoughts and reasons in our mind that we cannot find anything wrong with what we are doing. We come up with reasons to justify our sin and take a bite of the apple which God has forbidden us to eat.

God has provided us clear cut commandments which we need to abide by. He has not given us in-between instructions that we should get confused whether it is a sin or not, right or wrong.

There is no gray area in God's word so we must not allow the devil to create one and give him any space to propose a doubtful question against God. Know God's word well so that when the devil asks, "Has God really said to not do this?", we can answer him confidently, "Yes, it is written...

Dear LORD, please help me to study and know Your word well so that I can speak against Satan when he entices me with things which You have forbidden. Help me not to allow him to put thoughts of doubts and questions against You but recognize his evil plan and stand up against him rather than to stand with him. In Jesus' name, Amen!

Remain constant - July 8

Blessed is the man who remains steadfast under trial, for when he has stood the test, he will receive the crown of life, which God has promised to those who love him. James 1:12

A thermometer gives a reading based on the atmospheric temperature around it. It fluctuates up or down, depending on how warm or cool is its surrounding. Some of us are like thermometers. The way we are—our mood, thoughts, decisions and desires are changed according to who is around us or what is happening to us. Like the thermometer, we vary our outlook and do not remain constant. People and circumstance determine what we are like and we easily get influenced by it.

But instead of being like a thermometer, we ought to be like the thermostat who remains steady at the set temperature. It does not matter how hot or cold it gets; the thermostat does not change. It causes the thermometer to change but it does not change itself. In the same way, regardless of what our situation is or how people behave towards us, we need to remain steadfast; manifesting God's image through us. God has instilled the values of the fruit of the Spirit which is love, joy, peace, patience, kindness, goodness, faithfulness, gentleness, and self-control in us and so it does not matter how our current situation may be, we should remain constant under our trials and temptations that we face.

Instead of fluctuating according to the people and circumstance, we need to set the tone and let others see and feel our constant flow of Jesus' love through us.

Dear LORD, please help me not to be ruled by my emotions, surroundings, and people. May I not be manipulated or pressured into things according to how I feel in the moment. Instead, teach me to remain firm and steady regardless of my situations. Always help me to be controlled by the Holy Spirit who leads me in all truth and holiness. I give You full control so take my life and let me live steadily in Your will. In Jesus' name, Amen!

Seat of honor - July 9

You prepare a table before me in the presence of my enemies. Psalm 23:5

An enemy does not necessarily have to be a person. It comes in many forms such as a thing, place or a situation. One form of enemy for me is my career. I don't know how or why I chose to do what I do nor have I gained much deep passion for it after working in this field for so many years, but I'm doing what I need to do and have been successful in it so far. I cannot confidently say that I understand all aspects of my job but whatever I am assigned to do, I do it faithfully and effectively. It is God who gives me the wisdom and ability to accomplish my tasks and places me in high-standing with my peers and superiors. It is not something I earned or deserve but only due to God's favor and grace upon me that I am at where I cannot be on my own. This is an example of the meaning of "He prepares a table before me in the presence of my enemies". My workplace is my battlefield, but God allows me to fight through all my tasks and gives me success in all that I put my hands to.

We all have certain enemies that we struggle with each day. But if we trust in God and do our best faithfully, He enables us to do what seems impossible for us. He fights our battles with us and while we remain amid our enemies, He gives us success and "prepares a table for us" to sit in the seat of honor. Where we are weak, God's strength pulls us through, and we can rest in His favor. He removes all doubt, fear, worry and low confidence out of us and causes us to stand tall and shine for Him even in those places where we do not belong.

Dear LORD, thank you for making me capable where I am unable. Thank you for lifting me up from lower to higher places and giving me the honor which I do not deserve or have earned. It is only Your grace and favor upon me which allows me to stand fiercely in the midst of my enemies. In Jesus' name, Amen!

You are enough - July 10

"My grace is sufficient for you, for my power is made perfect in weakness."
Therefore, I will boast all the more gladly of my weaknesses, so that the power of
Christ may rest upon me. 2 Corinthians 12:9

The most mysterious person I know is myself. I just do not understand me! I learn new things about myself and find out different strengths and weaknesses in me as the day unfolds. More often my weaknesses are more than my strengths as they are revealed to me when I face certain situations and challenges. I realize that I am not as strong spiritually or morally as I ought to be. I end up failing miserably at those things which I know that I should not do or say. I can relate to Paul when he said that he does not do the things that he should but ends up doing what he should not. Every time I realize I did something I shouldn't have, I feel ashamed and ask God, "Why am I like this?, Why can't I ever get it right and why do I always fail You?"

When I feel like a failure yet again, God reminds me that He is aware of my frailty and wants me to experience His grace which does not hold my sinful nature against me. He makes it clear that all I need is His grace to keep me going in my disappointments. God knows that I am weak, and it is in my weakness that I learn more about God's love and convicts me to repentance and get it right with God. And as I receive God's forgiveness, I understand how much He loves me which in turn makes me try harder to please Him.

Dear LORD, thank you for reminding me that no matter how many times I fail,
You never get tired of it and give up on me. As my sin grows, Your grace also
grows much higher and forgives me of all my iniquities. I praise You as although
I may be weak, Your strength shows up in me and helps me to keep moving for-
ward in You. In Jesus' name, Amen!

Breakthrough - July 11

Fight the good fight of the faith. 1 Timothy 6:12

Sometimes we cannot understand why and what is happening when we go through certain trials in life. The more we try to run away from it, the more it chases after us. And the more we try to move towards something, the farther away it seems to get. One thing for sure though in times like this is to recognize who is behind it all. The devil feels threatened by our success and spiritual growth, so he tries to stop us by any means possible. When a breakthrough is about to happen in our marriage, family, health, career, school, church, or anything else which results in God's glory, the devil attacks that specific situation in order to stop us from moving ahead. He puts stumbling blocks in our way to make us fall, causes friction in our relations and holds us down by sickness or bondage so that we are unable to move forward and fulfill our purpose.

The devil does not give up easily and gives us a hard battle to hold us down, but we too need to fight the good fight of faith and not give up. We need to be prepared and fight on our knees with prayers for our marriage and our children, against our illness and circumstances. The victory has already been proclaimed by God; we just need to fight through it. It is like knowing the end of a movie, but we still watch it entirely, or knowing which team won yet we watch the whole game. In the same way, God has already won the battle for us, but we still need to go through the process of fighting so that we understand what we went through and how much God accomplished through us.

When we get on our knees, God stands up for us and the devil gives up as he cannot stand against our God. So be encouraged and rejoice in suffering as your breakthrough is near!

Dear LORD, no matter what the devil throws against me, help to remember that my breakthrough is near and that is the reason he is trying to stop me. Please give me the courage to fight all the way and not give up. Thank you for the victory that has already been won, I claim it in Jesus' name, Amen!

Spiritual blindness - July 12

...*"One thing I do know. I was blind but now I see!" John 9:25*

When the blind man was bought to Jesus for healing, he could not see Jesus yet because he did not have eyesight to see. But Jesus saw him!

We all must know of people in our lives who are spiritually blind, this may include our own self. Due to the lack of spiritual vision, some are oblivious to Jesus and the need for Him in their lives. We worry whether our loved ones' eyes will ever be opened and if they will see Jesus. But whether they see God or not, He sees them and is willing to open their eyes.

Oftentimes we wait to come to God because we think we need to first "clean ourselves up" and then approach Him for healing. But God wants us to come to him just as we are! If we could already save ourselves, why would we need a savior? It is the sick who need a doctor, not the already well. It is the blind who need vision. Jesus understands the reason behind our blindness and feels our pain. He sees our struggle with spiritual battle and wants to help. We may be blinded by our sins, but He knows this sickness and wants to heal.

Therefore, let us bring our blind to Jesus by continuous prayer and steadfast in hope. Jesus can and will open the eyes of our heart some day and we will see Jesus.

Dear LORD, please remove the scales off my eyes which blind me from seeing You. Please pluck out those things of the world that blur my vision so that I can clearly see the truth and the path You have set before me. Help me to realize the need for healing from spiritual blindness and call out to You. Thank you, LORD for seeing me even when I cannot see. Please open my eyes so that I can declare, "I was blind but now I see". In Jesus' name, Amen!

Walking in the rain - July 13

But let all who take refuge in you rejoice; let them sing joyful praises forever. Spread your protection over them, that all who love your name may be filled with joy. Psalm 5:11

Although it was raining heavily, I did not get wet because I had my big umbrella opened and held it up as I walked in the rain. If I stayed under the protection of the umbrella, I remained dry even if it was pouring rain all around me.

Storms do come in life and it rains both on the righteous and the unrighteous. The difference though is in how we handle it. Those who do not believe and do not have faith in God, get drenched in their storm because they do not have refuge to run into. But for those whose trust in our God, Jesus Christ, run to Him and are safe. He is like an umbrella to us when we walk through the storms of life. It does not matter how bad things get around us, if we trust God and walk under His protection, the winds and blows of negative circumstances cannot harm us. The rain could be heavy and scary but if God is over us, it cannot destroy us. It may splash us a little with some doubt and fear but if we hold on to the umbrella tight, it cannot knock us down as God shields us from the downpour and covers us as we walk right through the rain.

Storms are bound to come now or later in life, but it is important to be prepared and carry our "Umbrella" with us. God is our refuge in times of trouble so let us ensure that we are ready with God's promises over us as we face the rainy season of life.

Dear LORD, You are my refuge and fortress in whom I find my shelter when hit by storms in life. You are my umbrella that keeps me dry when I walk through the rain. Please help me to carry You with me so that no matter when or how the enemy attacks, I am prepared to fight with You as my shield and shade. In Jesus' name, Amen!

Choose to be holy - July 14

But just as he who called you is holy, so be holy in all you do. 1 Peter 1:15

Once an orphan child gets adopted, he receives a new family name right away, but to be a part of the family and understand their traditions and values take time. As the child becomes more familiar and involved with the family, he learns from them and slowly becomes one of them by adjusting to their family values and rules.

Many of us believe that once we accept Jesus into our lives, we automatically become holy. We expect a miraculous transformation that takes place and we become a new person instantaneously.

Yes, we become a new person and receive a new identity in Christ but to be like Jesus takes effort on our part. Jesus is holy and if our aim is to be holy like Him, then we need to work at it. Holiness does not come to us naturally or miraculously; we must choose to be holy. We need to purposely make a choice to be holy and in all matters decide what we will do, such as lie or tell the truth, gossip or walk away, visit a website or not, change the channel or watch an inappropriate show, use foul language or shut our mouth, go where we are not supposed to or turn around.

It is our small and big, day to day choices that we make that help us to be holy. Holiness is to be set apart, so we must remove ourselves from the traditions and influences of the world and choose to follow the standards of God regardless of what others say or think of us.

When we have a desire for holiness, God convicts us and gives us courage and wisdom to know His right from wrong. But eventually the choice is ours to make – to be holy or not!

Dear LORD, help to understand that you have set me apart as Your vessel for Your kingdom. May I not blend in with the worldly patterns but be separated so that when people look at me, they can clearly see Christ in me. May I truly reflect Your holiness in me by the way I live my life. Help me to choose to be holy as You are holy. In Jesus' name, Amen!

Refined to be defined - July 15

See, I have refined you, though not as silver; I have tested you in the furnace of affliction. Isaiah 48:10

My husband makes the best tea. I love tea and it's the first thing in the morning I must have before I do anything else. I can make my tea in five minutes but when my husband makes it, it takes him so much longer to brew it and makes me wait until it is made to his perfection. He says that for the true flavor of the tea to come out, it must be heated well. I guess it's worth the wait to have such aromatic, flavorful cup of tea in the end.

In the same manner our true flavor comes out when we are in hot water so to say. God sometimes turns up our heat and makes us go through a purification process in order to make us pure and tasteful. The hardships and setbacks that we face in life sometimes are a result of God refining us to bring to surface our sins, filth, doubts and impurities that are clinging to us. He turns up the heat to test our faith and see how flavorful we truly are when we are heated under the pressure of temptations and adversity.

Therefore, if we feel that we are undergoing intense heat, it must mean that God is at work in us to cleanse and refine. The process may feel unbearable and too hot for us to handle sometimes, but if we desire to be holy as God is holy, we must allow Him to purify us so that we come out pure as gold and as flavorful as the tea He has designed us to be.

Dear LORD, if I desire to be like You, I must try and choose to be holy in all situations. So please put me through Your refiner's fire and remove all dirt and filth which come in the way of holiness. Give me Your strength to endure the heat as I pass through it and may I come out tried and true, pure, holy and flavorful as You intend me to be. In Jesus' name, Amen!

Praying with burden - July 16

Again I say to you, if two of you agree on earth about anything they ask, it will be done for them by my Father in heaven. Matthew 18:19

For the last few days, I had a sharp pain in my knee. Every time I bent it, especially going up or down the stairs, I felt the pain. I found myself limping a little, asking for help to get me up when I was sitting down, rubbing ointments to relieve the pain, worrying if the pain was there to stay and praying for God to heal me. I do not know why and how it all began but after a few days, my pain was gone. I now understand what my mom and others who have leg pains must feel like. So, when I prayed for deliverance from my pain, I prayed for them also, but this time and onwards being more heartfelt as I can relate to their pain.

When we tell someone "I can imagine what you are feeling or going through", we really do not understand it because we have not experienced it for ourselves. Until we have felt the pain ourselves, we cannot imagine what it is like. It is difficult to comfort others just by our words, but when we can relate and share our similar experience, it is more encouraging. Therefore, God sometimes allows us to go through certain circumstances because He needs us to be there for someone as their support system and genuinely relate to their pain. And when we pray for our own situation, God wants us to lift others with the same burden as we would for our own.

Selfless, sincere prayers made on behalf of others are more powerful and so we need each other to pray for each other. So, when we undergo certain circumstances, let us not just pray for our own deliverance but also for someone else who needs our prayer support.

Dear LORD, when You give me opportunities to pray for others, please help me not to pray just for the sake of praying but pray with a burden as if it is my own. Help me to understand that You allow me to pass through certain difficulties so that I can relate to someone else's pain and sincerely pray. Our prayers are more effective when we pray for others so may I be selfless and pray for others more than I pray for myself. In Jesus' name, Amen!

Behind the scenes - July 17

For the weapons of our warfare are not of the flesh but have divine power to destroy strongholds. 2 Corinthians 10:4

While the performers get the accolades for their acting, it is the Director, Producer, Editor, Cameraman, etc. who work behind the scene to make up the story and decide what will be displayed on the screen. They are the unseen forces that teach and tell the actor what to say and how to act. The actor follows the direction given from the background and brings it to the stage with their own acting skills to make the audience believe the story that is being presented. We, the audience get to enjoy only what is displayed on the stage and do not know what is going on behind the scene.

Similarly, we only see what is displayed to us in the physical world but so much is happening behind the scene spiritually. Just the way there exists a physical world that we live in and observe with our eyes, there in an existence of a spiritual world which we cannot see. There is a constant battle between God and Satan over us. Oftentimes Satan overpowers us and influences to do the wrong because he tempts us with the physical things which we are vulnerable to. We are fleshly minded and so we easily fall into his trap. God, on the other hand, teaches us to keep our eyes above and beyond the physical world and look to Him with an eternal purpose.

When we watch a person display hatred, lust, pride, anger, bitterness and all other evil acts, it is due to the direction of the devil whom they have chosen to listen to. But when we choose God, we can see the display of fruit of the Spirit which is love, joy, peace, patience, kindness, goodness, faithfulness, gentleness and self-control.

We need to take heed to our actions and choose whom we obey and follow. Our actions, words, behavior and attitude which we display in our physical world tells a lot about who our Spiritual master is. So, let us be aware of the spiritual realm and decide whose side we are on in the battle.

Dear LORD, please open my eyes to see the battle that is taking place in the spiritual world. Help me not to support the devil by doing things that take me away from You but rather stay close to You and fight against the devil with all my might. Thank you for rescuing me from Satan's stronghold. In Jesus' name, Amen!

Digging deeper - July 18

Because your heart was responsive and you humbled yourself before God when you heard what he spoke against this place and its people, and because you humbled yourself before me and tore your robes and wept in my presence, I have heard you, declares the LORD. 2 Chronicles 34:27

A quarry is a type of open pit mine in which construction stone, rock, sand, gravel, or slate is dug out from the ground. This requires careful digging and removal so to not touch or damage the precious material. Once it is excavated from the ground, the material is often exploded into smaller, finer parts to use for construction.

Our heart is like a quarry. In it, many of us have hidden our passion and talents underneath the surface of a hard heart. We might be afraid or too arrogant of using our God-given abilities, and so we bury our treasure deep within, hoping to never utilize it. Some of us are too stiff and will not give into God's will and power over our lives. We feel as if we do not need God and continue to live in our own way of thinking and belief. We try to run away from God but the further we run; the more God chases us.

Because God loves us and knows our worth, He will never give up on us or stop digging. He will continue to dig and dig into the depths of our heart until we are discovered. Then He blasts our heart to break the stubbornness that is within us and make us humbler and more receptive towards Him. The process of excavating our heart maybe painful as it requires to be shoveled, pulled apart, cleaned and blasted but it is exciting to see what is awaiting us when God is through us.

So, if we feel as if we are being dug out and about to explode, take heart and be prepared as the breakthrough is at hand for the most beautiful, precious gem to be revealed.

Dear LORD, I ask you to reveal to me the precious treasure that is stored in my heart that can be used for You. Please dig deep within and excavate the true gem in me which I hide beneath the stress of this world. Remove from me any unrighteousness and sin that hinders me from You. My purpose in life is to bring You praise so please help me to use the talents You have put in me to display Your glory. In Jesus' name, Amen!

Walking on water - July 19

But Jesus looked at them and said, "With man this is impossible, but with God all things are possible." Matthew 19:26

Occasionally we find ourselves drowning in our circumstances. We can barely keep our heads above the deep waters with no base to hold us down. The more we try to get to the shore, the deeper we seem to get further away from it and do not know if we can ever get out.

When the situation seems impossible for us overcome, God tells us to do the impossible. He asks us to walk on water! That is to walk on the water of faith. The winds could be strong around us; the waves might be high and rough underneath us but if we keep our eyes on Jesus, He helps us to walk above the waves. When things get rough and unsteady, we need to keep our faith strong in the LORD and trust Him to get us to the other side, even if it seems impossible to us. If we reach out and hold on to Jesus, He establishes our feet on the surface of the roaring waters and allows us to stride through it without drowning in it.

So, no matter how overwhelming our current situation may be, we need to have faith that is able to see beyond it. Our God is the God of impossibilities who walked on water and is calling us to do the same by faith.

Dear LORD, I am drowning in my sin and it feels overwhelming to swim out of it. The more I want to get out, the more it sucks me in. My only hope is You who is standing in the middle of this storm and calling me out. Please build my courage to stand up and grab Your hand as You pull me out. Just the way You walked on water, teach me to walk also above the surface of my sin and hardships. Plant my feet firm on Christ the solid rock so that I cannot be drowned. In Jesus' name, Amen!

For this reason I remind you to fan into flame the gift of God, which is in you through the laying on of my hands. 2 Timothy 1:6

To start a fire naturally, we need to first lay down some dry twigs and layers of small branches and logs. Then we light a match and set it afire. The flames begin to spread a little at a time and we soon have a nice fire. After a while we see the fire dying off as the logs get burnt up. In order to keep the fire going, we need to keep fanning and adding more logs and branches until they are set aflame and we have a roaring fire again.

We all know of folks who could be burning out of their spiritual fire they once had. Children particularly, begin to question and doubt God as they start to grow up and have a mind of their own. They are easily influenced by ungodly friends and media and lose their fire for God whom they used to have before and trusted with all their dear little hearts. We, ourselves could be in this position. When we received Jesus Christ into our lives, our hearts were on fire for Him. We were ready to live and die for Him, jumped at all opportunities to serve Him and kept going like the energizer battery. But while being so busy doing things for the LORD, we do not have time to add more log to our spiritual fire and eventually find ourselves slowly losing our fire that once burnt so strongly.

When we notice the fire fading out, we need to fan it back into flame. We need to keep fanning by spending quality time with God in praying, speaking God's promises over our lives, keep trusting and not giving up. The bigger the fire we desire, the harder we must fan. It may take a lot of effort, energy, and patience to re-ignite the diminishing fire but if we do not give up fanning, the fire will set ablaze once again!

Dear LORD, please reignite in me the fire that I used to have for You. May I not become so busy doing work for You that I ignore the diminishing flame within me. I pray for a fresh anointing of the Holy Spirit once again and fan me back into the flame which you had set me on fire for. In Jesus' name, Amen!

It always works out - July 21

Commit your way to the LORD; trust in Him, and He will do it. Psalm 37:5

As a multi-tasker, I was dealing with five different situations at the same time. I was trying to figure things out about how and when I will be able to accomplish everything I was trying to manage for the day. After many back and forth text messages, phone calls, and running around from here to there, all things got done by the end.

Before starting the day off, I brought all my plans and concerns in prayer before God and asked for His help to figure things out with everything that I had to deal with. I planned and made my efforts to the best of my ability, sometimes leading to frustration and exhaustion. But because I submitted my concern to God, He helped, and everything fell in its place eventually. I realized that things do work out somehow, even better, especially if we reach out to God for help. I felt silly for worrying so much and running around physically and mentally while I should have trusted God to begin with and just taken it easy.

We may plan and try but when we allow God to come alongside us to help, He works it out for us. He sends the right people to assist us, clears out confusion and even extends time for us to accomplish it at the right time. God always has the best planned for us and He unfolds His agenda one at a time.

So, let us remember that God always works it for us at the end of the day no matter how difficult it may seem for us. We just need to submit our agenda into His hands and allow Him to work on it instead of us over-working ourselves.

Dear LORD, would You please help me to seek You first and submit everything into Your hands before I put my hands to it. When I have You by my side, there is nothing that I cannot do so help me to wait on You to give me the wisdom, strength and the skills I need to accomplish a task. I commit my plans and work into Your hands; bless it and use it for Your kingdom. In Jesus' name, Amen!

Under control - July 22

Whoever is slow to anger is better than the mighty, and he who rules his spirit than he who takes a city. Proverbs 16:32

Some folks are very easily ticklish, while for some, it would take a lot of tickling efforts to make them laugh, myself being one of them. I do not necessarily get tickled easily, it all depends on my mind and mood. If I want to laugh, I will but if I have my mind set on it, I will not laugh no matter how hard anyone tries. It is called self-control. It is about having control over the mind on what we allow or not allow to control us.

Self-control plays a key role in our spiritual walk also. It is one of the characteristics of the fruit of the Spirit which we as Christians must have. It is the ability to recognize sin and have the heart and mind to not fall into it. We make a conscious effort to say no and walk away from something or someone who brings us down spiritually. It's easy to lose self-control when we are tempted or wronged, but if we firmly stand in the heated moment and not let that overcome us, we become the master over that sin, instead of it mastering over us. But if we cannot take control and let ourselves loose, we become like an unguarded city without walls who welcomes its enemy to come in and take over.

According to the Bible, to have self-control is not just about having dominion of the mind and body over certain things but it is a matter of the heart and putting ourselves under the control of Jesus Christ. When we hand over the power of our lives to Jesus, we come under His authority and He becomes the controller. It is His truth that reigns in us and convicts us to take control over the sinful matter before it takes control over us!

Dear LORD, please help me to have control over my heart, mind, mouth and body and not let it run lose according to my emotions or circumstances. May I be spiritually controlled and in everything, only act according to the conviction of the Holy Spirit. May I bring myself under the submission of Christ and display the fruit of the Spirit in my life. Please help me overcome my weakness and teach me to be disciplined. In Jesus' name, Amen!

SEAL for Christ - July 23

Through you we push down our foes; through your name we tread down those who rise up against us. Psalm 44:5

Navy SEALs are the most elite US Military Special Operations warriors trained to carry out specialized, intense warfare. They undergo the harshest military training to operate in all environments (sea, land, air) for which they are named – SEALs. It is amazing to hear stories of how they handle the toughest combats and come out successful in their missions.

It inspires me to want to be a SEAL also and before anyone laughs at this, I realized that I am already one, a Christian SEAL that is! Being a true Christian too requires training, discipline, resistance, and determination to fight the fiercest battles that Satan rages against us. We are in a spiritual warfare where the devil is attacking us personally and our families. The battle is fierce, and God needs strong soldiers to fight with Him. He is searching for prayer warriors who can pray their way through any situations. Despite all odds, circumstances or seasons of life, God needs SEALs who can withstand pressures of life, resist the devil, remain faithful till the end and overcome any obstacles.

It is not easy to be a SEAL for Christ. It requires us to lean into discomfort of the world, stand up for Jesus when everyone is against Him, have a strong will power to basically let go off our own will and submit to God's authority. If we are willing to be a warrior for Him, God trains and equips us also. He does not leave us on our own but goes before us and fights with us to win this spiritual battle. Will you be an elite warrior for Christ?

Dear LORD, help me to realize that I am engaged in a spiritual warfare which requires me to be vigilant and be ever ready to stand against the devil. Please help me to be a prayer warrior whose prayers can move mountains and equip me with your armor to go and fight with the strength of the LORD in me. In Jesus' name, Amen!

Just relax- July 24

Be still, and know that I am God. Psalm 46:10

I am the type of person who cannot remain idle. I like to be busy and need to be doing something. If there is anything pending that needs to be done, I am not able to relax until I have taken care of it first.

I treat my problems in the same manner. When something is wrong or is bothering me, I just cannot be still and wait for God to work it out. I must do something about it and am unable to rest or be patient. I look for immediate solutions and try to figure things out right away. I may say I trust God but at the same time I do not wait for Him to act. When we behave such way, our restlessness only proves that we do not trust God enough to let Him handle it.

It comes natural for us to worry, overreact and overthink our circumstances but we need go beyond the natural and trust in God's supernatural ability. We are limited to a certain extent to help ourselves, but when we acknowledge who God is and how much more He can do, we are able to rest and relax while He works on our behalf. God may not move at our pace or the way we think He should, so we might feel a compulsion to help God out by doing things ahead of Him. But we need to realize that God has a master plan behind it all and His ways are much better than ours, and His timing is exactly right. So instead of fidgeting around with our problems and be overcome with worry, fear and restlessness, let us truly learn to be still. When God says, "Be still" He means that we need to stop whatever we are doing, relax and allow God to take care of it.

Dear LORD, help me to realize that You are God and I am not. Let me allow You to handle my problems instead of taking matters in my own hands and exhausting myself over it. Life is much better and easier when You are in it, so may You be the LORD of all in my life. I submit my life and its issues into Your hands, deal with it as You please. In Jesus' name, Amen!

Watch out for schemers - July 25

I urge you, brothers and sisters, to watch out for those who cause divisions and put obstacles in your way that are contrary to the teaching you have learned. Keep away from them. For such people are not serving our Lord Christ, but their own appetites. By smooth talk and flattery they deceive the minds of naive people. Romans 16: 17-18

Manipulators are people who control or influence others in a clever or crooked way. They have a way of getting people to like them, believe and do things their way by working in subtle, indirect ways. Their intention is evil from the beginning but hide it very well behind a mask in order to fool people.

The biggest manipulator that we need to be aware of is the devil. He deceives people by putting on a front which is attractive and unsuspecting. He modifies things around according to our needs so that it becomes alluring and hard for us to resist. By slightly twisting the word of God, the devil lures us into believing that there is nothing wrong in what we are doing. He comes up with multiple reasons and excuses that make us reason against God. We even begin to question God and His truth while accepting devil and his lies when we succumb to his influence.

When we let our guard down or are not vigilant to his tricks and games, we can easily be deceived by the devil. So, it is vital that we are rooted well in God's word to be able to discern the truth against the false and not allow ourselves to be manipulated by the manipulator.

Dear LORD, please help me to be vigilant and not fall for the wolf in sheep's clothing, the devil who comes to deceive me in different forms and shapes. I know that he is the father of lies so I pray for a sound mind and clarity to know Your truth and not become a prey. Give me the discernment to know the difference between good and bad, right and wrong. May I always remain grounded in You. In Jesus' name, Amen!

Then he said to them, "You like to appear righteous in public, but God knows your hearts. What this world honors is detestable in the sight of God. Luke 16:15

Reputation means what others think of us. Although we may say or act ignorant about it, we do care about our impression in front of people. We take careful measures to ensure that we carry our name well so that no one can find anything against us. We feel ashamed if we are caught doing something wrong as it reflects our character and exposes our sin not only to God but to people, which seems to matter to us more than what God thinks.

We should not wait to feel shameful about our wrong doings until someone points a finger at us. We should already be convicted and feel ashamed in the sight of God for sinning against Him, whether we are exposed by people or not. We can hide and do things behind the back of others, but we cannot say or do anything that God would not see or hear. We can fool people by putting on a front or a good show, but God knows us inside out. Our secret sins can be hidden from people but there is no place on heaven or earth we can escape from God's watchful eye. Our sin is already exposed to God beforehand and so we ought to make it right with Him first then everyone else.

God already knows it all so let us not wait to be convicted of our sins until they are visible to others. Or, let us not be so concerned with our status in front of people and engulf ourselves in impressing and fooling others that we become ignorant of the one who sees us and weighs us by our hearts, not reputation.

Dear LORD, may my only desire be to please You and not people. Help me not to worry about what others think of me but only what You think. Teach me keep my heart pure and be right with You so that one day when I stand in front of You, I will hear from Your mouth, "Well, done my good and faithful servant". In Jesus' name, Amen!

Spiritual hunger - July 27

Blessed are those who hunger and thirst for righteousness, for they will be filled.
Matthew 5:6

When a person is hungry, they become angry also. Thus, the word "Hangry" is used for someone who is angry because they are hungry.

When we are hungry, our focus is on food and when we will get to eat again. Really nothing else takes away our attention from it until we are fed. Our hunger for food causes us to be agitated and the only thing that can satisfy us is when our tummies are full.

The way we feel hangry for physical food, we should have the same craving for spiritual food also. Our hearts should crave for God daily and until we meet with Him through our quiet time of prayer and Bible reading, we should become restless, having a strong desire and hunger that none other than God can satisfy. We ought to be hangry for God and His righteousness. There should be a burning and aching in our being to please God and live righteously for Him. Just the way Jesus became angry and drove out the money exchangers from God's temple, a godly anger must stir up in us when we see and do unrighteous acts.

Physical hunger satisfies the body, Spiritual hunger satisfies the soul. Both are necessary so let us not be concerned to only fulfill the physical appetite while our soul is starving.

Dear LORD, give me a hunger for Your word and increase my appetite for the spiritual food which only You can satisfy. Help me to be restless until I sit at Your feet and am filled with You, the bread of life. I have tasted and seen how good You are so help me to share and tell others about You so that they too can experience You for themselves. In Jesus' name, Amen!

My own test - July 28

Each one should test their own actions. Then they can take pride in themselves alone, without comparing themselves to someone else. Galatians 6:4

While taking a final exam in Chemistry class in college, one of my so-called classmate friends was not prepared much for the test and decided to cheat by sitting in the row behind me at one level higher in the lecture hall. He would lean over and copy as much as he could from my paper. Lo and behold, he failed miserably as he later to found out that all our questions were different on the exam sheets that were handed out.

Our life is like a test. God has given each one of us a specific purpose to accomplish for Him. As we try to fulfill this purpose, we are faced with circumstances and temptations that test us to the core with our patience, faith, and integrity. We all have our own share of individual questions and struggles that we need to find our answers to by God's help who teaches and prepares us for our exams.

But often instead of keeping our eyes on our own test paper, we focus on that of others and either try to copy them or outdo them in their skills, talents, looks, success and status. We waste our precious time comparing ourselves to others and end up missing out on the wonderful opportunities that are set for us only.

We need to remember that our questionnaire is not the same as the person next to us. We will never pass the test of life if our focus is on what others are doing rather than concentrating on our own. Our life is our own and God has appointed us individually to be and do according to His master plan. We cannot cheat God by handing Him other's answer sheet, He knows which set of questionnaires He has given to us individually so we will have to give account of our own. Therefore, let us be prepared to answer God based on our own test sheet.

Dear LORD, please help me not to try to make others' calling my own and compete with others. You have placed me here with an agenda and purpose which is my own so teach me to concentrate on my task and not worry about what others are doing. May I be focused on my own calling and excel in the work You have called me to do. In Jesus' name, Amen!

Indulgence in sin - July 29

Let those who love the Lord hate evil, for he guards the lives of his faithful ones and delivers them from the hand of the wicked. Psalm 97:10

To be tempted is inevitable for all of us. The devil takes full advantage of our weakness and leads us to fall for those things or people whom we are vulnerable about. He does not waste his time on getting us to sin in those areas which we really do not care for to begin with. He comes after those things which we are trying to get away from as the devil knows that these are our weak points and he can get us to sin as we are vulnerable toward these.

In order to get away from our sin, we need to have a hatred for it. Until we despise our own sin, we cannot be saved from it. We cannot indulge ourselves in the sin and expect to be freed from it. The moment we realize that we are starting to enjoy a sin, we also ought to have a godly desire to get away from it. Often, we acknowledge our sin but we ourselves really do not do anything about it. We pray for deliverance but also continue in it while "waiting" for God to deliver us. But remember that God will not deliver us out of something which we ourselves do not want to.

Only when our love for God is greater, and to do His will is stronger in us, then only we will be rescued. Therefore, let us pray for a change of heart and have a hatred towards that which causes us to stumble and fall. Our willingness to please God causes Him to move and free us from the tempting situations. God helps us stand firm and resist the devil so that he will flee from us as we too desire to flee from him.

Dear LORD, create in me a hatred for the sin which I am involved in. Only until I come to my senses and desire to be freed, that I be freed. As You open the prison doors for me, please help me to truly walk out and not continue to live within the confines of the bondage. Thank you for Your rescue and deliverance as whom the Son sets free is free indeed. In Jesus' name, Amen!

Best friend - July 30

Greater love has no one than this, that he lay down his life for his friends.
John 15:13

Many claim to have hundreds of friends on Facebook. But statistics show that less than ten percent of these are true friends; the rest are mostly acquaintances. An acquaintance is a person who we know of slightly but have no close relation with. We know of them and it would not make much difference with their presence or absence in our personal life. A true friend is, someone who is close to our heart, knows us personally, is trustworthy, and whom we can rely on to come through for us even at a moment's notice without hesitation.

Many do call Jesus their friend but in reality, He only fits the category of an acquaintance. They may know of Jesus but do not know Him personally. He exists in their life as someone they are aware of and it probably does not make a difference to them whether Jesus is in their life or not.

Although we may have hundreds of "friends" in this world, Jesus is the one true friend that we cannot lose or miss the privilege to have. He is always there for us, willing to carry our burdens, share our sorrows, and loves us so much that He even laid down His life for us. What a friend we *can* have in Jesus!

Therefore, if He is not a friend yet, let us accept Jesus' friend request and make Him our lifelong friend whom we cannot live without.

Dear LORD, may my relationship with You not be as an acquaintance but a friend who knows me and loves me just the way I am. What a friend I have in Jesus who bears all my sins and grief! What a privilege that I have in my friend, Jesus Christ who carries all my pain and burden. Thank you, LORD, for always being there for me. May I cherish our friendship which binds us together in love. In Jesus' name, Amen!

No place like home - July 31

But our citizenship is in heaven. And we eagerly await a Savior from there, the Lord Jesus Christ. Philippians 3:20

When we return from a long vacation, there is no feeling like being in our own home and bed. It does not matter how good the vacation is or how luxurious other beds are, but the comfort that we feel sleeping in our own bed and walking in our own home cannot be compared to any other. There really is no place like home.

Similarly, there will be no comparison to what we will feel when we reach our ultimate home in heaven. Our life on earth is a journey or a vacation, but eventually we all will return to our real home where we belong with our heavenly Father. Even if life is good here on earth and we have the finest of everything, the best is yet to come. God has prepared a place for us which we cannot imagine how grandeur it will be and unlike anything we have seen on earth. The satisfying feeling of being in God's presence and entering His kingdom will be the most gratifying feeling ever. We may not realize it right now but when we are there, we will experience the joy of being really at home.

Dear LORD, as I voyage through this earth, let me not forget that my real home is in heaven where You are. My life on this earth is only as a temporary resident but my permanent residence is with You, so help me to be prepared to come home when this journey is over. Hold my feet on the path which You have laid out for me. May I not swerve to the right or to the left and get off the track which leads me to You. In Jesus' name, Amen!

August

Only if God is in it - August 1

..."If your Presence does not go with us, do not send us up from here". Exodus 33:15

Oftentimes after we have already decided to go somewhere or do something, we ask God to bless our plan and to be with us. We tell Him that we need Him but basically after we have made our plans and decisions already.

But foremost, if God's opinion matters to us, we should ask God to decide for us the next course of our path. Before we go any further, we need to ensure that it is from God and only if He will come along with us in our venture, then only we would move forward otherwise we need to stay put where we are. Our feet should not move before God makes His move first.

As we make big or small choices in life, we need to learn to pray for a heart to feel God's presence, ears to hear His voice, and wisdom to follow Him wherever He leads. And when we do so, not only does God prosper us but comes alongside us to be with us and helps us every step of the way. We experience His peace and are not afraid of stepping into new boundaries as we trust and are confident that God will provide us with all necessary means to be where He wants and what needs to be accomplished in and through us.

The only thing we need to be certain about is whether God is in it or not. If not, we cannot dare to make a move without God going ahead first!

Dear LORD, please help me to seek Your will in everything before I execute my plans. Only if my plans are in alignment with Yours and only if Your presence and blessings will be in it, may I move forward. I choose not to do anything without Your consent so may I pursue Your counsel first. In Jesus' name, Amen!

God's timetable - August 2

...for He who promised is faithful. Hebrews 10:23

Sometimes we feel that God has forgotten His promise when we do not see anything happening which we are waiting on. We assume that God does not care about it and He will not fulfill it. We even doubt ourselves and think that we might have misunderstood God's promise words and that it was not what we He may have meant.

It took Sarah twenty-five years to become pregnant after God gave Abraham the promise of making him the Father of many nations. Sarah became impatient in the meantime and tried to hurry God's promise by making her own decision and messed up. It took David seventeen years to become the King after he was anointed by Samuel. Unlike Sarah, David went on as usual trusting God, and not making his own assumptions or taking actions until the fullness of time came according to God's plan.

Most of us are like Sarah. When it seems to take too long from God according to our clock, we pace around frantically, thinking of the many what if reasons. We try to help God fulfill His promise by telling Him how to do it and taking our own actions, which we find out later is not what God had in mind for us to begin with. We need to be more like David. Although he knew he was the chosen future King, he did not let that get to his head in pride, nor tried to hurry in climbing up the status ladder on his own. He remained still and did what he needed to do as God shaped and prepared him over the years to take on this huge role.

If we too are awaiting God's fulfillment on a promise, let us not be like Sarah and be in a haste to get it fulfilled right away. There is a reason for waiting. While we are waiting, remember that God's promise still stands as He is preparing us for greater and better things. His timing and plans are simply perfect, so let us not push God to move while He is moving us along just at the right pace.

Dear LORD, please help me to accept Your timeline and not rush You to do anything before its appointed time. Help me to be patient and allow You to mold me as You prepare me to receive the blessings You have in store for me. Give me a willing heart to follow Your timetable and agenda, not mine. In Jesus' name, Amen!

Stop it in in tracks - August 3

"Watch and pray so that you will not fall into temptation. The spirit is willing, but the flesh is weak." Matthew 26:41

Sometimes our life turns upside down in a matter of moments and we cannot understand what and how it happened. Then there are times when it turns disastrous but in subtle and sweet ways. Before we even realize how and when it occurred, the damage is done and irretrievable. This often occurs in the form of temptation. Temptation is a trial which comes along our way where we have a choice to be faithful or unfaithful to God, our self and others. It tests us on those things which we are vulnerable to already. The devil knows and uses our weakness by constantly luring us into those things which are difficult to withstand. He does not leave us alone and continues to entice us with showing pleasures of that particular sin, and the moment we fall for it, he disappears and leaves us to deal with the consequences.

Therefore, it is important to recognize temptation and stop it in its tracks before it goes any further. If we allow ourselves to dwell on it, sooner or later we give in to it. The Bible acknowledges that we all experience temptation and being tempted does not make one guilty. How we handle it when we are tempted is what matters. Just how we allow temptation to feed into our mind, we have the power to cast it out also.

Prayer is the key to resisting temptation. When we find ourselves in situations where we know we are being tempted, we need to turn that thought right over to God and allow Him to divert our attention back to Him. God gives us power to resist so be wise and overcome temptation with God's wisdom and His strength.

Dear LORD, it is good to know that You can relate to temptation as You also were tempted. Thank you for showing us how you dealt with it. Please help me to do the same and resist the devil by using Your word as my strength and power. May I not fill my mind with thoughts that lead me into temptation but fill me with Your Holy Spirit that saves me from falling into sin. In Jesus' name, Amen!

Ready to return? - August 4

"When he finally came to his senses, he said to himself, 'At home even the hired servants have food enough to spare, and here I am dying of hunger! I will go home to my father and say, "Father, I have sinned against both heaven and you. Luke 15: 17-18

It did not make sense to a son to live under his father's authority, roof and protection. He wanted to be independent, so he demanded the portion of his still alive Dad's will and went away. He spent all his money on his so-called friends, partying away until he used up everything. Once his money was gone, all his friends left him also, and no one helped him in his time of need. When he finally came to his senses, the son realized what he had done and how good he had it in his dad's house. So, he decided to go back home. Instead of his father being angry at the son, he ran towards him and welcomed his prodigal son back with open, forgiving arms even before the son could say sorry.

Many of us like the prodigal son want to be on our own and think it nonsense to live under God's authority and protection. We think we are capable enough to make it on our own and do not need God, until we come to our senses and realize that we are nothing without God. Some of us still hesitate to come back home to Him even after we are convicted of our sin as we are afraid that God is mad and would not accept us back.

But God is not a God who holds grudges or is unforgiving. As soon as He sees that we are repentant, He hurriedly runs towards us and welcomes us back.

Therefore, if today you feel like the prodigal child who has left God to be on your own and now are ready to come back but not sure if you can, let me assure that Yes, you can! It is never too late to turn around, God is waiting with open arms!

Dear LORD, thank you for loving me so much and not holding my sins against me. Please help me to understand that You are always waiting for me to return to You and will accept me the moment I am repentant. So, help me to come to my senses, turn from my sinful ways and come back home to You. In Jesus' name, Amen!

Flow against the current - August 5

For I do not understand my own actions. For I do not do what I want, but I do the very thing I hate. Romans 7:15

We are naturally born with sin so evil is who we are for real. Evil thoughts, desires and actions are not taught but come naturally to us as humans because that is in our blood from the beginning. To be good is not natural, therefore we must train and teach ourselves to be one. Toddlers do not need to be taught to lie or be sneaky at a young age, rather they need to be trained to tell the truth and be honest. Although we desire to do good, we most often end up doing the opposite because that is what we are drawn to do. The devil uses our sin nature to tempt us even more and make evil things desirable which are not good for us. And so, we end up doing things we do not want to do and not do what we are supposed to do. It is easy and is the natural order of things, but God calls us to do the very opposite.

Once we come to realization of our sin and need to repent, we must flow against the current of the natural towards the supernatural. To do so requires willingness first then discipline and self-control. We need to have control over our heart to not allow evil desire to flourish; we need to master our minds to shut off unclean thoughts, ideas, imaginations and discipline ourselves to not act on what comes to us naturally.

It is difficult to swim against the current but with God's help, we can overcome our sin. We need to pray for our blind eyes to see and realize where we are headed and turn around to go with God instead of going with the flow.

Dear LORD, I am a sinner in need of sanctification. I was brought forth in sin and sin is what I know to commit. But You have called us to be holy so please put Your supernatural ability in me to resist temptation, be disciplined and self-controlled to not fall into sin. As difficult as it is to go against the sinful nature, I can do anything through Christ who gives me strength; therefore, I will go against my sinful nature in the strength of the LORD. In Jesus' name, Amen!

It's God's job, not mine - August 6

Do not judge others, and you will not be judged. For in the same way you judge others, you will be judged, and with the measure you use, it will be measured to you. Matthew 7:1-2

Some folks cannot rest until they point out someone else's fault. It is as if they have the God-given right to correct others and walk around with God's stick in their hands, ready to discipline. They are quick to judge, give advice on how to be better and make others feel bad, while portraying themselves as "better than thou".

It is not our duty to take it upon ourselves and chastise others on behalf of God. Our duty is to lift them up in prayer and allow God to handle them. Yes, we can surely talk in privately and let them know about our concern for them but by no means we must pass judgement. By reprimanding others, we may think we are helping God, but rather we end up bringing judgement on ourselves as we all are sinners in need of God's grace.

It is God's job to discipline all of us according to our own deeds. The only God-given right we have is that of asking for forgiveness, not handing out discipline. We need to remember that the rod we use against someone else, will be the same one God will use against us. Therefore, before we go out chastising others, we need to be certain that we ourselves are clear in God's sight.

Dear LORD, please remove from me pride and self-righteousness. Before I point fingers at someone else, please help me to look at my own sin. Give me understanding that just because I sin differently than someone else, I am no better. In Your sight, a sin is a sin so please help me correct mine and be found right in You. In Jesus' name, Amen!

Cramming at the last-minute - August 7

...they stood outside, calling, 'Lord! Lord! Open the door for us! But he answered, 'Truly, I say to you, I do not know you.' Therefore keep watch, because you do not know the day or the hour. Matthew 25: 11-13

At the end of every school year, we notice many students studying harder and doing extra work in order to make up for the missed assignments and to give their best on final exams as every point makes a difference in passing or failing. They wait till the last minute to get serious about their studies while neglecting its importance throughout the school year. If they had been vigilant from the beginning, they would be confident of their result and not need to be fearful of missing the mark in the end.

In the same way, many of us know very well about our sinful life and need to make a change but we ignore it for now. We become overconfident in ourselves and think that we will deal with it at the end and will surely make it. We assume we still have time to make up for the all the wrong we have done and will repent later.

But let us understand clearly that last minute is not guaranteed to any of us. We may be close to it but might not get a last chance to repent and end up missing our mark with God. Therefore, it is important to work out our salvation and be prepared ahead of time so that we do not have to fear our end. The door may get closed on us while we are cramming at the last minute, so let us seek God while He may be found and receive His forgiveness while we have the opportunity.

Dear LORD, You have told us to be prepared for Your coming as the day and hour is unknown. Please help me God, to ensure that I am in right standing with You so that when the final time is at hand, I am ready for You. May I not neglect this grace period You have given to me to get my life in order according to Your standards. In Jesus' name, Amen!

LORD, it is time for you to act, for these evil people have violated your instructions. Psalm 119: 126

Enough is enough is what we say when we cannot take it anymore. My husband and I sometimes find ourselves in certain situations where we cry out to the LORD and question why He allows us to go through some tough trials. We hit rock bottom and feel as if we have come to the end of our rope and cannot hold on any longer. We beg God to stop and tell Him to hurry in making His point that He wants us to get.

While we cannot understand why God allows us to face some difficult trials, God has a lesson that He teaches us through each one of them. The stronger and faithful that we are in Him, the harder the lessons He wants us to learn to make us even stronger in God.

We know that "God gives the hardest battles to His toughest soldiers" so if we are His faithful servants, we must be prepared to fight some of the hardest spiritual battles. Only warriors are placed in the frontlines of the battlefield as they are tough enough to handle it. In the same way, God puts His faithful warriors in the frontlines of the spiritual battles.

But through it all, we need to be assured that as we fight, God fights with us. He comes alongside us as the Commander and equips us in every way to overcome the attacks of the enemy. The harder the battle, the stronger the LORD makes us and gives us the strength to endure. Although it may seem fierce and unbearable, the reward for hanging in there and trusting God through the hard times is much greater. Therefore, let us not give up and lose courage. If God is for us, come what may, we can overcome!

Dear LORD, as I face difficulties and trials, please increase my faith and may I rely on Your power and strength to overcome them. Help me not to run and hide but rather face them with confidence that You are with me every step of the way. And if God is with me, who can be against me! In Jesus' name, Amen!

Personal Brand - August 9

Therefore be imitators of God, as beloved children. Ephesians 5:1

C ompanies spend millions of dollars on advertisement to endorse their product. They use a symbol, slogan, or a person which associates their product to it. As soon as we see or hear it, it reminds us of the product. Such as the big yellow arch of McDonald's reminds us of burgers and French fries and makes us feel hungry to go there.

In the same way, each one of us has an individual brand associated to us. Our personal brand is what makes others think about us when they see or hear something about us. Our walk, talk, dress, choices and reactions, all matter and people brand us based on these. What we put out there associates us to others.

If we call ourselves Christians, Jesus Christ should come to mind to others when they see or hear of us. Since we profess to be followers of Christ and His teachings, Jesus should be reflected through us in everything. Love, joy, peace, patience, kindness, goodness, faithfulness, gentleness, and self-control put together is the logo which should describe us as a Christian person.

So, when others think of us, can they associate these qualities to us? If we ask others to describe in one word which makes them think of us, what would it be? What is our personal brand? We need to proudly endorse Jesus in our lives that draws others towards Him.

Dear LORD, please help me to live my life in such a way that when people look at me, they can clearly see Christ in me. Teach me to live a godly life and may my words and deeds reflect You. Let me be a true representation of Your name. In Jesus' name, Amen!

Inner Beauty - August 10

Charm is deceitful, and beauty is vain, but a woman who fears the LORD is to be praised. Proverbs 31:30

Magazines are filled with articles and photos of what a beautiful woman should be like. The human standard of beauty is defined by how you look, weigh, height, clothes, makeup and hair. Billions of dollars are spent each year on beauty products and plastic surgery to make one look beautiful. While there is nothing wrong with looking good and presenting oneself nicely, this is not what defines true beauty. We can put on a "mask" and deceive people by the way we look, talk, and walk but we cannot deceive God. We may look at each other's outer appearance and determine what he/she is about, but God looks at our heart and determines how beautiful we really are. It does not matter to Him what kind of clothes we wear or what we look like from the outside, but He cares about how much we love Him and how much God means to us. People may praise our external beauty, but God praises our beauty from within.

While we care for our physical appearance, we need to care about our character even more because our character is what determines who we really are like as a person. Outer beauty will come and fade away, but inner beauty is here to stay. So, let us not allow magazines and media to determine how beautiful we must be. Instead, we need to look at God and allow Him to beautify us by His own beauty radiating in us. That is what matters-inner beauty!

Dear LORD, help me to measure my worth by my internal beauty and not with my external appearance. Please help me not to engulf myself in looking good on the outside for people's praises but may I be focused on who I am as a person in Christ. May my inner self be more beautiful than my outer. In Jesus' name, Amen!

What can I give thee? - August 11

The sacrifices of God are a broken spirit; a broken and a contrite heart. O God, you will not despise. Psalm 51:17

If someone pays for us one time, we usually pay for them the next time around. We reciprocate what was given to us by giving back. In the same way, we try to do that with God also. Although we would never be able to repay him back fully for how much he has done for us, we feel the need to do as much as we can in return. We think that the more "work" we do in His name, the closer we are to repaying God back. Therefore, we try to get involved in many church related activities and often force ourselves to follow the Christian religion strictly.

God does not expect us to pay Him back nor does He require any kind of sacrifice in order to gain acceptance with Him. The only thing God asks from us is that we appreciate the depth of His sacrifice and realize that if it were not for His love and grace, we would not be forgiven from our sins. If we can accept this fact, it should lead us to repent and quit our sinful ways. Once our heart is in the right place, we will not feel obligated to repay God back, instead we will submit to Him with love for His sacrifice. That is all God desires from us –not a sacrifice but a humble heart which is grateful and loves Him back.

Dear LORD, please help me to understand the depth of Your love and the sacrifice You have made for me. There is nothing I can give You back for what You have done for me. All I can offer You is my humble and grateful heart. Please accept it and use it as it pleases You. In Jesus' name, Amen!

Equipped to fight - August 12

The laborers carried on their work with one hand supporting their load and one hand holding a weapon. Nehemiah 4:17

W e can all agree that living our life is a challenge. In order to keep up with our daily living, we are busy making money, providing for our family's needs, entertaining ourselves through several activities and socializing. All these keep us occupied 24/7 and we do not have time for anything else. We complain that life is hard and basically do whatever we can to survive with both of our hands full.

As much as physical strength is needed for the hustle and bustle of life, so is spiritual strength. It is necessary to uphold ourselves through prayer as we go through life's ups and down. Prayer is our weapon that we need to hold on one side as we toil to make a living. We must not underestimate the power of prayer and ignore its importance. The devil, our enemy, is always on the look out to mess up our life, so we in turn need to be equipped to fight against him. While we work with our physical hands, we need to gird ourselves with the sword of God's powerful word through prayer.

By praying in all circumstances, claiming God's promises over our life, and trusting God to fight the battle on our behalf, we can overpower the devil through our prayer. With God's strength in us, we can continue to live our life like how God has intended for us. Nothing can bring us down if we are equipped well. So, while we work with one hand physically, let's ensure that we are holding onto Jesus' hand from the other.

Dear LORD, as I live my life, may prayer be my source of strength. Help me not be too busy with the things of life and ignore my prayer life. Teach me to have my priorities aligned so that meeting with You through prayer is my top priority. Help me to listen and heed Your instructions as You guide me through life. In Jesus' name, Amen!

Treasures in jars - August 13

Now we have this treasure in jars of clay to show that this surpassingly great power is from God and not from us. 2 Corinthians 4:7

Clay jars are created by potters who take the raw clay, shape and mold as they desire. They then paint and decorate the jars for whatever purpose they have in mind. In ancient times, clay jars were used to hold valuable documents and things for safe keeping. However, clay jars were temporary holding places as they were breakable and did not serve any other purpose than to hold valuables in it.

We are like jars of clay in whom the Holy Spirit dwells and gives power to live by God's word. God is our potter who created and molded us in the perfect shape as He desired to store His purpose into us. We hold God's spirit in us so while we are alive, we are to safeguard this treasure He has entrusted us with. The physical look of our jars may be good for display but what we have stored internally is what gives us the value. So, our main purpose is not about only taking care of our outward physical appearance but mainly to be clean and spotless from inside. Since we are a temporary holding place for God's treasure, our jars will be broken one day when we have served our time on earth and called home to God. He will then look within us and determine how well we did with the treasure that He gave us to hold.

Let us ensure that our jar is clean from inside out so that God's treasure within us remains just as beautiful and powerful as He gave us.

Dear LORD, thank you for choosing me to be the jar in which You have placed Your treasure, the light of the gospel that displays the glory of Christ. Please help me to truly shine Your light so that people can see Christ in me. May my jar continue to be filled with Your presence and overflow with Your love. In Jesus' name, Amen!

In the book of life - August 14

Heaven and earth will pass away, but my words will never pass away.
Matthew 24:35

Many of us have the perception that the Bible is an old history book. The events in it took place about two thousand years ago and so we read it as if the events are done and the Bible is finished. It is not the end though. The Bible story has not reached its end yet. The fulfillment of the end of the age is the portion of the Bible that we are currently in as the story is continuous to this day. We are living in the "church phase" of the Bible where God is still building up His kingdom. Before He ascended to heaven after His resurrection, Jesus made a promise that He will come back!

Therefore, we need to be prepared for God's return and tell those who have not heard about the good news of Jesus yet. God does not wish for any of our names to be left out from His book of life, therefore He is delaying His return to give all an opportunity to accept Him.

At the end of it all, God will search for our names in the book of life which will determine our final destiny. Will your name be in it? If you are not sure, then it is not too late yet. God is giving us a chance to still believe in Him, but do not wait too long otherwise we may miss the opportunity eternally.

Dear LORD, I know that Your coming is remarkably close. The warning signs of Your return are blasting all around us so please help me not to ignore it but seriously tell others about You so that they can repent of their sins and have their names written in the book of life. Thank you, Lord for saving me. I pray for the salvation of my unsaved loved ones. Please break their stubborn stony hearts and create in them a new heart that is willing to accept You as their Lord and Savior. In Jesus' name, Amen!

Reconstruction - August 15

He is before all things, and in him all things hold together. Colossians 1:17

Little children do not like anyone else to touch their toys. As soon as they get one, they are eager to carry it and assemble it on their own. They do not even like help from their parents as they think they know it all and can manage to build their toy.

But after multiple tries when it still falls apart and they cannot fix it by themselves, the children come crying to their parents to put the broken pieces back together and fix it. We too behave like little children in front of God. We think we know it all and do not need God's help in building our lives. We think we know what we are doing and enjoy it ourselves without His assistance until things in life start to fall apart. Then after we realize it is out of our control to fix it, we bring our broken pieces to God.

And just like a parent who does not get mad but rather is glad to help, our heavenly Father is eager and willing to help put our broken pieces back together. We may have made a huge mess and have many broken pieces that seem like cannot be put together anymore and we feel wasteful about ourselves, but there is nothing which God sees as a waste. There is nothing that God cannot join back. He is the glue who holds us together and will not let us break and be thrown out. He is our maker and knows how to fix us.

So, let us bring all our broken pieces to God, show Him the mess we have made and let God fix it. He is the one who created us, so He is the one who knows best where every part of us belongs. Let God construct us back together if we have torn it apart.

Dear LORD, sometimes I feel too torn apart to be mended together. I have nothing left of me but broken pieces. I still bring these to You because I know that You can turn this mess into something beautiful. You can turn my brokenness into happiness so take them, LORD and glue me back together with Your love and forgiveness. Assemble me in a new way so that I can be a useful vessel for Your kingdom. In Jesus' name, Amen!

It's all about You, Jesus - August 16

And calling the crowd to him with his disciples, he said to them, "If anyone would come after me, let him deny himself and take up his cross and follow me. Mark 8:34

We usually relate a Christian person as who goes to church, takes communion, prays, and carries a Bible with them. These are outward features that others notice in a Christian. But the more important qualities of a Christian are the attitude, character and standards that we live by. The way we speak to others, our reaction towards adverse circumstances, our integrity, and our way of daily living determines who we truly are in Christ. If we have accepted Jesus Christ into our lives as our God, then He should be reflected through us in and out. As followers of Jesus, we should be imitators of Him by living and loving like He does. We ought to deny ourselves and put Jesus before us. This means to put aside our own selfish ways and pleasures to live according to how God tells us to.

But many of us become so engulfed in pleasing ourselves that we become our own primary focus. Instead of denying ourselves, we deny Christ and put ourselves, our goals and desires first. We live for ourselves and compete, defeating the whole purpose of Christianity.

Our goal as a Christian must not be to impress people by our Christian title and showmanship but by how we really live up to it. If Christ is missing from our Christianity, can we truly call ourselves Christians?

Dear LORD, I thank you for the privilege to be known my Your name. Please help me not to take this lightly but may I earnestly carry Your name with honor and give You the due respect by my way of living. Help me to understand that to be a Christian is not about how much I do for You, but it is all about You, Jesus! So, in return for Your love, the least I can do is put my selfish desires away and put You first in my life. Please help me to do so, In Jesus' name, Amen!

Cry baby - August 17

You keep track of all my sorrows. You have collected all my tears in your bottle. You have recorded each one in your book. Psalm 56:8

My children think of me as a cry baby. I do cry easily, but my tears are an expression of my affection towards a person or situation. Tears roll off my eyes simply as my heart wells up with either happiness or sorrow. Often though, sad tears are shed more as I have a soft heart which aches easily for others, particularly for the elderly, children, and for animals these days ever since we have our little dog, my precious Teddy bear. Even when I hear about a struggle or issue that someone is going through, my heart pains and cries on their behalf.

Some folks resist crying because they feel it shows their weakness. So, they hold those tears back and not allow anyone to see their vulnerable side. But tears in fact represent a big and strong heart that is full of emotions for oneself and for others. God has given us tears to express our love and internal state. If we did not need tears, God would not have created them. As senseless as it may look to others when we cry, God sees our heart from it. Every tear that we shed matters to Him. He knows us intimately and sees what causes us pain and what brings joy to our hearts. God keeps an account of every tear to reveal to us one day what each tear meant to Him and what He did about it.

As we express our emotions through tears, know that God values them, collects them in a bottle and will turn them into a river of blessing for those whom they were shed. So, let the tears roll freely and allow God to catch them!

Dear LORD, thank you for giving us tears through which we express our love and concern for each other. Help me not be afraid to shed them when I am feeling happy or feeling hurt as You see the joy and pain of my heart through these. Thank you for considering my tears important and storing them. In Jesus' name, Amen!

Small beginnings - August 18

His master said to him, 'Well done, my good and faithful servant. You have been faithful over a little; I will set you over much. Enter into the joy of your master".
Matthew 25:21

Sometimes, we may feel as if we are carrying the burdens of the entire world on our shoulders alone and in order to satisfy the needs of everyone, we do whatever we can to accomplish as much as we can and how ever we can. We rush around taking giant leaps, shortcuts and jump from here to there while missing out on learning and enjoying the little steps that bring us to our goal.

Often our dreams do not seem to be fulfilled because we dream too high. There is nothing wrong with bigger dreams but for them to become a reality, we must start small. We can set a goal but to get there requires for us to take each step one at a time. We cannot just become a CEO of a company, a pastor of a mega church, or an NBA player without starting small first and then moving up to bigger things. It involves hard work, practice, patience, and faithfulness as we go through the process. As we take each step, God tests our faithfulness in little things and then blesses us to go to the next level. If we take shortcuts and to try to make it on our own, we can be sure that we will not last long if God is not the one who put us there. He has called us to take it one day at a time, doing the best in whatever is set before us, and being faithful in our little duties first in order to accomplish bigger things.

Like Josh Wilson sang, "A tiny rock can make the giant fall". So, let us take a grip of the tiny thing in our hand first before we aim for the giant.

Dear LORD, please help me not to despise my small beginnings but give You my best in all that You are calling me to do, little by little. Help me to stay focused on You and not compare myself to what others do. You have placed in me a specific mission to accomplish so may I serve You faithfully as You lead me to a higher purpose according to Your plan for me. In Jesus' name, Amen!

Never forget - August 19

I will recount the steadfast love of the Lord, the praises of the Lord, according to all that the Lord has granted us... Isaiah 63:7

When we face sickness and trials in life, we come closer to God as we realize that we do need Him, as basically He's the only one who can deliver us after everything we've tried and may have failed on our own. We then become more focused on God, fervent in prayer, Bible reading, and get humbler with God and with others. During the moments of trials, we take a better grip on our tongue and attitude and are more resilient against temptations lest we fall and are afraid that God would not deliver us.

But soon afterwards once we have overcome trials and things fall back into place, we kind of go back to our old self and ways. We start to slowly forget God's goodness and how He delivered us when no one else could. We use God in our weaknesses but put Him aside when we think we are okay on our own.

Friends, we should never overlook what God has done for us no matter how long it has been or how well we are now. We should not allow anything or anyone to come in between us and God now as we would not allow it to happen when we needed Him before. The same control we had over our sinful nature then should be intact once our trials are over also. Just the way we would like others to remember us and what we did for them in their time of need, God too expects the same from us. He desires that we remember His goodness and what He has done for us. Therefore, let us not forget God's faithfulness from before by becoming unfaithful to Him now.

Dear LORD, thank you for giving me the privilege to call to You for help. Thank you for being there for me in my time of need. If it were not for You, where would I be! So, may I never forget what You have done for me no matter how long ago it was. In Jesus' name, Amen!

Faltering faith - August 20

Now all glory to God, who is able, through his mighty power at work within us, to accomplish infinitely more than we might ask or think. Ephesians 3:20

We generally say that we trust God but often only up to a certain extent. We put a limit on God and a limit on how much faith we have in Him. When things seem beyond our control, we think that they are out of God's control also and thus our faith falters. If things seem reasonable to us, our faith stays strong but when things do not go the way we think or plan, we end up doubting. We forget that God does not work within our limitations. He is not bound by any boundaries nor is there any limit to how far He can extend His hand of grace. Our end is just God's beginning. When we are ready to give up hope for something, God shows up and proves us wrong. When it comes to trusting God, we need to think beyond our own capacity and remember God can do far more than what we can even imagine. There is nothing that He cannot accomplish nor is He limited by any human factors.

Dear LORD, when doubts arises in me, I ask you to arise my faith even higher. Please open my spiritual eyes that can see beyond my human limitations and see what You see. Help me to understand that Your hand is not too short to save but can reach beyond my restrictions. So, may I allow You to go to those places on my behalf where I cannot and save those whom I cannot reach. Please lead me to a faith that is without borders, a limitless faith, like my limitless God. In Jesus' name, Amen!

All creation - August 21

For this reason I say to you, do not be worried about your life, as to what you will eat or what you will drink; nor for your body, as to what you will put on. Is not life more than food, and the body more than clothing? Look at the birds of the air, that they do not sow, nor reap nor gather into barns, and yet your heavenly Father feeds them. Are you not worth much more than they? Matthew 6: 25-26

Another precious life had been added in my life to worry and care for when we got our little puppy, Teddy. Before we got Teddy, I could not relate how people could get so attached to an animal and never imagined myself to get one. But now that we have Teddy, I cannot imagine him not being around. He follows me around like my little bodyguard as my husband would call him. I look forward to going home to hug and play with Teddy. Especially when we are away on vacation, I miss him so much and cannot wait to go back home. I constantly worry what he might be doing without me.

While these thoughts are going on in my mind, I am reminded that this is my heavenly Father's world and He cares for all creatures, even as small as a sparrow. We, humans are created in God's image and He has a special care and bond with us compared to other creatures, but nonetheless, God cares for all His creation. There is nothing that He does not have His eye on, and no life goes unnoticed by the Creator.

So whomever we love, whether it's a human or any other creature, let's entrust everything under God's care because if anything matters to us, it also matters to God, and He makes every provision for all of His creation to be cared for.

Dear LORD, thank you for caring for me and all that I love. You have created this earth with such perfection that all creatures are precious in Your sight and taken care of. Thank you for this beautiful world and all that is in it. In Jesus' name, Amen!

But I have this against you, that you have abandoned the love you had at first. Remember therefore from where you have fallen; repent and do the works you did at first. If not, I will come to you and remove your lampstand from its place, unless you repent. Revelation 2: 4-5

There was a famous scene in a movie where someone approached the main actor standing in a queue and asked whether he was standing in the line like was supposed to. The actor's response was "Wherever I stand, is where the line starts". The meaning of it was that he does not need to be told where the line is or stand behind anyone in a queue.

In many churches, we see a queue of "preachers" standing in a line to go up on the pulpit to preach. They believe that the only place to share the gospel is to stand behind the pulpit in a church and in front of a house-full congregation. Whether they could be anointed or not by the Holy Spirit, many compete to get on the stage to speak because they believe their power and knowledge can only be displayed from a few feet above the rest and need the validation of the audience to tell them how well they spoke.

Sadly, many churches have lost God's favor because they have left their love for Christ and have started to love themselves. Instead of focusing on the spiritual well-being of the church a whole, they focus more on being well-known individually. And for the pursuit of getting ahead, the congregation suffers, and the church dies as it becomes spiritually malnourished. As a part of a church, we may get lured into these things, but we need to know that a church is a place to worship along with true worshippers of Christ. God recognizes his faithful worshippers and uses them as his mouthpiece regardless of the place or people. When God's anointing is present, standing in a queue for pulpit is not necessary; the preaching starts from wherever we stand.

Dear LORD, please help to remember that You are my first love and may it be my goal to love You always and foremost. May my heart be focused on You and be in alignment with what You want me to do. Help me know who I am in You and be willing to stand and please You alone wherever You place me. In Jesus' name, Amen!

Soar like an eagle - August 23

But those who wait for the LORD shall renew their strength; they shall mount up with wings like eagles; they shall run and not be weary; they shall walk and not faint. Isaiah 40:31

An eagle has a few distinct characteristics that sets it apart from the rest of the bird category. It flies much higher than the rest of the birds. The eagle does not like to bicker and dispute with other birds, so it stirs clear from them to avoid conflict and competition. It knows what it is capable of, so the eagle does not lower its standard to the others. Second, while the other birds run and hide from the storm, eagle fly right into it. The strong wind beneath its wing gives the eagle an extra boost to soar even higher, above the clouds and out of the storm. And while it is soaring, the eagle keeps an eye on its prey below. It does not lose its vision but is focused on what it is looking for.

If we want to ascend in our life with Christ, we need to soar like an eagle. There is no need to lower our standard and remain low with those who seek to bring us down. In the race of life, we often pull each other down rather than help up, so we must recognize who and what to stay away from. We must rise above to what God has called us as an individual. And as we rise and find ourselves amid the storm, instead of running away we can run right into it fearlessly knowing that God is with us. He gives us the strength that we need to rise higher and above the storm.

Dear LORD, You are the wind beneath my wings that helps me soar above the storms that I go through in life. Help me not to get discouraged and hide in fear but face the storm as I rely and wait on You to lift me up. Thank you for being my help, confidence and strength as I walk and run to towards my victory. In Jesus' name, Amen!

Impress or Influence - August 24

Live such good lives among the pagans that, though they accuse you of doing wrong, they may see your good deeds and glorify God on the day he visits us. 1 Peter 2:12

We usually aim to either impress people or influence people. When we try to impress others, we tend to forget who we really are and try to be someone who we are not. Our goal becomes for others to think highly of us than the reality. In the process to impress others, we lose focus of who we truly are. We get caught up in showing others how good we are rather than worrying about what God thinks of us.

But if our aim is to influence others, we must lead by example by doing good, but also not be afraid to show our flaws and shortcomings so that people can see the truth about us. We must do this so that we ourselves can learn from our mistakes and for everyone to see how God brought us out of the darkness and how far we have come along in Christ. We should be genuine in our testimony and be boastful about how much God has done for us, and not try to impress by telling how much we have done for God.

This is the way God wants us to live—to influence by being true to ourselves and to others, to be righteous and to walk uprightly in God's ways so that people can see our growth in the Lord and learn from us, despite our failures.

Are you an impresser or an influencer?

Dear LORD, please help me to be genuine so that when people see how mightily You have worked in me, that they may glorify Your name. Help me not to mislead others by only portraying my good but be open enough to share my shortcomings so that we can relate and help each other grow in You. As You have restored me, may I influence others and may my life be a testimony of a sinner saved by grace. In Jesus' name, Amen!

Wonder working power – August 25

Submit yourselves, then, to God. Resist the devil, and he will flee from you. Come near to God and he will come near to you. James 4: 7-8

Resistance is pushing back against something that is pushing from the opposite side. For example, if someone tries to break open the door from the outside, we push against it to keep it shut or place something stronger than the force which is being exerted from outside.

Satan is such an intruder who tries to break into our home, family, and life. And if we do not push back against him, we become his target. In order to resist his attacks, we must push back with a stronger force than him. And that resistance from our side is called prayer. There is power in prayer! Many think of prayer as nothing more than sitting with our eyes closed and saying some formal words. But praying is speaking directly with God and calling on His mighty name to fight back on our behalf. When we pray, we prompt God to act on His promises which He's promised for our good.

We may underestimate prayer but there is wonder working power when we pray in the name of Jesus. So, when the devil pushes hard to destroy us, our children, and homes, we must assert stronger force of prayer against the enemy. We need to be prayer warriors and hold that door tightly shut so that the devil cannot penetrate through. We must give the devil a good fight and he will eventually flee when we resist him with the strength of the LORD in us.

Dear LORD, teach me to use prayer as my weapon when attacked by the enemy. Help me not to succumb into fear and give up but rather fight fiercely on my knees with prayers that can break any chains or strongholds over me and my loved ones. Lift me up directly Your throne as I pray to You and may I tap into the powerful name of Jesus against whom none can stand. In Jesus' name, Amen!

Better late than never - August 26

So the last will be first, and the first will be last. Matthew 20:16

The Bible talks about two sons whom the Dad asked to do something. One son said he would do it and then did not do it while the other son who first flat out refused, eventually ended up doing what the father asked of him.

We can compare ourselves to these two sons and determine which one we can relate to. Many are quick to responding yes to God. Whatever the Bible says, they agree with it right away, but do not follow through. They like what it states and commit to it from their mouths but do not really do anything about it. They miss the mark as their love and service to God comes only from mouth but not from deed. Then there are folks who say no to the gospel first because they do not have any regard for God's word and feel self-sufficient without Him. But later, they come to their senses and realize the importance of obeying God and turn away from their sinful ways to follow Him. Their service to God really comes from the heart because they have realized the true meaning of obedience and now have regard for the one who asks.

So, if we are like the son who keeps saying yes to God but do not really do anything to please Him, our words are empty and meaningless. It is well to be the son who initially said no but did repent later. It is better to turn to God even later than to say yes first and turn away later.

Dear LORD, may I not just be a talker but be doer of the word. May I not just talk big and do nothing but teach me to be reliable and keep my word. Help me not make empty promises which I cannot keep and give false hope to anybody. Please convict me by Your Holy Spirit about those things which I refuse to do for You and make me come back with a repentant heart. In Jesus' name, Amen!

Wandering thoughts - August 27

Since, then, you have been raised with Christ, set your hearts on things above, where Christ is, seated at the right hand of God. Colossians 3:1

To take rest is good when we work hard, are sick and need to take a break. Our bodies and mind need it to refresh, re-energize, and be well for the next task. But being idle is just being lazy, not having any goal in mind, or motivation to work towards something. This leads a person to occupy their mind with nothing but unnecessary thoughts, imaginations and ideas. Idleness distracts and leads us into temptation and takes away our focus from what we value. It can turn dangerous as it does not take much to turn our thoughts into actions that lead to sinful activities and negative consequences.

We live in a sinful world and person who does not have a goal to strive for will end up doing something sinful. If our mind is empty, the devil is ever ready to fill it up with his sinful ideas as the saying "An idle mind is the devil's workshop".

Therefore, it is necessary to occupy our minds with godly thoughts and activities. Instead of having wandering thoughts, we should read God's word and ponder on His goodness. Instead of having unhealthy chats with others that mess with our minds, it is better to have meaningful conversations with God through prayer. We must not allow idleness to take away our focus of who we are in Jesus and what He expects from us as His child.

Dear LORD, fill my mind with thoughts of You. Teach me to immediately shut off those thoughts, ideas, imaginations and feelings that come to me which are impure and unholy. Please always help me to concentrate on You and listen to Your voice as You speak and teach me the way of life. Cause me to remain busy with You and not with the world. In Jesus' name, Amen!

A sin is a sin - August 28

God would surely have known it, for he knows the secrets of every heart.
Psalm 44:21

There are two types of sin that we all are guilty of. Sin which others see us commit and sin that no one else but God sees. We dismiss the sin that we commit from our heart, mind, and eyes as "not a big deal" since we really do not act on it. But whether we act on it or not, a sin is a sin whether committed externally or thought of. The secret sins are more dangerous though because they are devious. We deceive others as they see us righteous on the outside while internally lays our unrighteousness that they cannot see, thus are fooled by our act.

We may escape the eye of people with our secret sins but cannot expect the same from God. He knows our every thought and motive and will judge us based on what we are from the inside. And so, it is necessary to take charge of our heart and mind and not even entertain a sinful thought. We need to discipline ourselves to shut off the sinful thought the moment it enters in. The devil is good at brining evil and lustful thoughts in our mind and we need to be vigilant to shut it off as soon as we think of it. We must not allow it to grow lest it deepens and makes it harder to root out. Let's be quick to confess and get rid of the sin big or small, open or secret, the moment we feel convicted of it.

Our Father up above is looking down below so be careful little eyes, mouth, mind, and heart what you see, say, think, and feel!

Dear LORD, please help me to be mindful not only of my actions but my thoughts. Teach me to take captive every thought that is not from You and dismiss it in the name of Jesus. Please remove from me the spirit of falsehood, lust and perversion that corrupts my mind. May the Spirit of truth penetrate and fill my heart with Your righteousness. In Jesus' name, Amen!

Thank you in advance - August 29

On the day I called, you answered me; my strength of soul you increased.
Psalm 138:3

We all have some prayer request that we might be waiting for an answer to. We pray regularly for it and wonder when or if God will ever hear our prayer. The fact is that God does hear our prayer and is already at work on it before we even bring it up to him. He is aware of all that concerns us and does not wait for us to act until we reach out to Him. He is already on it by aligning things, people, places and paths for us. God has a plan and purpose behind everything He does so while we try to figure out things on our own, God is on the move.

Therefore, let us wait for the breakthrough that is coming our way. When God's timing is at hand, nothing we have done or not done can stop Him from what He is doing. His way is perfect, and He is our good, good Father who looks out for the best for His children. Our concerns are His concerns also and our prayers are already answered before we even appeal to him. It is just a matter of trusting God for His timing and His will to be done in our lives. So, when we pray and ask for certain things, know that God knows about it already and thank Him for answering prayer before we even see the results.

Dear LORD, thank you for going ahead of me and paving the way before I even walk on it. You know my future and have already set things for me. Before I bring it to Your attention, You are aware and working on it already so teach me to be thankful for answered prayers prior to seeing the results. In Jesus' name, Amen!

Righteous anger - August 30

Now that you know these things, you will be blessed if you do them. John 13:17

Many of us are too nice or afraid to speak up when we see something being done unfairly either at home, workplace, church, etc. We are afraid that by speaking up, it will make matters worse. Or as Christians we feel that it is not biblical to get angry, so we sit back quietly allowing ourselves to be mistreated and letting the unfairness continue. We try to keep a peaceful environment and hold people together, so we do nothing to address the negative situation.

Being bothered and calling out unjust things is called righteous anger. As nice as Jesus was, He got angry and started throwing things out of the church that corrupted His holy temple. He could not stand to be a part of the circus and regardless of the consequence, He did what was right and needed. Jesus demonstrated what righteous anger is by not getting angry at the people directly but at their sin which they were partaking in.

It goes the same for us; when we know of unfair things, we should not be fearful of the consequences and step aside. If we do not stand up, we contribute to the injustice and are no better than the ones who do commit it. Our silence is our compliance to it; therefore, we must tell the truth where truth needs to be told. If the Holy Spirit reveals the truth to us, we must not remain silent and look the other way, but must speak up as He gives us boldness to step up and speak with love and respect towards the unrighteous acts.

Dear LORD, please give me the wisdom to recognize the truth according to Your word and the courage to stand up against any unrighteousness. Help me not to worry about the consequence or hatred from people but to do the right no matter what. Help me to hate the sin but love the sinner and so please help me to act with love, and not sin even when I am angry. In Jesus' name, Amen!

Take the load off - August 31

Therefore do not worry about tomorrow, for tomorrow will worry about itself. Each day has enough trouble of its own. Matthew 6:34

Because we live and need to make a living, it is hard not to worry as the Bible tells us to. Worry is a part of life, but it should not rule our life. We should not allow our mind to constantly dwell on our difficulties or be overwhelmed with continuously thinking and being fearful with stresses of life. While we cannot ignore the needs and concerns, we have for ourselves and loved ones, these ought not consume our mind all the time and take away our peace. When we say we trust God yet worry, it is like carrying a heavy load on our back and sit with it still attached on our back instead of taking it off our shoulders and laying it aside.

When we do feel worried about anything, we should turn it over the LORD. He too is concerned for our needs and is willing to take it off our shoulders. The matter is in our hands though whether we allow Him to carry it or still try to hold it ourselves.

Feeling worried is inevitable but we need to know that God is greater than all our worries. Nothing that concerns us is hidden from Him or is He not capable of handling. Therefore, when worry comes in, let us point it directly to God and let Him handle it.

Dear LORD, I bring to You all that bothers me. You have offered to carry my burdens so please help me to give it to You and not take it back once I have submitted it into Your hands. Please help me to trust You and allow You to take care of everything that is heavy on my heart. Fill me with Your peace as I rest and wait on You to meet my needs. In Jesus' name, Amen!

September

Time is at hand - September 1

And if I go and prepare a place for you, I will come again and will take you to myself, that where I am you may be also. John 14:3

We are not able to wrap our mind around some of the things that we see and hear these days. Unimaginable things are happening, and these are nothing but signs of the end of age. People do not take these signs seriously but for those who believe in Jesus can relate to the happenings around the world and know that His return is near; nearer than we think. After His resurrection, Jesus ascended back up to heaven and said that He will return to come get His people to be with Him. He did not give us an exact date or time but surely gave us signs to look out for as an indication of His time coming near.

The signs are getting louder and louder and we need to take it seriously. It is better to be ready than to be caught off guard and miss the opportunity. Those who truly know Him and have accepted Jesus as their personal God, will He take with Him. The rest of us have a long-awaited ultimate judgement to pass through. No money or status will be able to rescue us.

We need to pray for spiritual awakening in our hearts and blinded eyes to see the reality of things to come.

Let us not take it lightly–Jesus is coming soon!

Dear LORD, please help me to heed the warning signs of the end times and warn others of Your return. Help me to step out of my comfort zone and share the good news gospel to as many people as I. Please open the eyes of my blind loved ones who are living in ignorance and procrastinating on their decision to accept You in their lives. Soften their hearts and create a desire in them for You. May their faith not be an extension of my faith but truly be their own. In Jesus' name, Amen!

Heart transformation - September 2

I will give them an undivided heart and put a new spirit in them; I will remove from them their heart of stone and give them a heart of flesh. Ezekiel 11:19

It is exceedingly difficult to change anyone's mind. No matter how much we try to convince, most of us are stubborn in our ways. We feel that we are right and so we do not want to listen to each other. The world teaches us that we all have a right to our opinion so none is right, nor none is wrong. We are self-willed, do as we please and think as what suits us. Particularly when it comes to religion, many have their minds made up regarding God and no matter how much we try to shed the light of truth, it does not permeate through their hearts.

We might be discouraged and give up on the individual as there may be no hope for a change. But we forget that the God who put the heart in us is also capable of changing it. While we may not be successful in breaking one's stubbornness, God can easily do it. He can make the heart of stone melt and change one's attitude to desire and follow Him.

So, when we do not have any hope for someone to change their ways, let us take them to God, the Ultimate Heart Specialist to do what He is best at – Heart transformation!

Dear LORD, I pray for my loved ones who are living in stubbornness against You. They are set in their ways and self-righteousness. Would you please melt the heart of stone and put a new heart, willing and ready to accept You. Bring them to their senses to understand who You are and their need for You in their lives. Apart from You, we can do nothing so please break our pride and humble us to receive You. In Jesus' name, Amen!

Trust and obey - September 3

For now we see in a mirror dimly, but then face to face. Now I know in part; then I shall know fully. 1 Corinthians 13:12

When God asked Noah to build an ark, it did not used to rain then. The concept of rain was something new which was never seen or heard of. God watered the earth from below with mist coming up from the ground. Although Noah had no idea what it all meant, he obeyed God and did exactly what he was instructed to do. Noah was probably made fun of and ridiculed by his fellow men but he paid no attention to what others had to say, he simply trusted God and obeyed His directions.

Sometimes what God calls us to do may be unheard of or beyond our imagination and ability. But like Noah, if we trust God, we do not need to know and see everything first before we choose to trust and obey. God has a grandeur plan for our lives and reveals to us step by step as we follow His leading. His thoughts towards us are much better than what we can possibly think of.

Therefore, if there is something in our life which seems beyond belief, we should believe God nonetheless, and do what He says. There is a fulfillment of promise awaiting us when we choose to obey even when we do not understand.

Dear LORD, please help me to accept Your calling as You ask me to do certain things without questioning or doubting. Help me to trust and obey as Your ways are much higher than mine and Your plans are beyond my comprehension. May I not worry about the input of others, but faithfully serve in whichever way You need me to. In Jesus' name, Amen!

Situation Room - September 4

Let us then approach God's throne of grace with confidence, so that we may receive mercy and find grace to help us in our time of need. Hebrews 4:16

There is a room in the White House called the Situation Room where top Security Leaders and Advisors meet with the President to discuss and make strategic plans for the security of the nation. It is a highly secure room and talks are highly confidential. People who are invited in the Situation room are limited to only the ones that are important to the matter.

I call my prayer time, the "Situation Room" where I am invited to meet with the King of Universe to personally and confidentially discuss and seek His advice on battles of my life that I fight in my own little world. This is the place where I can approach God's throne of grace and let it all out without any fear. This is the place where I find peace, encouragement and guidance on how to handle situations.

We all have battles with issues such as addiction, sickness, marital problems, children, peer pressure, financial concerns, temptations, depression, etc. that we fight individually. And praying is like going to the Situation Room to speak to God and seeking His guidance on how to deal with our problems. God's Situation Room is open to all and we are all important enough and invited to meet Him. And when we come out of the meeting, God does not send us back out empty handed to combat the problem in our own way, but fully equips and gears us up to fight the battle we are facing with Him coming alongside us every step of the way. Have you visited your Situation Room today? No appointment is needed, just walk in and discuss the problem with the Commander in Chief.

Dear LORD, thank you for allowing me to approach Your throne with full rights as your child. You do not cast anyone out who come to You so here I am God, with all my struggles and fear. Please help me to pay attention as You speak and heed Your instructions on how to tackle my enemy. In Jesus' name, Amen!

Long drives - September 5

He leads me in paths of righteousness for his name's sake. Psalm 23:3b

When driving to an unfamiliar location, there are four things that we rely on – the Driver, Car, GPS and Road. We trust that the driver knows where to go and how to drive the car. We believe that our car will function properly, that the roads will be smooth and marked correctly for us to go through, and our GPS will give us directions on which way to take in order to get us to our final destination.

In the same way there are four things that we rely on as we travel through this life. We are the driver of our life who has the control of deciding where we want to go. If we decide to live as a Christian, Jesus Christ is our vehicle on whom we rest and rely. He becomes the mediator between us and the road that leads us to our eternal home. The Holy Spirit is our GPS who gives us directions in every area of our life. He shows us which way to go, where to make a U-turn if we get off track and brings us back on our path. Our Heavenly Father is the only road on which we travel that leads us to our destination. He marks the way for us all the way up to where we meet Him at the end.

Just as we trust our car, roads, and GPS to take us where we need to go, we need to put our trust in God who goes with us and guides our path through life. But the decision as a driver is in our hands to choose whether we allow Jesus to take control and be our mediator, Holy Spirit to be our GPS, and God the Father the road that leads us to heaven.

Dear LORD, I give you the control of my life. Please take over and lead me in the paths of righteousness. May I follow the conviction of the Holy Spirit who is my helper through life and stay focused on the destination, my eternal home, to meet with You. In Jesus' name, Amen!

All is well - September 6

...Do not be grieved, for the joy of the LORD is your strength. Nehemiah 8:10

We all face certain circumstances where we feel weak and defeated, not knowing how we will make it through. It is hard to smile and be cheerful when things do not seem to be going well in life.

When we have lost our strength, we can rely on God's power. When we feel hopeless, we can be hopeful in God. Our situation may seem rough and we may keep running into closed doors, but we need to be assured that God is working on our behalf, making a way where there seems to be no way. He will open doors that lead to even something better. So while we can't see the future ahead of us and we may not have enough strength of our own to make it through the trial that we face, knowing that God is with us should be enough to bring joy to our hearts.

Being joyful is not just an emotional feeling and it does not depend on our surrounding circumstances. Rather it's a peaceful state of heart which knows that all is well even when it doesn't seem like it, because the God who holds our future is the one who loves us and has the best planned for us. So, when we feel weak, we ought to rely on God's strength and put our hope in Him as He turns our sorrow into joy.

Dear LORD, to know joy is to know You. When I have You, there is nothing that can stand against me so please help me to rejoice in all circumstances as You have all my situations under control. I submit my anxiety, fear, doubt and worries into Your hands. Please turn these into peace as I trust You to be with me and help me through every difficult circumstance that I face. In Jesus' name, Amen!

Foggy climate - September 7

Your word is a lamp to my feet and a light to my path. Psalm 119:105

Foggy weather is one of my favorite atmospheres. It is like heaven on earth and feel like I am walking in clouds. Sometimes the fog is so dense though that we cannot see more than a few feet away and if driving, we need to turn on low beams just to be able to get a clear vision of what is a little ahead. We drive slowly through it relying on our lights to pave the way for us some distance at a time.

We basically walk through life in foggy atmosphere. We cannot see what is far ahead of us, nor can we go back and trace exactly what we left behind. In order to see ahead we need light to guide our path and that light is God's word, the Bible. The Bible is the lamp which teaches us right from wrong and directs us in every matter as we journey through life. This world is a very dark place and in order to be able to make the next move, we need to need on to hold on God's word very near to us, right at our feet to guide our next step.

Like in the days of past without GPS, we would study our maps closely and memorize the routes to take us to our desired destination; in the same way we need to study God's word closely and memorize scripture words to help us stay on path to our final destination.

It's not enough just to read some Bible passages leisurely just to check it off our daily chores, but it's essential that we take time to get to know God intimately and trust in Him as He takes us through life. We may not be able to see clearly but if we have God's light directing our steps, we will not stumble nor fall.

Therefore, let us embrace God's word in our heart and allow Him to pave the way in life, one step at a time.

Dear LORD, thank you for Your word, the Bible which gives me light as I walk through life. Please open my mind and give me listening ears to hear You speak as You talk to me through the Bible. Help me to hold Your word dearly to my heart as it is the light that shines and makes me know the right path. In Jesus' name, Amen!

Fully girded - September 8

Therefore, put on every piece of God's armor so you will be able to resist the enemy in the time of evil. Then after the battle you will still be standing firm. 14 Stand your ground, putting on the belt of truth and the body armor of God's righteousness. 15 For shoes, put on the peace that comes from the Good News so that you will be fully prepared. 16 In addition to all of these, hold up the shield of faith to stop the fiery arrows of the devil. 17 Put on salvation as your helmet, and take the sword of the Spirit, which is the word of God. Ephesians 6: 13-17

For every Christian, there is a spiritual warfare going in and around us. We are engaged in this battle and it's absolutely necessary that we are well equipped and ready to fight for our body, mind, and soul.

As big as Goliath was, there was something missing from his gear and that's where David was able to target and hit him right on the spot.

Goliath represents the devil and he is on a look out to see where we are exposed for him to attack. If we leave any open space and are not properly geared up, Satan throws a blow right where we are weak and vulnerable. As this Bible verse teaches, we must put on the full armor of God, the whole armor, not partially. We cannot be covered in some areas and not in others but we need to be completely covered from head to toe with God's truth, righteousness, faith, and peace all over us so that the devil cannot find the slightest area to penetrate through.

No matter how big and strong the Goliath may be in our life, if we learn to consistently pray in every situation and throw back Bible verses against every attack that comes towards us, he cannot harm us if we are wholly girded up and leave no room. Therefore, it is important to pray and know our bible verses by heart! These weapons are more than enough to fight back.

Are you equipped and ready?

Dear LORD, thank you for the armor You have provided for me to put on to protect myself against the enemy. Please help me not to leave any room for the enemy to penetrate through but be fully girded. Teach me to be grounded in Your word so that I am prepared to use it when I am attacked. With Your help, I can face any giants that come against me. In Jesus' name, Amen!

Sinking in sin - September 9

He lifted me out of the slimy pit, out of the mud and mire; he set my feet on a rock and gave me a firm place to stand. Psalm 40:2

Mostly every day before I get out of bed, I make up my mind about something which I will do or not do. But the next thing you know I have failed myself and end up doing the exact opposite of what I had in mind to do. I start all over again the next day and find myself failing yet again in some way or the other. I feel stuck in sinking sand and keep going deeper underneath instead of coming out. The more I try to better myself, the more I feel pulled down and continue to struggle.

The devil feels threatened when he sees us coming closer to God and so he does everything he can to hold us down. He ties us up in chains of temptation of whatever our vulnerabilities are and makes it difficult for us to resist. The harder we try, the heavier he makes the ball and chain that we keep being pulled instead of breaking free.

It is tough to pull ourselves out by our own strength but when we rely on God, His strength overrides our strength. If we reach out and grab God's hand, He is mighty to save and permanently break any chains that bind us. In order to be rescued though, first we need to recognize the quicksand of sin which we are in and seek help. The more we ignore or play around with it, the harder it becomes to come out.

So when we find ourselves sinking in our sin, instead of struggling with it on our own and feeling frustrated, cry out to God for help and take a hold of His stretched out hand which can pull us out and establish our feet on solid rock, which is Christ himself!

Dear LORD, I am crying out to You for help to rescue me from my sin. I am unable to do it on my own and feel helpless. The more I try, the more I feel trapped. Please forgive me for letting You down. I thank you for not giving up on me and holding my sin against me. Please come to aid and deliver me so that I can be made new and live for You alone. In Jesus name, Amen!

Lukewarm Christian - September 10

I know your deeds, that you are neither cold nor hot. I wish you were either one or the other! So, because you are lukewarm—neither hot nor cold—I am about to spit you out of my mouth. Revelation 3: 15-16

I hear people complain about the weather all the time. We complain when it is hot, and we complain when it is cold. We like to be right in the middle, otherwise we are uncomfortable and unhappy.

In the same way, many of us like our relationship with Jesus to be just about right. We like our Christianity to be lukewarm. We like to be in close enough proximity to God in case we need Him some day. But we do not like to be too close either that it would make us uncomfortable and alter our earthly living. We like the best of both worlds, spiritual and earthly so we keep ourselves in the middle. We pick and choose what we like about Jesus and only follow certain things while we choose to ignore the ones that make us come out of our worldly comfort zone.

But Jesus has clearly warned us against being a lukewarm Christian. Either we are for Him or against Him. If we consider ourselves Christian, then it needs to show by our walk, talk, and deed in every way. And if we are cold towards God, we need to examine ourselves and turn up our spiritual thermostat. If we ignore Him now, there will be a non-retractable day when Jesus will finally give us the cold shoulder and spew us out.

Dear LORD, please help me to make up my mind about my relationship with You. I understand that I cannot be a part of both worlds as friendship with the world is enmity with God. I would rather have Jesus so please help me not to follow the patterns of the world but be heavenly minded and live my life according to how You want me to. In Jesus' name, Amen!

We will rebuild - September 11

"The bricks have fallen, but we will rebuild with dressed stone... Isaiah 9:10

In the movie, "London has fallen", within moments different places in the city were simultaneously attacked and bombed by the enemy. Various bridges, churches and buildings collapsed, and everything came tumbling down. Mostly every wall was broken down to pieces. But even after such a disastrous experience, a few weeks later it was shown that the city was coming back together. The news reporter in the movie said, "We may have been broken but we will rebuild".

Sometimes in real life, we may feel that we have been attacked from every direction. The enemy has attacked our home, marriage, children, health and finances. We could relate to Job from the Bible whose life turned upside down within moments. Everything that he loved and owned was broken into and destroyed. We too may have lost everything and have come to the end of our rope feeling hopeless, ready to give up and give into the enemy's hands.

But as trying our times may be, they are not meant to remain with us forever. The devil may have infiltrated through us, our loved ones or our possessions but we must not allow him to keep us in defeated state. He may have broken us down but there is nothing that can stop us from rising again. We must fight and take back what the enemy has taken away from us. We must rebuild the walls of our home and family that the devil has torn down. With the hedge of protection of Jesus Christ and His blood we need to seal our lives and homes. Even if everything may have been destroyed, with God's help and our own willingness, we can rebuild and restore our broken walls once again stronger than ever before.

Dear LORD, sometimes I feel as if I have fallen and do not know if I can get up again. But I know that You would not allow me to remain collapsed and let the devil win over me. So, thank you for giving me the courage to get up and regain all that the enemy has stolen from me. I give You my shattered pieces, please take them and help me rebuild what has been broken. In Jesus' name, Amen!

Generational blessings - September 12

For the Lord is good and his love endures forever; his faithfulness continues through all generations. Psalm 100:5

We are aware of the legacy of a generational curse. It is our negative personality, behavior or some action that we blame our heredity and past generations for. We excuse our stubbornness by saying that we are born like that and cannot change. We accept it as our unfortunate inheritance in life and live with it. We generally focus more on the generational curse but leave out the other important inheritance – the generational blessing!

While religion and faith in God is becoming less and less important to us during this generation, most of our forefathers lived their entire lives solely on faith. They spent hours on their knees pleading for God's mercy and blessings for their children and children's children, which we are reaping now. We may not acknowledge it, but it is the prayers of our parents, grandparents, elders and past families that are sustaining us currently. It is their blessings over us that are being passed down to our generation. Satan may try to destroy us by a generational curse, but it will be broken by our generational blessings which is promised over us. Prayers and petitions have been made on our behalf and we need to continue to pass them down to our future generations so what we sow now will be reaped later.

Our God is a promise keeper and if He promised it, He remains faithful to its completion. God is not bound by certain time periods but sees through His promise throughout all generations. So don't be disappointed by a generational curse that might be over you or accept it as your lot in life, allow the generational blessing to overpower it and reap the goodness that has been in store for you.

Dear LORD, please help me to break the chain of the generational sins that may be passing down from one generation to the next in my family. May I not accept it as my inheritance but with Your help, be freed from it. Teach me to draw the line and not carry it forward to my children. I thank you for my parents and forefathers whose prayers of blessings I am reaping now. Help me to do the same for my children and generations to come. In Jesus' name, Amen!

Exit door - September 13

Then the Lord knows how to rescue the godly from trials, 2 Peter 2:9

When we are faced with temptation, we usually raise our white flag up in surrender before even trying hard to resist it. I believe the reason why we quickly give in is because deep down we want to enjoy the sin, so we commit it and then blame temptation for it. To submit or resist temptation is in our power. As hard as it may be, God always provides a way out for us, but the choice is ours. God has a will for us and so do we. In order to align our will with God's, we need to be self-controlled and disciplined.

When faced with temptation, instead of looking for excuses to go for it, we need to look for ways to get out of it. By asking for God's help before we fall makes more sense than to ask for His help once the sin is committed and the damage is already done; as it's easier to stay out of a mess than it is to get out of it.

So, if we are ready to fall, let us fall at Jesus' feet first and look for the exit door which He has already opened.

Dear LORD, please help me not to look for excuses to sin. May I not allow the devil to twist my arm into sinning but help me to truly resist temptation. Thank you for providing a way out each time. Please help me to run to the exit door as soon as I feel the temptation coming on. In Jesus' name, Amen!

Whether you turn to the right or to the left, your ears will hear a voice behind you, saying, "This is the way; walk in it." Isaiah 30:21

When we need to finish a project, prepare for a test, or make a decision about something, in the beginning we may feel insecure, incapable and afraid that we don't know what to do or how to go about doing it. But if we pray for it and rely on God, He gives us the wisdom, skill and ability to accomplish it. When we are confused and do not have an answer to our problem, God puts ideas in our mind which enables us to solve it. Often, we think that our issue is insignificant in God's sight and so we do not bother going to Him with everything. But God cares about everything that concerns us, big or small. If it matters to us, it matters to Him and He would rather have us turn to Him for help right away than to struggle with it. Nonetheless we aim to handle it on our own till we run out of other options. But it should be the other way around. Our first and only option is God. When we turn to God, there is no need to turn anywhere else. He longs to help us but does not force Himself on us. He allows us to try in our own ability until we realize our need for His help. He waits patiently for us to run to Him like how children run to the parents to fix something when they cannot fix it for themselves first.

If there is something which needs to be done but we are not sure how to accomplish it, let us turn to God. We can ask Him for help from the beginning and then watch for ideas and answers popping up in our mind telling us which way to go and what to do. This is the voice of God directing our steps, so let us listen!

Dear LORD, please help me not to rely on my own understanding but come to You with all that concerns me. You have the words of life so help me to tune into You to hear Your voice direct me. Thank you for being readily available to help whenever I call to You. In Jesus' name, Amen!

Walk by faith not by sight - September 15

But when I am afraid, I will put my trust in you. Psalm 56:3

What are you afraid of the most? For me, it would be my children's future. They are already faced with so many challenges while they are still young that I cannot even comprehend what it will be like for them in adulthood. The world seems to be losing its moral values and it is becoming even more difficult for our children to apply the godly principles we teach them at home once they step out into the world. The devil seriously is like a roaring lion always on the lookout for children and families to devour. His goal is the destruction of Jesus, his prime enemy, so he strongly pursues after especially those of the Christian household and makes it very difficult to stand upright in this upside down world.

Being fearful is a natural, physical state of the mind which none of us are exempt from. But *when* we find ourselves in this state, we need to turn to God for help and counteract fear with trust. Although it may be difficult to believe in what we cannot see yet, we need to trust God regardless. Just the way He was and is with us through our ups and downs and challenges in life, God will be with our kids. The way He saved us, He will save our future generation also. As their days are, so will their strength be to respond against the vile acts of Satan.

So, when we feel insecure and afraid about our unknown future, we need to remember who holds our future and trust God with all our heart.

Dear LORD, when fear of the uncertain future grips my heart, may I find my peace in You, the one who holds the future. Help me to walk by faith and not by sight of the things that are in front of me currently. Increase my trust in You and may I hold on to You tightly as we go through different phases of life. In Jesus' name, Amen!

You say, "I am allowed to do anything"—but not everything is good for you. You say, "I am allowed to do anything"—but not everything is beneficial. 1 Corinthians 10:23

We live in a pretty much a free society today where everything goes and is acceptable. No one bothers to confront someone because we are told to mind our own business and not meddle in other people's lives for the decisions they make and how they choose to live. So, we let people be and do whatever pleases them.

We make thousands of decisions each day based on our wants, needs, desires, influence of others, and circumstances. Our decisions determine our character. For those who fear God and have moral values, base their decisions on what they believe and have learned. They live by integrity in all areas of their lives and make decisions on what is right and wrong according to God's standards. Then there are folks who do not have any regard for God nor hold any moral values. They do as they please selfishly regardless of how it affects them or the people in the sphere of their life.

We may not need to justify our decisions to each other, but we certainly must do so with God. We may not be accountable to each other but are accountable to God in the end. Paul has said in the Bible that everything is permissible but not everything is beneficial for us.

So, while we make decisions based on our own thinking, let us consider the will of God, the integrity of our heart, and the pros and cons of all that we do and say.

Dear LORD, please help me make my decisions based on Your word and expectation from me. Give me a sound mind and clarity so that I am aware of what I am doing. Help me not to be influenced by what the world teaches but by what You have instilled in me. May my life be pure and true so that I can stand faultless before Your throne. In Jesus' name, Amen!

Online shopper - September 17

How great are your works, O LORD! Your thoughts are very deep! Psalm 92:5

I am not much of an online shopper. I would rather go to the store and physically see, feel, and try on something before I buy it. But while I was looking for something online recently, I realized how easy it was to go shopping virtually through hundreds of stores and buy whatever I need without walking through isles or driving from store to store. I did it right from the comfort of my chair at home. Plus, I could expect the items to be delivered right at my doorstep within the time frame which I choose to receive them.

Many of us treat the answers to our prayer like online shopping too. We call ourselves the customer, and God as the deliverer whom we go to get our necessities and desires. We choose the things that we want, add them to our cart, check out as if we earned them, and expect God to deliver at the time we set for Him. But God does not run by our clock nor is He limited to any human timing to deliver. He works according to His schedule and at His pace. Our rush order does not mean an emergency for Him also. We may think He is late, and we pace back and forth impatiently, but God delivers right on time. He knows what, where, when and why we need certain things and will only give as He sees fit.

God's timing is perfect so when we go to God with our needs, we must remember that He does not just give us things at the time we expect but rather God gives us His best at the right time. Therefore, let us not rush God but trust His timing and we will not be disappointed when the answer to our prayer is delivered!

Dear LORD, I know that the fruit of patience is sweet so please help me to be patient. Help me not to put You on my timetable and expect a rush delivery but rather wait for You to deliver when the time is right. You know my needs and have always provided, so increase my trust as I rely on your provision. In Jesus' name, Amen!

Oil and water - September 18

Those who belong to Christ Jesus have nailed the passions and desires of their sinful nature to his cross and crucified them there. Galatians 5:24

Most of us want the best of both worlds. We like to have worldly and spiritual possessions at the same time. We change our priorities based on our need, desire, mood, atmosphere, and influence. When we are a part of the social crowd, we want to be like everyone else and behave differently than when we are in church or around other godly folks. Our walk and talk changes according to who we are around and what is happening in our sphere. But once we have decided to follow Jesus, our lives cannot remain the same. We cannot belong to both worlds and jump around. If we call ourselves Christians and truly have committed our lives to Jesus Christ, then we must give up our old self and live a new life in Him. All our old habits, desires, and attitudes need to change according to God's likeness. We need be identified with Christ with all our being and not just some here and there. If we believe that Jesus was crucified on the cross for our sins, then we need to crucify our old sinful nature on that cross also, receive a new life in Jesus, and dedicate to living the rest of our days here on earth to God.

It is not easy to live in this world and not be a part of it. But we must be like oil and water. Although they both are in the same pot, they do not blend in together. Oil surfaces on water and does not mix in and so we as Christians can be in the same pot but need to surface on a different layer.

Dear LORD, please help me to realize that once I have invited You in my life to be my LORD and Savior, I must give up my worldly pleasures and find my pleasure in You alone. Teach me to recognize and get rid of my worldly desires that cannot blend with Your values. May I not live my life with double standards but be firmly rooted in You and be set apart for Your kingdom. In Jesus' name, Amen!

God's word cannot change - September 19

Blessed are those whose ways are blameless, who walk according to the law of the LORD. Blessed are those who keep his statutes and seek him with all their heart; they do no wrong but follow his ways. Psalm 119: 1-3

As times are changing, we are also expected to change with the new world ethics. What once was unacceptable is now the new norm. In order to fit in, many of us put our Christian morals on the line. We might be ok to hurt God's feelings but not people, so we go with the flow and change our attitude based on what is acceptable these days.

Times may change, technology may change, and people's outlook may change, but God does not change nor does His word take on different meaning to fit into today's world standards. What is written in the Bible stands firm to this date as it did years ago. People may twist God's word to make it applicable or non-applicable to our times and situation today, but the truth of God's word cannot change no matter what we think. If God was against it then, He is still against it right now. Just because we change, we cannot expect God to change His mind as well.

If we consider ourselves followers of Jesus, then He is our moral guide, not people. It should matter to us what God's word says and we are to abide by His teachings. Let us not manipulate God's word to fit our fancy and force Him to accept our wrong as right.

Dear LORD, You are the same yesterday, today and tomorrow. Your word is also the same as it was the day You spoke it. People's attitude towards You may change but may I remain firm in my faith. Thank you for Your never-changing love and promises. I have experienced You in a real way and know that You are alive so please help me to stand up for You no matter what others say. In Jesus' name, Amen!

Love in action - September 20

But if anyone obeys his word, love for God is truly made complete in them. This is how we know we are in him: Whoever claims to live in him must live as Jesus did. 1 John 2: 5 – 6

Loving someone is not just a matter of heart and words. It is not enough just to feel the love, but it requires work for it to flourish. When we love someone, we make time for them, look forward to seeing them, make sure that we do not hurt them and do our best to keep them happy because their happiness becomes our happiness. We proudly show off our love for them and want others to see it.

When we say we love God, we demonstrate our love for Him and to others by not only believing in Him but by gladly obeying His word. We show our love for God by action, not just words. Our love for Him creates in us a desire to want to make Him happy and so we do our level best to follow Him and do what He says. We take pride in associating with God and our love for Him becomes evident by the way we live according to His standards. We cannot just say we love God if our life does not show it. It must match up internally and externally; spiritually and physically. The way we behave and live our life must align with our belief in God.

If we say we have love for God, but it does not show, then can we say we are in love with God?

Dear LORD, You demonstrated Agape love by giving Your life as a ransom for my sin. There is no higher love than this, how can I repay You back? The only thing I can do for You is to give You my life as an offering and live to honor You. God is love, help me to love also. In Jesus' name, Amen!

Selfless giving - September 21

Bring the full tithe into the storehouse, that there may be food in my house. And thereby put me to the test, says the Lord of hosts, if I will not open the windows of heaven for you and pour down for you a blessing until there is no more need. Malachi 3:10

To tithe is to freely give one-tenth or more of one's income annually to the Lord through His Church. Tithing is not an option, but a commandment given by God to His people for His people in need. It is an act that requires us to not be selfish but selfless and help others besides our own.

When it comes to spending money on our self or for a social cause, most of spend our money generously without giving much thought, such as buying expensive clothes, food, purchasing lottery tickets, parties, etc. But when it comes to supporting a cause for a charity or church need, many of us think twice about giving our hard-earned money. Somehow, our budget comes into consideration then and we recalculate to conclude that we cannot afford to give as we have many expenses to meet.

Some of us do not bother to give at all by using the excuse of our money being mishandled by the church or organization. But it is not the case every time and it should not stop us from doing what God has called us to do. We must do our part and allow God to handle the rest. To give our tithes is to willingly give God back a little portion of the abundance He has already given us. Out of our blessings we bless others, so we need not be stingy in giving but give selflessly.

It's blessed to give than to receive and when we do give freely, God does not hold any of our blessings back but freely returns double-fold and even more to us.

Dear LORD, thank you for giving me all that I need and much more. Please help me not to be greedy or selfish and hold my blessings just for me and my family. Help me not to look out for my own interests but the interest of others and help in whichever way I can. It is my honor and duty to share with others with what You have blessed me with so may I give with all my heart. By giving to others, I am giving it back to You; please accept it and use it to further Your kingdom. In Jesus' name, Amen!

Satan's target - September 22

Be alert and of sober mind. Your enemy the devil prowls around like a roaring lion looking for someone to devour. 1 Peter 5:8

Perhaps because I eat small portions of food at a time, I feel hungry more often. I get hungry easily and am always on the lookout for food. I can just finish a meal and soon after, I am ready to ask, "When are we eating again?" It just seems like I can never get enough of food to eat, especially junk food.

The devil too is always hungry. He is like a hungry lion always on the lookout for his next prey. His hunger is for people, especially the godly folks, whom he can attack and bound them under his authority. The devil is threatened when he sees people coming closer to God so he does whatever he can to make us his target. He lures us into temptations of our weaknesses, brings doubt and fear in our mind, and throws stumbling blocks in our way to stop us from moving near to God. The moment we let our guard down, the devil is ready to attack.

Therefore, it is important for us to be vigilant and be on the lookout to not fall as the devil's victims. And the way to be vigilant is first by knowing who we belong to. If we say we are for Christ, then we need to ensure that we must fight against the devil and not with him. Often, we get confused by not knowing right from wrong as the world teaches us one thing and Bible the other. We need to know God's word well to be able to recognize the devil's lies and not give him any room to penetrate in our heart and mind to deceive us into anything.

Just as the devil is on the lookout to gobble us up, we ought to be on guard against him and not become his next game.

Dear LORD, please always help me to be alert so that I do not become Satan's target and sin against You. May I have the discernment to know the difference between right and wrong according to Your word so that I am not deceived. Give me a hunger for Your word and righteousness and may I only be satisfied with You, my living bread and water. In Jesus' name, Amen!

Emotional Roller coaster - September 23

Every good and perfect gift is from above, coming down from the Father of the heavenly lights, who does not change like shifting shadows. James 1:17

We find ourselves on an emotional roller coaster occasionally. Our mood depends on what is happening around us. One moment we could be on cloud-nine, but then it does not take us long to fall flat on our face the next moment when something goes wrong. If all is well and good, we are happy and ready to praise God but when something is not going so well, it is hard to get our praise on.

God has designed our bodies to feel all sorts of emotions and to have mood swings is just a part of being a human. But regardless of our emotional roller coaster, one thing that needs to remain steady is how we feel about God. Our thoughts and affection towards God must not depend on how we feel on a given day. Our feelings cannot be the determining factor about who we are in Christ or what He means to us. It does not matter what we go through in life, whether good or bad, our relationship with Christ should not be compromised for anything. We ought to be confident of our love for Him just how His love for us remains constant and unchanging.

God understands how and why we feel certain things. He knows what makes us happy and causes us to be anxious, but as long as we know that God does not change and that He's got us no matter what we face and feel, we can praise Him in every emotional state.

Dear LORD, help me not to allow myself to be ruled by my emotions, environment or any person's manipulation. May I not let these determine my feelings and faith in You. No matter what my physical, mental or emotional state may be, may it not affect my spiritual state. Please help me remain steady in You regardless of my situation or sentiment. In Jesus' name, Amen!

Don't grumble - September 24

Give thanks in all circumstances, for this is the will of God in Christ Jesus for you.
1 Thessalonians 5:18

Standing in front of a jammed pack closet full of clothes, my daughter was complaining that she had nothing to wear to school. I understand that it is a feminine thing and a girl just cannot have enough of clothes, shoes, or makeup.

While helping her pick out the clothes, it made me realize that we do the same with God. He gives us everything that we need yet we complain that we do not have enough of this or that. We whine about what we do have and ask God to give us better things that fits our demand. For example, instead of appreciating the decent jobs which God has given us to provide for our livelihood, we groan about the workload, hours, commute, boss, and colleagues. We do not feel satisfied with the closet-full of clothing that we already have but we demand certain colors, styles, and material. We take what we have for granted and the more we have, the more we want, and better.

There is nothing wrong of dreaming about bigger and better things, but we should be appreciative of what we do have. Instead of focusing on one little corner that may still have room for more, we ought to be grateful for the abundant blessings that we already possess. We do not earn or deserve any blessings on our own, yet God chooses to bless us because of who He is. And when we choose to complain instead of being thankful, we disrespect God's goodness.

Dear LORD, rather than grumbling about what I do not have, please help me to appreciate what I do have. Help me not to pick and choose my blessings because everything I have is better and more than what I can do for myself. May I never overlook my blessings but be humbled and gracious for all that You continue to bestow me with. In Jesus' name, Amen!

Strength to strength - September 25

They go from strength to strength, till each appears before God in Zion.
Psalm 84:7

Due to a pinched nerve in her spine, the pain in my mother's legs made it difficult for her to walk. We were worried about her as we were planning a two weeks trip to Israel, which we heard from multiple people beforehand that it requires a lot of walking on rough roads. Not sure of how she could handle it, we put our trust in God and committed my mom and others with health/walking issues into God's hands and off we went. Lo and behold, we witnessed God's strength working in each one of them. A much healthier person even laughed and said that the ones with health issues were walking faster than him. We still cannot understand how but, they went from strength to strength each passing day and experienced all of God's goodness in the Holy Land. We all returned safe and sound, healthy and refreshed in the Lord.

God works in ways which we cannot fathom. We do not necessarily need to know everything in advance before we put our trust in God. Before figuring out all the details and then deciding to put the rest in God's hand, we need to put all in God's hand first and let Him handle the rest. If we have faith in God and wait for Him, He can make the impossible happen for us. Trust is having faith without seeing it first. So, if we choose to look at our circumstances and act accordingly, it is not faith and we are bound to fail. But if we keep our eyes on Jesus, He holds our feet firm on His foundation and puts His spirit in us to accomplish the impossible.

Dear LORD, oftentimes just by looking at my weaknesses, I feel like giving up before I even begin. Please help me to see beyond my natural eye and know that You are with me and equip me in every way as I need it according to my days and my needs. Help me to rely on Your strength when I am weak and feel Your power working in me when I am powerless. Thank you for your encouragement that I can do all things through Christ who gives me strength. In Jesus' name, Amen!

Lost and found - September 26

For the Son of Man came to seek and to save the lost. Luke 19:10

In the story of the Shephard leaving his ninety-nine sheep in order to look for one lost sheep is an analogy of Jesus searching for one person who is lost even if He still has the rest of the ninety-nine. He cares for each soul and every one of us is precious, and we each mean a lot to God.

Many of us put ourselves in the crowd of the ninety-nine and not the lost one. We feel safe and secure in the crowd as we know our Shephard and have an intimate relationship with Him. But even when we consider ourselves found and steady, we can end up going astray and find ourselves lost sometimes. We may think we know our Shepard's voice very well and are confident in our walk with Him, but if we take our eyes off God or close our ears from hearing His voice, we are likely to detour from the course and wander off. Fear and doubt start to seize us as we think that the Shephard has lost track of us and will not come looking for us. But thank God that He keeps count of each one of us and knows us intimately to feel our absence. Even if we have disobeyed Him and wandered off the track, God does not leave and punish us for our waywardness. He knows the harm and danger that we put ourselves in and because of His love and care for us, God comes searching for us.

Therefore, if we feel like the lost sheep today, rest assured that we are not alone, but the Shephard is coming to our rescue. He will not rest until He finds us so do let us not consider ourselves lost when God has declared us found in Him!

Dear LORD, many times the devil puts thoughts of doubt in my mind to question Your love for me due to my sins. But thank you for the reminder that You would never leave me nor forsake me even when I go away from You. Thank you for not giving up on me but coming to find me no matter how far I have gone. Please help me recognize Your voice, return and follow You as You lead me. In Jesus' name, Amen!

Playing with fire - September 27

Can a man carry fire next to his chest and his clothes not be burned?
Proverbs 6:27

My phone was charging in the kitchen while I was cooking. When it rang, I picked up to talk on the phone while I was nearby the stove and did not realize that the cord had come in the way of the stove and caught on fire. I immediately noticed it and blew off the fire from the cord before it touched the wires or caused any damage. Had I not seen it; it would have been disastrous. Fire is dangerous and if we are not vigilant around it, it can cause irreversible damage.

In the same way, sin is dangerous and can be deadly. Just like fire, some of us like to play with sin. We do not think of it much and toy around with it until sometimes it is too late to stop its consequences. Too often we think we can entertain sin and temptation in our heart but not fall into it. We feel confident in our self-control and think we know how far we can allow ourselves to go. But before we know it, the little spark of sin spreads from an "innocent thought" to a full-fledged transgression, burning us up and anything that comes in between.

Therefore, if we know our vulnerability, we must avoid those occasions, people, or places where we might find ourselves playing with the fire of sin. If we fail to do so, we set ourselves up for failure and compromise the holiness to which God has called us. We need to be vigilant of the dangers of sin and keep ourselves away from its path if we desire to not get burned.

Dear LORD, teach me not to entertain sin in my heart by thinking that I have full control over myself to not allow it to turn into action. The moment I let my guard down, I know that temptation can overpower me and lead me into sin, so please help me God, to stay away and not be in harm's way. May I not be overconfident in myself but be vigilant and not put myself in those situations where it can be hard to resist. In Jesus' name, Amen!

Intolerable conditions - September 28

He gives power to the faint, and to him who has no might he increases strength.
Isaiah 40:29

Recently we took a memorable trip to Israel and had one of the best times of our lives. As fun as it was, we did face some challenges which now seem minor, but at the time seemed unbearable. While crossing the border from one country to another, without access to baggage carts, we had to walk over half a mile with our heavy luggage in hand to get to the next tour bus which was waiting for us on the other side of the border. Not only were we responsible to carry our own luggage but that of the many elderly who were also with us, who could not carry their own. As we were walking back and forth, hauling so many heavy bags, we felt our strength diminishing and the task just seemed endless and our energy depleting. Yet slowly but surely with the help of each other and God's strength in us, we dragged all the bags across. What seemed like an unbearable task was accomplished somehow. And now that we look back on it, we laugh about it and are even ready to do it all over again as the excitement and better times that awaited for us at the next border were worth the discomfort we endured.

As we go through challenging situations in life, we may feel like it is intolerable and do not know if we will make it through. We basically are ready to give up as the end of our tough time does not seem to be anywhere near the end, and we do not have strength to carry the heavy burden that is laid upon us. But as we pass through the rough road, we need to remember that God is with us through it all. He equips us with His powerful spirit and strength to make it to the other side. Our current pain will be worthwhile when we look back on it and see it turn into joy someday. What we are ready to give up turns out to be our biggest accomplishment as we see God work in us.

Dear LORD, as my circumstance feels unbearable sometimes and when I don't have the strength to go on, help me to remember that what I cannot accomplish on my own, I can do it with Christ who gives me strength. I will not give up but keep moving forward with Your Spirit working in me. In Jesus' name, Amen!

Trimming time - September 29

"I am the true vine, and my Father is the gardener. He cuts off every branch in me that bears no fruit, while every branch that does bear fruit he prunes so that it will be even more fruitful". John 15: 1-2

It is good to trim our hair every few weeks to cut off the split ends and dead hair in order to make room for fresh, healthy hair to grow. Some do not like to do this often as they feel the hair length gets shorter. But trimming is necessary and only helps the hair to grow faster and healthier.

Similarly, God prunes us regularly so that we become spiritually healthy. He cuts and removes those things, habits, or people away which are harmful for us and bring us spiritually down. God is the gardener of our life and He knows who and what hinders us from growing in Him, and so He prunes those branches in us that do not produce fruit.

The process of pruning does not feel good and brings discomfort to our lives but if we want to grow in God and fulfill our purpose, we need to be pruned. We need to allow God to remove us from our comfort zone and plant us in those places and amongst those where we can flourish.

If we feel we are dying spiritually, we ought to pray for God to run through the garden of our lives and trim those edges off us that prevent us from growing. It may hurt to see some part of us being cut off as we might be accustomed to it, but if it will not go, neither will we go any further with God.

Therefore, do not allow yourself to die slowly, let God bring life back into you!

Dear LORD, help me to be still and allow You to remove some people and things from my life that are not good for me. As much as this process hurts, help me to know that it is necessary for You to make room for bigger and better things. Increase my trust as I wait and watch You make me grow in You. In Jesus' name, Amen!

Even if I think about it - September 30

You have heard that it was said, 'You shall not commit adultery.' But I tell you that anyone who looks at a woman lustfully has already committed adultery with her in his heart. Matthew 5: 27-28

M any of us think of a sin as a sin when we actually commit it physically. We do not count what is going on secretly in our heart and mind as sinful. If it is not seen by anyone or has any consequences, we do not consider it wrong.

But in God's eye even if it is thought of, it is a sin. It does not matter to God whether we have acted upon it or not, but if it is something that we have done in our hearts, it is as good as being committed.

Most of us are concerned with our godly image on the outside so we ensure that our words and actions are pure in everyone's eyes. We also try to convince God with our clean and outward behavior. But we cannot hide from God what is truly going on inside of us. He weighs our every thought and measures us according to the purity of our heart, not our physical actions.

So, we need to be careful with what is going on in our head. We need to have a control not only on our words that are spoken and deeds that are done, but more importantly on the thoughts and motives which are within. If sinful thought starts to arise, we ought to shut it off right away as allowing it to pass through our mind is same as doing it.

Dear LORD, I pray for purity not only on the outside but from within as You see the intent of my heart first before my action. Please help me to control my wandering thoughts and bring them under Your submission. Break me free from the spirit of lust and pride that seek to make me impure. Blot out my transgressions and create in me a clean heart, O LORD. In Jesus' name, Amen!

October

Freedom by confession - October 1

Then I acknowledged my sin to you and did not cover up my iniquity. I said, "I will confess my transgressions to the LORD." And you forgave the guilt of my sin. Psalm 32:5

The phrase "Ignorance is bliss" means what we do not know cannot hurt us. We find ourselves applying this to our sins also. We avoid scriptures that speak of our sins and rationalize our behavior. Some sins just seem pleasurable for us, so we act in ignorance and enjoy them to the fullest. We try not to worry about the consequences when we are living in sin and hope to deal with it sometime later.

People who are in right standing with God are the ones who feel convicted of their sin and instead of avoiding it, they bring it up to God right away to confess, repent, and ask for help to overcome. The moment they commit the sin, they understand what they have done is wrong and have an urgency to get it off their chest. This is a measure of a righteous person in God's eye.

The Bible clearly teaches that confession is bliss, not ignorance. The more we ignore something, the bigger and difficult it becomes to deal with. It starts to weigh heavy on our hearts and sooner or later, we end up paying for it. But the sooner we realize and confess our wrongdoing, the quicker God's mercy is to forgive us. He cleanses us and removes our sin far from us, never to be brought back up again.

Dear LORD, please help me to deal with my sin as soon as I commit it. May I not ignore it and put it off till later to indulge in it longer. But as soon as the Holy Spirit convicts me, teach me to confess it and repent of my sin. As a child of God, may I not hold on to any impurity and unrighteousness but cast it off right away and receive Your forgiveness. In Jesus' name, Amen!

Unseen Pilot - October 2

It is better to trust in the LORD than to put confidence in man. Psalms 118:8

Many folks have a hard time believing in God because they cannot see Him. They have the "I need to see it to believe it" type of an attitude towards God. Yet for most part, all of us are quick to trust and believe in things we cannot see such as the Pilot of an airplane. We get in the plane, sit down, relax, watch movies, eat, drink and sleep in mid-air with full confidence that the aircraft will take us from one place to another without ever seeing or meeting the Pilot who controls and flies the jumbo jet. We do not ask for His credentials or to see him face to face before we trust him with our lives for the next few hours. We just take the Airline's word for it and assume that the Pilot must have the expertise, knowledge, experience, and is fully capable. So, we just put our trust in the Airline and the Pilot and get on the plane without seeing or checking the engine.

In the same way God exists, but why do we have such difficulty believing in His existence? Why are we reluctant to get on board with Him? Why do we try to find our own way while He is the expert who can navigate our life through the storms, depths, heights, and unknown paths? God is the one who gives wisdom to man to achieve things in life so while we can put our trust in man, wouldn't it be better to trust in GOD who is the creator of man himself?

Dear LORD, Your word says "blessed are those who have not seen yet believed". Please open the eyes of my faith to see You, feel You and know that You are here. Help me to never doubt Your existence as I have experienced You in my life and am confident that You are God and are with me. In Jesus' name, Amen!

For God's eyes only - October 3

On the contrary, we speak as those approved by God to be entrusted with the gospel. We are not trying to please people but God, who tests our hearts. 1 Thessalonians 2:4

In the beginning of the first church, husband and wife, Ananias and Sapphira cheated by only brining a portion of their offering. They lied by saying that they brought everything while they held some back for themselves. They did this to look good in front of their church members. It was the praise of the people they were seeking instead of God. By keeping their eyes on who was bringing what and what kind of accolades others were receiving, Ananias and Sapphira became greedy for praise and cheated, resulting in both of their deaths.

Many of us are greedy for praise – not more so from God but primarily from people around us. In order to be complimented, we go extra lengths to do something where our good deeds get noticed by others. Our eyes remain on people and how to outdo others instead of focusing on God and doing things for Him with a clean heart.

When we bring our offering to God, whether it is of time, talent or money, we ought to bring it to God with humbleness and gratefulness. It should not be with the intention of receiving accolades from people but with the intent of pleasing God. Our goal should not be about being noticed and only doing things when others see us but rather continue to do good even if no one notices. God sees everything we do, in private or in open; He knows the intention of our heart when we do it and rewards us accordingly.

We can fool people, but we cannot fool God so in everything we do, we should do it for God. It is His praise that we need to seek and not that of people.

Dear LORD, as I strive to serve you, would You please help me to do it for the growth of Your kingdom and not for the promotion of myself. Help me not to do good for the sake of receiving praises from people or with the intent of expecting only blessings from You, but rather do it because I love you and want to give you back some of it. You have said to not let one hand know what your other hand is doing when we give, so please help me to give in secret, knowing that You know and that is enough for me. In Jesus' name, Amen!

Silence is strength - October 4

...In quietness and trust is your strength... Isaiah 30:15

The Bible teaches us to "Do unto others as you would have done unto you". While the worldly philosophy is "Do unto others as is it done to you". We are taught to treat people like for like, get even, fight and speak back. If we do not retaliate, it is assumed that we are giving permission to be walked all over and taken advantage of. We are considered inferior or weak if we do not stand up for ourselves. However, it is the opposite. It is easy to blurt out anything, but it is difficult to hold it back. It is not difficult to do evil for evil but to do good in return for evil, requires will power which many of us struggle with. We often become quick-tempered and do or say something right back as if to prove our point or bravery against someone.

But to remain silent takes courage. To hold back our flesh in heated moments takes self-control and discipline. It is more courageous to not strike back when treated unfairly, walk away from a fight or remain quiet when spoken against. Being quiet is not a sign of weakness but rather of strength and for those who possess this quality are considered as peacemakers. By choosing to be silent, they put out the fire rather than spreading it.

God sees all and knows who does what to whom. So why bother to fight for ourselves and make it worse? Instead trust God and allow Him to handle it by His strength and way.

Dear LORD, please teach me to hold back my tongue and attitude when I have been wronged. Instead help me to demonstrate Your way of forgiveness by not holding it against anyone and let it go. You see me heart so may I allow You to fight on my behalf and plead my innocence to those who come against me. In Jesus' name, Amen!

So teach us to number our days that we may get a heart of wisdom. Psalm 90:12

There was a bouquet of fresh flowers in a vase on my kitchen table. While eating breakfast, as I looked at the flowers I thought about the journey of the flower. I do not know where its seed came from or whose garden it was planted in. It must have been selected by a gardener and made ready to be put into someone's hand who brought it to us as gift. Now it sits on my table, adorning my kitchen with its beauty and fragrance.

A flower blossoms only its season, brings gladness to a heart whose garden it blooms in, spreads its beautiful fragrance around wherever it is placed, and is only here temporarily, until someone plucks it out or it withers away.

Our life is like a flower. We are brought into the world for an explicit time, in a season or era where we are needed for God's purpose. He plants us in a specific family and location for a specified amount of time. While we are here, our purpose is to bring joy to those around us and spread our beautiful fragrance of love. We need to make the best of the time allotted to us and ensure that our lives enrich the lives of others. Our presence should bless others and we become the reason for someone to smile when they see or think of us.

Just as a flower, our season on earth is only temporary, so whatever purpose God has put us here on earth for, let us not waste our time and miss out on the opportunities to spread and share our love and appreciation while we have each other. And let us be wise with our timing and choices so that at the end our journey, we leave behind a fragrance and beautiful memory for those whose lives we were placed in.

Dear LORD, thank you that You have given me my own individual fragrance to spread in my world. May my life be like a flower whose beauty and fragrance brings joy and sweet memory to those around me. Teach me to spread Your love by spraying it on me so that when people come near me, they will see and smell You all over. In Jesus' name, Amen!

Just as I am - October 6

Watch out!" Jesus warned them. "Beware of the yeast of the Pharisees and Sadducees. Matthew 16:6

Jesus refers to "yeast" frequently in the Bible in His teaching. When we add yeast to our dough, it makes the bread rise. Just a little is enough to cause the lump of dough to expand; too much of it causes it to burst and fall apart. When Jesus talks about yeast, He refers to the teachings of the religious leaders who go around telling people how to be "religious". They are more concerned about obeying laws and rituals rather than focusing on the salvation of the people. Jesus warns about this as He clearly sees the leaders missing the point. The goal should be to draw people near to Jesus and not push them away by demanding religion over relationship.

Indeed, rules and etiquette are needed in the right amount for a church to exist, but when that becomes the focal point, it causes the congregation to fall apart. It misleads one to think that in order to obtain God's love and forgiveness, we must follow some strict regulations or else we are not worthy to approach His throne.

Jesus invites everyone to come to Him "Just as I am". He is the same God everywhere and knows us internally, and so He does not expect us to first whitewash our outer selves before we come in His presence. It does not matter what sin, shame, attitude or attire we have on, all God wants us to do is come with our filth and receive Him.

If God has not instilled any methods on who or how to worship Him, neither should we. Instead we ought to encourage each other in Christ to build up His kingdom. Let us not allow rules set forth by religious leaders to stop us from receiving God's love, come, just as you are!

Dear LORD, thank you for the invitation to come to You just as I am. You do not require approval letters from religious leaders about how good I have been in following Your laws and regulations. You only see the humbleness of the heart and that is the only requirement to come to You so please help me to bring to You my repentant heart and not any other sacrifices or offerings. In Jesus' name, Amen!

Whoever says he abides in him ought to walk in the same way in which he walked.
1 John 2:6

I was in the process of organizing my kitchen and decided to put labels on all the spices in the cabinets. Some spices look like each other and are hard to tell what they are just by the looks of it while some are obvious and did not need a label. But to be consistent, I labeled all the spices regardless.

We too carry a label on ourselves. Often two labels, one as what people see us as and the other as what God sees us. We could call ourselves Christians and ensure that we display all the right characteristics of a Christian by going to church, doing charity work, saying our prayers, reading the Bible and talking to each other in Biblical terms. We align ourselves in the right positions according to the worldly standards and put ourselves on a showcase as a good Christian amongst others, if not better. However, our internal features could be misleading as we really are not what we portray ourselves to be. Our looks, fragrance and texture can be total opposite of what is inside of us than what we display to others.

What is within us is what defines the true us. It does not matter what our worldly label is, how attractive our outer appearance may be or where we place ourselves on a worldly display case. Our real identity is about what we really are like when someone comes close to us and gets to know us from deep within. Our true color might be dull, our fragrance could be stinky, and we could be bitter when tasted. According to God, only one label is necessary and that is who we are as a person in Christ. If Jesus Christ is who we have chosen to follow, then He must be represented through us in every aspect of our lives, internally and externally. Our walk, talk, and motive should align with our only label as a true Christ follower if we call ourselves a Christian.

Dear LORD, please search my heart and point out those flaws within me that are not a representation of You in my life. May I not be labeled as a Christian if there is nothing in me which displays Christ in me. Help me to represent my identity in You and be the person who is truly labelled as one – A woman of God!
In Jesus' name, Amen!

Culture vs Religion - October 8

Him only shall you serve. Matthew 4:10

Many of us mistaken religion for culture, especially in a foreign country. We engage in many activities assuming it is a cultural thing but fail to understand that much of it stems from religious beliefs. Yoga which has gained much popularity lately is used as a form of exercise that is based on the Hindu philosophy of union between our consciousness and that of the spiritual world. The Navratri festival in India is another example where folks enjoy traditional outfits, dancing, and partying till late night. During this festival there is an image of an idol placed in the middle which folks dance around. Indirectly, many participate in this idol worship without even knowing or understanding the difference between culture and religion. Similarly, many of us dance away for fun at parties and do not even realize that some dance songs are nothing, but worship songs dedicated to different forms of idols. There is nothing wrong in music and dancing but inadvertently we may end up chanting praises to some god and not even realize it amidst our partying.

Therefore, we must be vigilant and think twice before we participate in any cultural activities. We must not be deceived and blindly do as others just for the sake of fun and culture. It is a devil's way of engaging us in idol worshipping indirectly by portraying it as culture rather than religion. We must examine the different ways people worship other gods and ask for the Holy Spirit's help to distinguish whether it glorifies our true God or some other man-made god.

Dear LORD, help me not to be deceived in worshipping any other gods. Make me aware about the religious backgrounds of other religions before I engage in any cultural activities. Help me not to be so engulfed in the fun of it that I come up with excuses to participate. You are the one and only true God so may I worship You alone and represent You in all my conduct. In Jesus' name, Amen!

Beautifully wrapped - October 9

Outwardly you look like righteous people, but inwardly your hearts are filled with hypocrisy and lawlessness. Matthew 23:28

For my Birthday, I received a package in the mail. After I opened the big brown box, there was a smaller, beautifully wrapped gift box inside. Just by looking at the impressive package, I was excited and expecting a nice present. When I carefully opened the gift box, there were just a couple of wipes of perfume samples sent from a company I must have signed up for to receive free samples. There was not much inside as much was presented on the outside of the box.

Some of us are like a beautifully wrapped package from the outside. When people look at us, they get impressed by our looks, personality, status, fame, and overall presentation. We even wrap ourselves nicely in our religious attire to make others think how godly we are. But truth be told, when seen closely, there is not much to us from the inside as much as we portray on the outside. We are more superficial than we truly are internally. We spend so much of our time and energy to ensure that we look good and impress others by our outward appearance but we don't pay as much attention to what we are from the inside, which is more of a concern to God than anything else. God does not see us as people do. The only thing that impresses him is what our heart is about towards Him and others.

So, if we truly desire to be holy and righteous, our heart needs to be pure above all else and our inward should match, maybe even more, than what is on the outside.

When people examine us closely, do they realize that there is not much to us than we make ourselves to be? Or are we truly as beautiful inwardly as we are presented from the outside?

Dear LORD, please help me to focus on my inner beauty more than being concerned of what I look like from the outside. Help me to understand that true beauty is what is inside so may I spend my time and energy to keep my heart pure and holy. Help me not to wrap myself outwardly with attractive covering while the inner is dirty and full of unrighteousness. May my internal and external presentation be compatible and acceptable to You. In Jesus' name, Amen!

Blind leading the blind - October 10

And if the blind lead the blind, both will fall into a pit. Matthew 15:14

Recently, the FaceApp had gone viral. It takes your current face and shows what you would look like as aged. Its accuracy is so realistic that the craze to see how we will look old in the future had everyone hooked on it. This app had spread like a wildfire and was a new trend that people followed. As fun as it was, it had some cyber security issues that were discovered, and many folks stopped using it and regret ever using it.

How often we all fall for the "trend" without thinking much about it. Since everyone is doing something, we just assume there is nothing wrong in it and go for it also. We have lost our ability to reason and blindly follow others without understanding what is right or wrong, harmful or safe.

The number of people who do not believe in God has significantly dropped also as now the popular trend is to believe you are your own God, and there is no such thing as higher spiritual power. Just because it is popular does not mean it is good for you. We need to experience God in a personal way so that we can decide for our self. God does exist and if we truly seek Him, we will find Him and not be disappointed.

We have become like blind leading the blind, so let us not just follow the popularity trend and end up regretting our decision to believe in Jesus as God. There is something about the name Jesus, so check Him out and see for yourself. Don't let others determine who you should follow and lead you astray from the truth.

Dear LORD, please help me not be swayed by what others teach me about You. I know who You are and who I am in You so let that be enough for me to follow You. May I not be a follower of the worldly patterns but be a leader who can lead others to You. In Jesus' name, Amen!

Countless times - October 11

Then Peter came to Jesus and asked, 'Lord, how many times shall I forgive my brother or sister who sins against me? Up to seven times?' Jesus answered, 'I tell you, not seven times, but seventy-seven times'. Matthew 18:21-22

We humans get offended very quickly and hold grudges against each other over little matters. We like to take revenge and do like for like. Maybe as Christians, we let it go a few times but do wonder when enough is enough and is time to retaliate. In the Bible, Jesus said to forgive an offense of someone seventy for seven times which totals to 490 (not 77). Every Hebrew word has a numeric value so 490 adds to the word "Tamim" which means to perfect, complete, or finish. Therefore, Jesus basically implies that we ought to forgive each offense as many times needed in order to bring to completion the offender to not commit that sin anymore, or for us to not hold it against them any longer. The point is to forgive countless times to bring one to full restoration.

Jesus himself demonstrated forgiveness by taking our sin upon himself and restored us to completion when He said, "It is finished". We have been fully forgiven in Christ and are no longer under the bondage of sin. However, it does not mean that we have received freedom to continue in our sin but are free so that we can move forward to being a better person in Christ.

So, if Jesus has taught us to forgive as many times necessary, how much more does He forgive us? His grace is unlimited and never says enough is enough. Even if we fail countless times, God continues to show us His mercy as He knows we are a weak vessel and in need of continual forgiveness.

Dear LORD, thank you for not keeping a record of my sins. In the LORD's prayer I do ask You to "forgive us our trespasses as we forgive those who trespass against us", then how can I expect You to forgive while I cannot forgive others? So please help me to do the same with those who have offended me and forgive like you do. In Jesus' name, Amen!

Childish or childlike - October 12

I tell you the truth, anyone who doesn't receive the Kingdom of God like a child will never enter it. Luke 18:17

Toddlers love to play with pots and pans rather than their toys at that age. They grab anything that comes in their hands including sharp items and run with it without realizing the potential of harm it can cause. And when parents grab it away from them, they cry and fuss for not getting what they want. This is called being childish, not knowing better, having a lack of maturity, yet demanding. Being childlike on the other hand is when a small child makes a jump from the bed or sofa with full confidence that the parent is near and will catch them. They know the parent will not let them get hurt and without understanding or thinking it through for themselves, they just trust the parent and take a plunge innocently.

Our faith in God can be childish or childlike. Often, we ask for things without really understanding whether it is good or bad for us. We see only in the present; it seems appealing and must have it right away without realizing the potential harm that lies ahead. Since God knows better, he allows us to whine and cry but will not give into our childish demand and give us something which we ask for immaturely.

A childlike faith is trusting God in all circumstances. It is to take a plunge into something unknown to us but being certain that God will catch us. It is having confidence in God that He loves us and will not let His child get hurt. This is maturity, to simply trust God in His strength and timing to hold us up without our input or knowledge in it.

Many of us would agree that we behave childishly when it comes to trusting God. But the Bible teaches that we must be childlike to enter the kingdom of God.

Dear LORD, please forgive me for my childish behavior in many ways and demanding things from You in my own understanding. Rather, give me a childlike faith to trust in You in all conditions and accept what You do for me. Thank you for being my heavenly Father to catch me and hold me through life. In Jesus' name, Amen!

Payback - October 13

Not a result of works, so that no one may boast. Ephesians 2:9

I asked my son to pick up something from a store and when he came back, he told me how much I owed him. He had the audacity to ask me for money back which was not even half of what I had just paid for his fast-food meals. It made me angry and laugh at the same time, and it also made me realize that I'm not much different towards God when it comes to asking Him in return for the things, I've done for Him.

We are quick to forget how much God does for us. We beg and plead for His help but as soon as mission is accomplished, we do not even take time to thank Him. We forget God's goodness until we need Him again. On the contrary, we expect God to remember every little work that we have accomplished for Him. We expect him to pay us back for the time and energy we put into others or for His work. God does notice everything we do and will not hold back His blessing towards us but is it essential for us to remind Him or demand a payback as if we have earned it?

No matter how much we do for God, cannot compare to what He does for us. So, it is unnecessary to bring our works in His face and expect a payback. If anything, we ought to be grateful for His grace and love towards us while we are unlovable and undeserving due to our sins.

We need to count our blessings that we have received from God instead of making God count our little works that hold no virtue in comparison to how much more God does for us.

Dear LORD, help me to be grateful for my blessings instead of acting like I deserve them. There is nothing that I can do that can make up for what You have done for me, so may I never use my accomplishments and try to make them comparable to You. It my honor to serve You so please help me to do so without accepting anything in return. In Jesus' name, Amen!

Busy doing nothing - October 14

For it is by grace you have been saved, through faith—and this is not from your-selves, it is the gift of God. Ephesians 2: 8

After my mom retired, every time that I call her on the phone and ask what she is doing, she usually replies "Busy doing nothing".

It feels like we too are busy doing nothing when it comes to our spirituality. We are preoccupied making a living and meeting the standards of the world that we lose focus of what is important. We become engrossed with our rituals and activities and miss out on the true purpose of our religion. Religion is the belief in certain faith. But being of the Christian faith is not just about belief in Jesus Christ, but it is to have a personal relationship with Him. It is about getting to know Jesus, not just knowing about Him. We must spend quality time in praying, reading His word, putting our faith in Him, and believing that we are saved by God's grace and not by our works alone. And because of our love and reverence for God, we have the desire to please and do His will which He calls us for.

So, when we are busy doing "things" for God and not busy building a relationship with Him, we too can say that we are busy doing nothing because our works alone do add up to nothing. Personal relationship with Christ takes precedence over our Christian chores and duties so we need to be mindful that we are not busy doing nothing rather busy doing something which has eternal worth.

Dear LORD, please help me not to become so busy doing charitable activities which You do not have any regards for. More than my sacrifices of work, You desire Me, so I give You my heart and my life to You. Please draw me close to You so that I can have a personal relationship with You and not just a religious belief. In Jesus' name, Amen!

Twist and turn - October 15

Have I not commanded you? Be strong and courageous. Do not be frightened, and do not be dismayed, for the Lord your God is with you wherever you go."
Joshua 1:9

Although life seems like a routine for the most part, we all go through days which are good and bad. Some days just go by like any other day and then suddenly, something happens that either changes the entire course of the days to come or even lifetime. Then there are days when everything seems to be going wrong and suddenly, everything works out and turns better to make our days more enjoyable.

Life seems like a roller coaster filled with sudden drops and lifts, twists and turns in an unpredictable way. At some moments we may laugh and feel the tickle in our tummy; at other times we may scream and are scared. But through the roller coaster ride of life, God is like our safety belt who holds us fastened to our seat. We know that we are safe because He holds us tight and will not let us fall off no matter how high or low, how straight or crooked our path may get. He gets us through the ride safely if we sit tight and hold on to God.

So if we feel as if life is going in all directions and are unsure about the next step, we can rest assured that the Engineer of our life knows every twist and turn and will not allow us to fall off the tracks. We just need to buckle up, sit back and enjoy the ride of life as God has us secured in the palm of his hand.

Dear LORD, please help me to hold on to you tightly as my life seems like a roller coaster ride sometimes. No matter how high or steep the fall, please help me to sit secured knowing that You are with me and will not allow me to be shaken. Thank you for your safety and protection through the journey of my life. In Jesus' name, Amen!

Hang on - October 16

We are hard pressed on every side, but not crushed; perplexed, but not in despair; persecuted, but not abandoned; struck down, but not destroyed. 2 Corinthians 4: 8-9

When we say that something is hanging by a thread, we mean that it is in a very uncertain state and is unlikely to survive or succeed. Oftentimes we are faced with circumstances in life that are almost ready to fall apart and there seems to be no more hope for our situation to ever get better. We feel as if we have fallen off a cliff and there is nothing but a twig that we are holding on to which can break any moment.

It is in these moments when we are afraid that the twig will not be able to hold us any longer and we can fall and crash at any time now, we need to realize that Jesus is the "twig" who we can grab and hold. Many of us do not have confidence in Jesus and believe that He is just an imaginary entity and cannot do anything for us. But if we give God a chance, He will prove us wrong. He is real and He can do anything if we put our faith in Him. There is nothing that He cannot deliver us from, there is no burden too heavy that God cannot carry, nor is there any storm that God cannot calm.

It does not matter how bad our current situation may feel like, God has promised that He would never leave us nor forsake us. We may doubt His promise based on our condition but He who promised is faithful and will pull us out of the pit. When the weight of the world pulls us down and the storms of life tosses us around, Jesus holds us by the hand and will not let us go. We can rest assured that Jesus has got us and will hold us tightly no matter how beaten up, crushed, or despaired we may be.

Dear LORD, when life feels overwhelming and I do not know how to sustain myself, please help me to see Your hand reaching out for me. May I grab Your hand which can pull me up and out of anything that is bringing me down. In Jesus' name, Amen!

Authority to cancel sin - October 17

"I, I am he who blots out your transgressions for my own sake, and I will not remember your sins." Isaiah 43:25

Recently we went back to a store to return an item. The customer service rep was not able to retrieve the item even after several attempts on her computer as the item was purchased before the 30-days return policy. She called the Manager who punched in her password and was able to override the system and took back our item. The store associate did not have the same access, only the Manager had the authority to cancel out my purchase.

We often try to cancel out our sin by our own effort or through a person such as a priest. We attempt to be "good" or do some good deeds for a while hoping that it will be enough for God to override our sin. We may even confess our sins to each other as if by doing that we can be forgiven. Surely, we can forgive for what we have done to each other, but we cannot forgive on behalf of God what we have committed against God. Until we confess it to God Himself, we cannot be forgiven. No one else or nothing we do can cancel our sin. Only God has the authority over sin! It is Jesus who paid the price for our sins, so the power has been given to Him only. When we approach God humbly and seek His forgiveness, He cancels our sin and does not recall them ever again.

Dear LORD, help me to understand that forgiveness of my sins cannot be earned by good deeds or erased in a confession box. Only You have the authority to cancel my sin so please override it by Your grace. Please help not to hold on to my sin but turn it to You before the grace period of repenting is over. In Jesus' name, Amen!

Fed up - October 18

Therefore, do not let sin reign in your mortal body so that you obey its evil desires. Romans 6:12

In order to be freed from the bondage of a sin or addiction, we need to have a desire for it. We need to hate our sin in order to be rescued from it. God does convict and make us aware of the sin but unless we are ready to give it up, He will not act. Until we are fed up and humbly cry out to God for help, He will wait for us. And the first step to freedom from sin is the realization of sin itself. We must come to our senses about it and acknowledge it as wrong. It should create a yearning within us to be freed and forgiven. God does not deliver us from something if we enjoy it. We may pray for deliverance but maybe we are not in a rush to be delivered and like to take pleasure in it before we call it quits. We deceive ourselves to believe that we are waiting for God to act but enjoy it in the meantime.

But if we truly recognize our sin and reach out to God, He forgives us and helps us out of it. He changes our heart and renews our mind to dislike our sin even more and be eager to get rid of it. God gives us courage to say no and step away when faced with temptation. He equips us with His strength when we are too weak to fight on our own. God knows the struggle with our sin and so if we are ready, He is ever ready to help us.

Dear LORD, it is not about when You will deliver me from my sin rather about if I want to be delivered. You have given me that choice so please help me to recognize my sin right away and come to You with a repentant heart. Thank you for the forgiveness of every confessed sin and setting me free. In Jesus' name, Amen!

Above all else - October 19

Seek <u>first</u> the kingdom of God and his righteousness, and all other things will be given unto you as well. Matthew 6:33

We all feel flattered when someone chooses us over somebody else. It makes us feel special when we are on someone's top of the list. Being first means we are of importance and the number one priority over anyone else. Many of us might say that God is the top priority in our life, but He could be just one of our priorities. We keep Him around in the vicinity of our life but not always on the top. We may plan on spending time in prayer but if something else comes up and so if we put off praying to later, then we've demoted God from number one to lower as the other activity just replaced God's spot.

In every given situation where we need to choose between God and other things, if we put God aside, then He is not our priority. It is easy to say that God is first in our life overall, but to choose Him first in all situations and always takes effort and discipline. It requires us to re-prioritize and re-schedule things in life. We may need to let go off some people or activities which replace God and take our focus away from Him. And when we do keep God as number one in our life, the rest just falls into its place as He is on top of everything and can handle the rest.

Dear LORD, help me consider my relationships and activities to determine where You stand in my life. Point out those things which take my focus off You. Please help me to make the necessary changes so that You are always my top priority. In Jesus' name, Amen!

One stone is enough - October 20

Then David said to the Philistine, "You come to me with a sword and with a spear and with a javelin, but I come to you in the name of the LORD of hosts, the God of the armies of Israel, whom you have defied. 1 Samuel 17:45

We all have giants of difficulties in our lives that we wish we could get rid of. We become like the Israelites that when we see the big and strong Goliath in front of us, we get discouraged and run off. But we need to face it like David. He was half the size of Goliath and did not have mighty armor or army with him. All he had were a few stones and a sling shot. But just one stone was enough to slay the giant. David's strength was not in his sling shot, but in God. He had enough trust in God that he stood up to the giant, knowing with full confidence that God would deliver him.

Sometimes we gather enough courage to stand against our adversary but instead of slinging our stone, we throw little pebbles and hope that it will go away. We pray here and there, allow doubts and fear to get in our way, feel discouraged and lose hope quickly. Instead, we need to have full trust in God that although we may be weak, He is mighty. We may feel powerless, but we must know that God is powerful. Our God is bigger than any Goliath we come across and there is nothing or no one that our God cannot defeat.

So, instead of throwing little pebbles from a distant at our circumstance, let's face the giant and pray with all our might, trust with all of our heart, and lean on God to direct us in throwing our stone to knock it right out.

Dear LORD, You are my rock on which I stand to face the giants that come against me in form of sickness, temptation and hardships. Please help me to face my foe with confidence, not in myself but in You who is mighty to save. May I use the stone of prayer that You have given me as a weapon to win over the enemy. In Jesus' name, Amen!

Meet me at my failure - October 21

But Peter said to Him, "Even though all may fall away because of You, I will never fall away." Jesus said to him, "Truly I say to you that this very night, before a rooster crows, you will deny Me three times." Matthew 26: 33-34

When Jesus told His disciples about His upcoming death, Peter replied confidently that he would never betray Jesus and would stick by his side. He was so sure of it and would not have it any other way; not even Jesus could change his mind at that moment. A few hours later though, Peter faced the truth and proved that he did not love Jesus as much as he said he did. Peter denied Jesus three times in one night in front of others! Yet Jesus did not hold it against him. Instead He met Peter at his failure and accepted his broken heart and a contrite spirit to start His church through Peter.

Sometimes we become overconfident in our self about our love for God and tell Him how much we will do for Him. We feel so sure of God's calling in our life that we operate under assumption of our own thinking and start doing things "for God". But God knows the extent of our love and He patiently waits for us to realize how much we really are in Him. Often, we talk big but when the time comes to act on it, we go in the opposite direction. And it is when we fail Him and realize the truth about our self, that God takes our failure and turns it into victory.

God knows us better than we know ourselves so let us not be overconfident and exaggerate our love for Him. He knows our heart and is okay with whatever we have to offer. God does not ask for great sacrifices or mighty works, only our humble heart. He can take a pebble and turn it into a rock like Peter when we give God our true self.

Dear LORD, please help me not to show off and talk big if I am not able to deliver. May I be truthful with myself and with You and give You only what I must genuinely offer. Accept it Lord and use it for Your kingdom. In Jesus' name, Amen!

Stay within the lines - October 22

Because of the LORD's great love we are not consumed, for his compassions never fail. They are new every morning; great is your faithfulness. Lamentations 3:22-23

When we try to teach little children how to draw, we start them off with a blank paper with traces on them so that they can follow the dotted lines and trace over the pattern that is already drawn for them.

In the same way, God gives us all a new day or a season in life as a piece of paper and starts us off with a marked pattern which He wants us to follow and trace over what He has in mind for us to do. He already has a picture drawn out, but it is up to us to recognize the pattern and follow His direction through prayer and reading God's word. We can either choose to stay within the lines of God's pattern and make something beautiful of our life, or we can go beyond the lines and make a messy picture.

And although we may mess up, like any good parent, God hands us another blank sheet to start all over if we come to Him with confession. God wants us to get better each time and gives us second chances to learn from our mistakes and re-try until we get it right.

Dear LORD, please help me to stay within Your will and trace my life over the pattern which You have drawn for me. Thank you for not tossing my mistakes away but teaching me through them and giving me another chance. May I get better each time and my life become a beautiful painting. In Jesus' name, Amen!

Buffet style - October 23

All Scripture is God-breathed and is useful for teaching, rebuking, correcting and training in righteousness. 2 Timothy 3:16

Buffet style restaurants are one of my favorites. Since its paid fully in advance to cover all the food at the different stations, I like to take full advantage of it and try out different types of food and stick to what amuses my taste buds while putting aside the ones I do not like.

It reminds me of how similarly we treat the Bible also. We think of it as some Scripture Buffet and pick and choose what we like and do not like about it. We choose verses to read and follow that make us feel good and work for our benefit, while we pass over the ones that discipline or rebuke us. We pick the ones which we want to apply to us and leave the rest for "others".

God's word is not a buffet. It is not meant to be glanced over and choose which scriptures to put on our plate while passing the others over to be wasted or eaten by others. Each and every word of the Bible is priceless as it is fully paid for by the blood of Jesus and meant to be applied individually to each one of us, thoroughly read, understood, enjoyed, and followed fully to satisfy our hunger for God.

Dear LORD, please help to understand that Your word is not for me to tear apart and decide what applies to me and what is meant for others. Please help me to accept it all together as You encourage me through it; and rebuke me in my sin. Thank you for the strength and wisdom that You give me to live by Your word fully, not partially. In Jesus' name, Amen!

If this be so, our God whom we serve is able to deliver us from the burning fiery furnace, and he will deliver us out of your hand, O king. But even if he doesn't, we want to make it clear to you, that we will never serve your gods or worship the gold statue you have set up." Daniel 3: 17-18

When our prayers are not answered in the way we hoped for, we may find ourselves asking questions like, "Why didn't God hear my prayers? Were my prayers not genuine? Was my faith insufficient? How much more did I need to pray about it?" The truth is that God does hear our every cry but does not necessarily give us everything that we ask for because He knows better than we do. Our faith might be strong enough to move the mountain, part the sea in front of us, or break down the wall, but it may be out of God's perfect will for our life and thus, He does not give it to us.

For each one of us, God knows what is best for us. He knows our future and knows what lies ahead on the other side of the mountain, sea, or behind the wall. And because He loves us so much and does not want to see us get hurt in the future, God sometimes does not move the mountain or break the barriers that we think are in the way. To us it may feel like an obstacle in our path, but God allows it to be there to keep us from further pain, and even as a detour to take us through a better path in life.

So no matter what we desire or face in life, we should be accept God's will as our best and have faith that of Shadrach, Meshach, and Abednego who trusted God and refused to bow down to adversity regardless of whether God would deliver them or not.

Dear LORD, even if my prayer does not get answered the way I want it to, I will not give in to the enemy's will but continue to trust You regardless, as Your thoughts and plans towards me are much higher and better than what I can imagine. Please help my faith to remain strong and not falter according to the hardships that come my way. In Jesus' name, Amen!

Doctor Fish - October 25

We were therefore buried with him through baptism into death in order that, just as Christ was raised from the dead through the glory of the Father, we too may live a new life. Romans 6:4

Baptism is basically an outward act which symbolizes our confession of Jesus in our lives. We are blessed to have been baptized in the Jordan River in Israel, the same river where Jesus was baptized. One thing that caught me off guard at the baptismal site which we were not aware of, is that in the water where we stand to get baptized, there are many tiny little fish that come and bite at your feet. It does not hurt but just have a weird, tickling feeling all over the feet. These fish are called Garra rufa, also referred to as "doctor fish" because they eat away dead skin found on peoples' feet, leaving newer skin exposed. They are also used in many pedicures these days as a foot massage/spa treatment.

What the fish were doing to our feet in the waters of the Jordan River truly symbolized the true intent of baptism. They served as a reminder of the work of the Holy Spirit in our lives. By immersing in water through this ritual, we publicly declare that we are putting our old self away and coming out as a new person in Christ. When we accept Jesus into our lives as our Savior from sin, the Holy Spirit convicts us of our external and the hidden sins and removes the impurities within us so that our new self can be exposed. Just how the little fishes gave us a little uncomfortable feeling, we may feel uncomfortable and feel a little biting pain of the Holy Spirit when he cleanses us. But His intention is for our own good, so if we are serious about our new life in Jesus, we must allow the Holy Spirit to work and cleanse us from all unrighteousness.

Dear LORD, thank you for purifying me from my external and internal sins which cause me to be spiritually dead. Please help me to allow You to work in my life, as uncomfortable or painful it may feel, to be purged of all impurities in my life and be renewed in You. May I put away my old self and live a new life in You. In Jesus' name, Amen!

And let us not neglect our meeting together, as some people do, but encourage one another, especially now that the day of his return is drawing near. Hebrews 10:25

Churches become famous around the holidays such as Christmas or Easter, but the attendance starts to decline slowly after the holidays are over. Classrooms become filled with children for Sunday school and many churches need to lay out extra seats or even rent bigger halls to accommodate the influx of people on these special days. Many people do attend regularly, some are not able to go regularly due to certain limitations, but some choose to stay home purposely or "watch" church online just because its more convenient. They however do not seem to mind getting dressed and go to church even for a social occasion or to celebrate the holidays.

Those of us who attend church primarily on holidays are considered CNE Christians – Christmas, New Year and Easter Christians who think going to church is only necessary on special occasions, but not the rest of the year. Is it alright to celebrate Jesus' birth and sacrifice on just one day and forget about it the rest of the year? Jesus must mean something to us every day that we ought to look forward to worshipping Him together with other believers on a regular basis. Irregular worship does not hold any merit in God's sight because He is not a God for certain occasions. He does not appreciate our occasional worship. We may feel good about ourselves to attend church, but it means nothing to God if we are there just to show our faces in a church building on holidays.

If we are serious about God, then our worship should include regular attendance in church to worship and have fellowship with other believers.

Dear LORD, please help me to make a better effort in being a part of a church worship on a consistent basis. May I not to come up with excuses from coming together with You and my fellow believers but be dedicated to church as I am with my work and other places. In Jesus' name, Amen!

After Your heart - October 27

The Lord looks down from heaven on the children of man, to see if there are any who understand, who seek after God. Psalms 14:2

Out of all the people in the Bible, I can relate to David the most. I pray each day to be a "Woman after God's own heart" as David was known as the "Man after God's own heart". David had a calling on his life from God which He was fulfilling but while under that calling, David made many mistakes. His heart was in the right place however, he succumbed to the human nature and ended up sinning on multiple occasions. But because of his love and reverence for God, David kept running back to Him with a repentant heart as soon as he realized that he had sinned against God. It hurt David that he had hurt God and each time that he sinned, David felt God's pain and begged for forgiveness. Therefore, God helped David to learn from his mistake and become bigger and better after his fall every time. God did not remove the anointing from David as He saw that David had a genuine heart for God and always tried to be the man who God wanted him to be.

As we call ourselves Christians, we too must have a heart like David and follow Christ with all our heart, mind and soul. God has placed His anointing on us and helps us to fulfill His purpose if we stay close to Him. God understands our sinful nature and does not turn His face away from us, instead He convicts us of our sin, looks upon us with mercy and inclines His ear towards us as we whisper a heartfelt apology. Even if let God down by sinning over and over, God keeps lifting us up each time as He sees in us a heart to please God and do what is right.

Dear LORD, I seek to be the person after Your heart. Create in me a clean heart, O God, and renew a steadfast Spirit within me so that I can be who You have called me to be. Help me to remain under Your anointing and fulfill the plan and purpose You have for me. In Jesus' name, Amen!

How great is the goodness you have stored up for those who fear you. You lavish it on those who come to you for protection, blessing them before the watching world. Psalm 31:19

We all have a daily course which we follow pretty much every day or at least on weekdays for most part. At a specific time of the day we are basically doing the same exact thing every day and that makes one wonder sometimes, if this is what life is about? Routine! At times we may feel bored about our monotonous life and complain that life is dull and uninteresting.

Instead of grumbling, we should be praising God for the routine because it means that all is well with our life. The daily routine is a blessing from God who continues to provide for our needs and life is sails smoothly without any major setbacks. Things could take a turn for the worst and turn our world upside down in a split second, changing our life, and forcing us to follow a new routine which may or may not be as pleasurable as the one we have right now.

So let's not take our daily, little blessings for granted, rather enjoy the routine and give God the glory for giving us another day to enjoy life in the same manner as we did yesterday, and hopefully to see another day of blessing tomorrow.

Dear LORD, as I perform my daily activities, help me not to complain but be thankful as they may seem insignificant today but, O, how precious they are! Help me to reflect about how different my life would be if even one of these blessings were taken away from me. So, may I have a grateful heart about every little blessing that You give me. Thank you for being gracious to me and giving me these blessings which some could only wish for. In Jesus' name, Amen!

Glue me back together - October 29

He is before all things, and in him all things hold together. Colossians 1:17

It made me feel good when someone from my family said that I was the glue that holds us together. Glue is something that we do not give much credit to, but it is critical for everything. It is an adhesive or substance that keeps things connected and joins broken things back together.

For my life, Jesus is the glue that keeps me together. I have felt many times like broken pieces and as someone who cannot be restored. Due to my sin and shame, doubt and fear, I have broken down and lost all hope. But just when I have hit rock bottom and been left with nothing but little broken pieces all over the place, Jesus comes down to me, collects my pieces, and glues me back together with his love, forgiveness, and hope.

Oftentimes, we feel beat up against many storms in life that we cannot hold ourselves together and fall apart in pieces. As we look at the debris of ourselves, we may be ready to throw it out and do not see a reason for anything good to come out of it. But let us remember that when we do not see any value in ourselves, God sees us as priceless. He does not give up and throw us out as hopeless junk.

All things hold together in Christ so it does not matter how many broken pieces we have fallen apart into; we just need to give those pieces to God so that He can restore and glue us back together.

Dear LORD, thank you for being the adhesive which holds me and my world together. Regardless of how many directions that I get pulled from to maintain my family, work, and all other things that I do, You hold me tight in Your arms and keep me together. Help me to keep the glue between us moist by my prayers, reading Your word, and staying close to You. In Jesus' name, Amen!

Jesus copycat - October 30

Be imitators of me, as I am of Christ. 1 Corinthians 11:1

A few days ago I asked my husband to do something and his reply was "I'm not Jesus, I can't do that" to which I replied, "I know You're not Jesus but you can be Christ-like".

The purpose of a Christian is not be Jesus, but to be like Him. No one can take the place of Jesus; He is the only God, and none can do what He did for us. But we as Christ followers are to imitate Him and follow His example in our daily living. We often excuse ourselves into sinning by saying that we are not God and due to our sinful nature, we sin. But while being fully human, Jesus demonstrated being sinless. He endured hardships, temptations, insults, and even died at the hands of sinful men. Despite all this, He did not sin and proved to us what we can be capable of. Jesus taught us to love sacrificially, forgive without limits, give without expecting, honor for insults, go the extra mile, be joyful, hopeful, and rejoice always.

It is not easy for us and neither was it for Jesus, but He did it and so can we by the help of His Spirit living in us. We are created in His image so we can be like Christ if we want. The key word is "if we want". The decision is in our hands to be like Jesus who gives us the strength to endure hardships, wisdom for right decisions, patience in trials, courage to walk out or be silent when insulted, and grace to forgive when treated unfairly. It is a matter of determination for us whether we want to be like Jesus fully or partially. With all our being, we ought to imitate Jesus if our aim and plea is to be like Jesus!

Dear LORD, please help me not to be an imitator of the world but follow You with my walk, talk and deed. Teach me to love and forgive like You. May I live my life in such a way that, when people look at me, they can clearly see Christ in me. In Jesus' name, Amen!

Fallacies - October 31

Have nothing to do with godless myths and old wives' tales; rather, train yourself to be godly. 1 Timothy 4:7

More than often we receive the type of messages on our phones which tell us to "forward this message to 10 people and you will be blessed tomorrow" or "money will come your way in the next 24-hours". Many people do believe these and pass it along right away and some do it because of fear that if they do not, they will have bad luck and something evil will happen to them.

These are called superstitions and the Bible warns against these types of things. We are not to fear and believe such things because they are simply not true. Believing and participating in such myths is going against God. Our blessings and curses do not come our way just because we follow or break some silly email chain. Nothing happens by luck or by following a superstition, but by God's will. Our times are in the LORD's hand and He has a plan and purpose for us which cannot change due to our misconceptions and rituals. The power for such is not within the fallacies but in the hands of God.

Therefore, let us be wise and not waste our time on counting the number of people we need to pass a mythical message to in order to receive a blessing or avoid bad luck. Rather, we should focus on the message of the cross and share that with others so that they can receive the eternal blessing from God.

Dear LORD, please teach me not to believe and blindly follow the myths and superstitions that people follow. Help me to understand that these are not from You but from the evil forces of the dark world which comes against me. May my hope not be built on luck and chance but on You, who knows my very being and causes all things to work for my good. In Jesus' name, Amen!

November

Just do your part - November 1

I planted, Apollos watered, but God gave the growth. So neither he who plants nor he who waters is anything, but only God who gives the growth. He who plants and he who waters are one, and each will receive his wages according to his labor. For we are God's fellow workers. You are God's field, God's building. 1 Corinthians 3:6-9

It is exciting to see the growth of the plants which we planted over the summer. All I did was plant the seed in the soil, watered it regularly and leave it out in the sun. Then patiently, I watched the little plants start to grow bigger and bloom with flowers and vegetables.

Like how we plant seeds in the garden, God asks us to plant spiritual seed in other people's lives. He does not require us to do much more than that. Yet, many of us do not bother to do even that much as we assume that it is not our responsibility to tend to their spiritual growth from beginning to end. We feel that it may require too much work or are afraid that the seed we plant may not bear any fruit, therefore we do not bother to do anything. We leave it up to someone else to do the job.

But God could be asking us to only plant the seed of introducing someone to Jesus and place them in the "Son-light". He may have other people in mind to water and nourish. All we need to do is our part and God can do the rest and grow something bigger and beautiful out of the little seed that we plant.

Dear LORD, please help me not to be shy or afraid to tell others about You but to step out of my comfort zone and share the good news about You to whomever You place in my path. May I not be concerned about what happens next but just do my part and leave it in Your hands to lead them to You according to Your time and will. In Jesus' name, Amen!

That's why! - November 2

Wait patiently for the Lord. Be brave and courageous. Yes, wait patiently for the Lord. Psalm 27:14

As a toddler, when our daughter would be in the middle of doing something and if we would ask her why she was doing what she was, she would reply "That's why". She would not elaborate further but continue in her little task until it was fully done and then finally tell or show us why she was doing it. In the meantime, we would just have to be patient and keep wondering what she was up to.

In the same way, we often do not understand God's way and may ask Him why He is doing what He is doing to us. It may not make sense to us and we want to know the reason why things are happening in our lives like they are. But God is a master artist who does not like to reveal His partial work. If He showed us His incomplete work, we may interfere with it by giving Him our advice and ideas on how He should do it, or even take the paint brush from God's hand and try to finish it ourselves in haste. We do not like to wait for God to show us His vision and so we take matters into our own hands and attempt to draw our own painting. And that is the likely reason why God does not disclose every little thing to us but rather have us wait and watch until He is ready to show us His finished work.

God is the painter, and He has a purpose behind everything He does. So, if we trust God, we ought to know that His plans and ways are much better than ours. And if our plans do fall apart, instead of being discouraged, we ought to be excited to see what better plans God must have. He will reveal it in due time so let us be patient and wait for God's complete work to be displayed.

Dear LORD, You are the creator, and I am the creation; You are the potter, and I am the clay so please help me to accept Your authority. May I not question You about everything that happens in my life but receive it gladly and be excited to see the beautiful, finished product that You are shaping me into. Help me to be patient and allow You to mold my life according to the master plan and purpose You have for me. In Jesus' name, Amen!

Gaper Delay - November 3

Make it your goal to live a quiet life, minding your own business and working with your hands, just as we instructed you before. 1 Thessalonians 4: 11

We were stuck in traffic yesterday evening but did not find out why until we got closer to the scene. It was nothing more than a car pulled over by the Police. But other cars were slowing down just to look at what was happening. This is called Gaper Delay. It is causes traffic jams because pass-erby's slow down to get a glimpse of the incident that is occurring on the side of the road.

In our journey in life we often get stuck in a traffic jam because we slow down to look at what is going on in other people's lives. Sometimes we lose focus of where we are headed because we want to know what is going on with others. Instead of keeping our eyes on the road that God has called us to walk on, we get busy minding into others' business and worry about what is happening in their lives.

When Jesus told Peter what to do, Peter wanted to know "What about him?" Jesus replied that it was none of Peter's business to find out what God will do with the other person. Peter simply just needed to follow Jesus and let God deal with others in His own way.

How about you? Are you more concerned about others while neglecting your own salvation? Is there a Gaper's delay in your life because you are slowing down to see the outcome of others' rather than your own? Let us pay close attention to our self and first make sure that we are right with God before we worry about others.

Dear LORD, teach me to keep my eyes on You and not others as I serve You. Help me not to waste my time being distracted by what others are doing but concentrate on my own life and my relationship with You. May I know my calling and do what You have You need me to do without worrying or comparing myself to others. In Jesus' name, Amen!

Half-hearted sacrifices - November 4

Devote yourselves to prayer with an alert mind and a thankful heart. Colossians 4:2

One morning I found myself anxious and rushing through our family prayer time in the morning. I could not help but check the clock multiple times while my husband read the daily devotional. It was almost time for the school bus, and we could be late if we did not leave on time. My mind was somewhere else while we were "praying".

This kind of praying is called a "ritualistic" prayer where we go through the motions but really our heart is not in it. Often, we do things for God just to check them off our list and make ourselves feel better. When we do such heartless deed, it is meaningless in God's sight. He'd rather not have us do it than to offer Him our half-hearted sacrifices, just how Cain's offering was not pleasing to God as he gave him a "whatever" portion, while Abel took his time and delighted in giving God the best of what he could offer. In the same way, we cannot expect God to bless our efforts when we know that we have not given Him our choicest offering that requires our time and attention.

In order to give our best to God, we need to have a desire to please God first and then have a plan on how to go about doing our best, such as wake up a little extra early to be able to fit in the quality time with God. God hears and sees everything we do but none of it holds any virtue for Him when we do not give Him our finest. So, let us make an effort that means something to us and to God!

Dear LORD, search my heart and point out those things which I do that are only for the sake of making myself feel better. Help me not to give you partial and half-hearted sacrifices as they do not mean anything to You. But in everything that I do, may I give You my best. May the words of my mouth and the meditation of my heart be acceptable and a pleasing aroma for You. In Jesus' name, Amen!

Point it out - November 5

Brothers, if a person is caught doing something wrong, those of you who are spiritual should restore that person gently. Watch out for yourself so that you are not tempted as well. Practice carrying each other's burdens. In this way you will fulfill the law of the Messiah. Galatians 6:1-2

Most of us are concerned with self-image and so we carry two different personalities. One is the outward person for the world to see as good and proper at work, school, church, or amongst friends and relatives. Then some of us have an inward personality which is pretty much hidden from the outside world but only reserved for our close ones, especially our family, to see and deal with such as anger, bitterness, pride, and hatred. We have become so good at switching between these personalities that we do not even notice what we are doing and end up deceiving others and our self also. We lose our identity and forget who we really are, unless someone points it out to us who sees both side of ours. It is not easy news to accept when someone does point out our shortcomings and it is not easy for the one breaking the news. But we need to hear the truth about ourselves to realize our double-standard life that we could be living.

Many times, we see and know things about our loved ones that are not right in the sight of God, but we are too afraid to say something in fear of retaliation or hurting their feelings. And so, we remain silent to keep the peace. But by keeping silent, we do not help but hurt the person even more because we allow the behavior to continue which leads them further astray and away from God without their realization. As God's children are called to build each other up so when we know of something wrong in a loved one, we should be courageous enough to talk to them with love and in private without being blunt or embarrassing them in front of others. And if the individual is truly a person of God, he will take heed to what is said and examine his ways to make it right with God and others.

Dear LORD, when I see my loved ones living in an unrighteous way, may I not look the other way and ignore it. Please give me boldness to confront and tell the truth so that they can realize it and turn from their evil ways. May I not be judgmental towards them but support with love to help them become a better person in You. In Jesus' name, Amen!

Punching bag - November 6

We are pressed on every side by troubles, but we are not crushed. We are perplexed, but not driven to despair. 9 We are hunted down, but never abandoned by God. We get knocked down, but we are not destroyed. 10 Through suffering, our bodies continue to share in the death of Jesus so that the life of Jesus may also be seen in our bodies. 2 Corinthians 4: 8-10

Thankfully, I have never been punched or kicked by anyone in my life. But for those who have had this unfortunate experience can attest that it hurts. Although I may not have been ever hurt physically in life, I have been spiritually attacked by the devil more times than I can count.

The devil feels intimidated when we come closer to God, so he does anything in his power to bring us down. The stronger that we get in the LORD, the stronger his blows come towards us. He uses us like a punching bag to knock us out. But like a punching bag that does not get knocked out, we too must resist his blows and come back against the devil to resist him with all our might. We need to put up a good fight and not give up so easily.

No matter what our struggles or circumstances may be, the devil has no power to overcome us if we do not allow him. He may be strong, but our God is stronger. No weapons formed against us can prosper when we have God on our side. He gives us the power and ability to stand up and fight against all odds. Despite of how many times we have been punched and kicked by the devil, we must rise from the ashes of defeat and stand up against the enemy once more. If we do not give up and resist him, the devil will eventually have to give up and flee from us.

Therefore, let us not become afraid when the devil attacks us, rather welcome it as an opportunity to let God show the devil who He is messing with.

Dear LORD, help me to be the person that when I wake up in the morning, the devil says, "Oh no, she's up!" May I not run and hide in fear of him but rather stand up against the devil and give him a good fight back. I know that You are with me so by Your power in me, no matter how many blows the devil throws at me, I can withstand him. In Jesus' name, Amen!

...For the battle is the Lord's, and He will give you into our hands." 1 Samuel 17:47

When trouble strikes, we shift our gear into survival mode and do whatever it takes to get through it. Because it is against us, we assume it is ours only to deal with, and so we run around frantically trying to figure out solutions to our problems. We lead ourselves to exhaustion until we finally realize that certain things are just not in our control. We may be the target that the devil tries to hit but his aim is towards God. Satan is on a spree to snatch God's children away from Him and does whatever he can to strike us down by hitting us with illness, family matters, job issues, etc. He throws any obstacle in our way to stop us from moving forward and increasing God's kingdom.

Nonetheless, our God is not just a so-called god. He is the Lion of Judah who will not allow His children to be snatched out from under His protection. He guards His children in His arms, which is the safest place that we can be in. When the devil strikes us, God takes is personally and fights with a vengeance like a mother lion who attacks anyone who dare come near her cubs.

Therefore, when we are targeted by the devil, let us remember that the battle belongs to the LORD and He has already won us! We do not need to panic but rather pause from running around, call out to God for help and be still and watch as God fights it out on our behalf.

Dear LORD, help me not to fear the attacks of the enemy as the victory has already been won in You. May I be fearless and confront the devil with full confidence as You will not allow me to fail and be destroyed by the enemy. Thank you always for watching out for me and protecting me under Your mighty wings. In Jesus' name, Amen!

Simple gestures - November 8

Rejoice with those who rejoice, weep with those who weep. Romans 12:15

We get excited when we receive an invitation to a party. We start planning out our schedules so that we can attend and think of what we will wear and such. Even if it is far in distance, we still go just to have a good time. But how much effort do we make in visiting someone who is sick or has lost a loved one? Many of us come with plenty of excuses not to go such as "I don't have time", "I don't want to bother them," or "I want to go but don't know what I would say". While some of these might be legit reasons, many times we use these excuses just to get out of it. It may not be a big deal to us, but it makes a big difference to the one who is going through rough times to know that there are people out there who do genuinely care. Only a phone call, text message or simply just our presence is sufficient to comfort someone. It does not matter whether it is a loved one or just an acquaintance, we can demonstrate God's love through this simple gesture.

If we can make an effort in attending a celebration, let us make a greater effort to be there in times of trouble also. Just the way it is more blessed to give then to receive; it is more blessed to be there for someone in times of grief then to be there to party with them.

Dear LORD, please give me a heart for the broken and be there for them in whichever way I can. Help me to be purposeful in my showing my affection towards those who are hurting. The least I can do is pray and give them Your comfort so help me to do so without any excuses. In Jesus' name, Amen!

For the word of God is alive and active. Sharper than any double-edged sword, it penetrates even to dividing soul and spirit, joints and marrow; it judges the thoughts and attitudes of the heart. Hebrews 4:12

Did you ever go to a restaurant and order soup expecting it to be hearty, meaty, chunky bowl of delicious soup but instead got a light, watered-down, imitation soup? Just by the look and taste of the soup we can tell that it is not what it is truly supposed to be like.

Oftentimes, we find folks who do the same with the gospel. There are "Prosperity Preachers" who pass out a watered-down version of the Bible to others. They only tell what others want to hear and leave out the vital information just because they are afraid to tell the truth and worry that people will not come to hear them. And there are also folks who like to receive only a watered-down version. They are called "Prosperity Followers". They pick and choose things from the Bible that only apply for their benefit but not those that rebuke their sin.

The Bible is not like a "strawberry picking farm" where walk with our basket and go through the field to pick and choose what we like and overlook the rest. It is meant to be read and applied in its entirety. The truth is hard to swallow sometimes but it is meant to rebuke and rebuild us so we must not water-down the Bible. It is a hearty food for the soul which God made especially for us, so let us eat God's word fully and not leave any leftovers.

Dear LORD, thank you for giving us Your word to live by the truth in it. Please help me not to apply the words which benefit me only but also take to heart the ones that rebuke and correct me. Teach me to abide by the Bible fully and not abuse it to make it fit my way of living. In Jesus' name, Amen!

No better than - November 10

Do not judge, or you will be judged. For with the same judgment you pronounce, you will be judged; and with the measure you use, it will be measured to you. Why do you look at the speck in your brother's eye, but fail to notice the beam in your own eye? Matthew 7: 1-3

When we listen to a sermon that sounds critical, we immediately apply it to others. We think that it pertains to someone else and so we nudge, cough, nod our heads, and say "Amen" loud enough to get their attention to let them know that they need to pay close attention to the message as it applies to the other. We even try to send the video or link to have them listen to the message later.

Oftentimes, we are quick in pointing fingers at others and criticizing for their sins but consider ourselves to be righteous. As righteous as we may think of ourselves, if we are not humble, it is not true Christianity. As Christ-followers, we should show humility and give grace to others as we have been given. We should never think a better and greater Christian than anyone else. We all sin and fall short of God's glory so we must consider our sinful ways first before we show others their faults and shortcomings. The scriptures pertain to us first so that we can apply these to our life before we go out and help others to be better. Similarly as in case of an emergency, the Flight Attendant instructs us to put on our oxygen mask first so that we are well enough to help others; in the same way we must be in right standing with God before we bring others to Him for judgement.

Therefore, in humility, let us apply God's word to our own actions so that we can lead others by our example into godly living.

Dear LORD, help me not to be quick in judging others while excusing my own sin. Convict me by Your Holy Spirit to see my own wrongdoing and repent of my ways before I point at someone else. May I have a humble heart and treat others with love as You love me. In Jesus' name, Amen!

Huger games – November 11

So I say, walk by the Spirit, and you will not gratify the desires of the flesh.
Galatians 5:16

The biggest temptation that I face most often is the temptation of food. I love to eat and get hungry easily. Especially on the days of fasting or just watching my diet, when I am the most vulnerable, the devil plays hunger games with me and uses those times to tempt me to the point of meltdown. He takes me up on the mountain to show me the vast kingdom of delicious food and gives me excuses to give in. If I give in, I feel worse and regret afterwards that I let myself down. But if resist it and stand firm, I feel good about it as it was worth the effort of not giving into my hunger pangs.

The devil is good at figuring out what our desires and weaknesses are and uses those things against us to break us. God allows the devil to tempt us, but at the same time He gives us the strength to resist the devil so that we become strong in the LORD. The devil may have the power to tempt us, but we have the power to resist. If we are serious about fighting against the temptation, God is serious about helping us out of it.

Temptation is extremely hard regardless of what it is. It comes in different forms and shapes for each one of separately. But the power to resist temptation comes only in one form, which is Jesus Christ! So when we are faced with a tempting situation, let us not take it lightly and give room for the devil to play mind games; instead we need to shut out the thought immediately by rebuking him in the name of Jesus.

Dear LORD, You know those things that are hard for me to resist so I need Your strength to overcome these temptations. Please help me to have self-control and not be lured into it. May I be vigilant and not put myself in places and situations where I am surrounded by my weaknesses. If I do not give in, the devil will give up so help me stand firm. In Jesus' name, Amen!

Light in gloom - November 12

The people living in darkness have seen a great light; on those living in the land of the shadow of death a light has dawned. Matthew 4:16

All human beings have and will walk through the "Valley of the shadow of death" at some point in life where we feel like there is chaos, discouragement, sorrow, fear, and the grip of death close at hand. We may feel afraid and alone as we walk through this dark valley.

For there to be a shadow, a light is needed for the reflection which means a light exists amid darkness. And God is our light! He is amid us and does not let us walk alone. He comes along with us as we pass through the valley, which might be dark but God's light shines on us and guides us out of it. He does not abandon and leave us there with dark, scary shadows of fear, worry and heartaches, but brings us out of it.

So, even though evil may lurk around to hold us in the dark depths, remember that we do not need to fear because God is with us as our light to lead the way and comfort us as we walk through and out of it. If God our light and salvation is with us, can shadows hurt us? So, let us not fear the shadows in the night but shine God's light so that they will not come near us.

Dear LORD, You are my Shephard who goes before me to lead the way. So even though I walk through the valley of the shadow of death, I will not fear for You are with me. May I rest in this assurance that no matter how difficult the journey of my life may be, You remain close beside me to shine and guide me all the way.
In Jesus' name, Amen!

Takeaway message - November 13

The unfolding of your words gives light; it gives understanding to the simple.
Psalm 119:130

A t the end of most training sessions or professional meetings, the attendees are requested to give their feedback and ask questions. They are also asked to reiterate the takeaway message about what they learned to ensure that they were paying attention, and that the session was useful for their role.

Similarly, reading the Bible is like attending a training session with God. Through His word, God speaks and instructs us on matters of our life and gives us an in-depth explanation of who He is. And so as we start to read the Bible, we should not do it as an obligation to God or as a part of our daily chore to cross it off the list, but with a desire and excitement to learn from God and about God himself. We need to fully engage in reading it carefully word by word and understand how it applies to us.

At the end of each bible reading session, we can ask God to clarify things which we could not understand, give our feedback and comments, and have a takeaway message from each passage that we read.

It is not enough just to merely read the Bible, but we need to dig deeply into it as God instructs us through His living and powerful word.

Dear LORD, give me wisdom to understand Your word clearly. Help me not to read it partially or interpret it by own thought process. But may I read this holy book in its entirety carefully so that I know the full gospel story and am clear about who You are and Your plan of redemption from beginning to the end. Let Your word come to life as I read it. In Jesus' name, Amen!

Against the flow - November 14

Enter through the narrow gate. For wide is the gate and broad is the way that leads to destruction, and many enter through it. But small is the gate and narrow the way that leads to life, and only a few find it. Matthew 7: 13-14

While walking in a busy street, it makes it a little easier if we had to walk in the same direction as everyone else. There are higher chances of running into people, being knocked down and getting nasty glares because we are coming in their path. They make us feel as if we are "weird" for walking one way while everyone else is going the other way. And for us also, it takes longer to get where we want to go because we are going against the flow of where everyone else is headed.

Similarly, our Christian walk can be described as going against the flow because it does not conform to the patterns of the world. When we say no to things which go against the word of God, we get stared at, knocked down, called narrow-minded, backwards, weird, etc. People might think that we are walking in the "opposite" direction, but they fail to realize that what they call "opposite" is the true and only way to God. If our heart is set on following Jesus, it should not matter to us which way the flow of the world goes. Our determination should be to follow God despite of what is said or thought about us. Even if we are alone and journey is hard due to the resistance of people who comes against us, we must not give up and turn around just to please people and fit in. We must keep our focus on Jesus and trust Him as He leads us through the path that is narrow but the right one.

Dear LORD, it is difficult to stand out in the crowd and be different than those around me. But regardless of what people think, help me not to give up but always remember who I am in You and keep walking according to Your word. And as I walk, let people see You in me and cause them to turn around also. In Jesus' name, Amen!

Call to me and I will answer you, and will tell you great and hidden things that you have not known. Jeremiah 33:3

In our world these days, everyone thinks they are right. We all are right in our own eyes. Once we have made up our mind about something, it is hard to change it. Even if we are wrong, we like to defend our decision and argue our point to make it right. We are unwilling to listen to the other party and no matter what they have to say, we look for fault in others just to prove ourselves right.

Many of us do the same with the word of God. As much truth that it contains, just because we have decided to not believe it, we look for errors in it. We question and judge everything in the Bible based on our opinion and that of the world. Although seeing, we become blind to the truth because of our arrogance and stubbornness. We try to disqualify God by fault finding instead of fact finding.

Our God is not a mysterious being who is so distant and unfathomable. Rather, He is close and personal to us that if we call out to Him, we can find Him. He does not hide anything but is willing to answer all our questions and remove any doubts we may have about Him. And once we know the truth about God, He sets us free from all our doubts and qualms.

So, if we have any questions about God that stop us from believing and trusting Him, we can just ask God to reveal the truth. Jesus is the way, the truth and the life, so there is no chance for disappointments for those who search for God with all their hearts.

Dear LORD, please open the eyes of my heart to see You clearly. Give me a sound mind and clarity so that I can understand and receive Your word by faith as You teach me. Allow the Spirit of truth to penetrate my heart so that there is no room for doubt about You. In Jesus' name, Amen!

Confess and abandon - November 16

Whoever conceals their sins does not prosper, but the one who confesses and renounces them finds mercy. Proverbs 28:13

For a sin to be revoked, three things are essential – confession, repentance, and forgiveness. God has already done His part of forgiveness beforehand by dying on the cross for our sins. The other two are our responsibility which God has left up to us to do. We must decide whether we want to receive the forgiveness which God has to offer. And if want to be forgiven, then we must confess and repent.

Confession is agreeing with God and accepting our sin without making any excuse or justifying it. Repentance is about regretting what we did and not wanting to do it anymore. It is not enough just to feel bad for what we have done, say sorry, and move on. We cannot continue behaving the same and being the same person once we have repented. We need to deliberately try not to commit the same sin again. We must make changes to our attitude and lifestyle as necessary to avoid falling for the same sin again. It requires self-control, discipline, and willful decision daily to withdraw ourselves from the temptation. It is not easy to change our behavior overnight but once we understand our error and are willing to change, God starts to transform us from within. He begins to renew our mind and gives us a different outlook. He puts a new heart in us to dislike what He dislikes and do what pleases Him.

Therefore, if we want to be rid of a particular sin, we should not only feel sorry about it but make a conscious effort each time to not allow ourselves to fall into the sin. We must put on God's armor daily and purge it out of our lives for good.

Dear LORD, thank you for offering Your forgiveness which you bought for me by shedding your precious blood and dying on the cross for my sin. Please help me to receive this forgiveness by realizing my fault and having a willing heart not to commit the sin again. I can overcome it and be victorious over my sin by Your power in me, so help me God! In Jesus' name, Amen!

Garbage removal - November 17

Set your minds on things above, not on earthly things. Colossians 3:2

Thank God for Garbage service. All we have to do is collect the trash from our place, tie it in a bag, throw it in the trash bin, and pull it up to the sidewalk for it to be taken away on a given day. It is as easy as that. Once it is put out there, it becomes the responsibility of the trash collectors to handle it and discard it where and how they need to. It is not our problem anymore and we do not ever have to see it again.

Wouldn't it be great if we could do the same with the trash in our mind? How good it would be for us if we could literally open it and empty out the junk that takes up unnecessary space in our brain? It sounds unrealistic, but we actually can. All we need to do is bring all our thoughts, worries, irritations, and impurities to Jesus through prayer. And He is gladly available to collect it and take it away from us to never see it again. God makes space in our heart so that we can be at peace and have room to be filled with His love. Just like the trash collectors who diligently come and pick up our dirty trash, our God does not care how heavy or "dirty and stinky" our trash is. He does not look at what is inside the trash but just picks it up and throws it out so that we can be clean and free again.

It is as easy at that. So, if we feel overwhelmed and our mind is full of junk but do not know where to dispose it, let us take it to the foot of the cross and Jesus will take care of it.

Dear LORD, thank you for offering to take away those things that add to my stress and cause me to be restless. Please help me to identify the waste and bring it You to be freed and cleaned. Occupy my thoughts with You and fill my life with Your presence in place of the garbage that corrupts my mind. In Jesus' name, Amen!

Learning from mistakes - November 18

For the LORD disciplines those he loves, and he punishes each one he accepts as his child. Hebrews 12:6

One of the good parenting skills is to discipline the children when they do something wrong. Most of the time, children just do not understand and keep pushing their limits until they get in trouble. And when they are corrected, get yelled at or are grounded, they may feel unloved and treated unfairly. But to the parents, it is necessary to do so in order to teach the children a lesson, keep them from getting into further trouble, and to train them to know and do better.

Our Heavenly Father treats us in the same way. Because He loves us, He sometimes feels it necessary to chastise us when we go astray on the wrong path. Because He wants the best for us and to be more effective for His work, God pushes us out of our comfort zone and takes us through the fire to mold us into perfect shape. When we undergo some hardships and trials, God may seem mean and unfair at that time, but later we do realize that His chastisement was for our own good.

Discipline is necessary for discipleship! Therefore, we must accept it and allow God to train us to be holy.

Dear LORD, please help me to understand that You train and discipline me as Your child the way I train my children. Although the punishment may seem harsh, it only builds me up in You, so give me the strength to endure and ponder on my mistakes to learn from it and become better. Remove from me my rebellious heart and make me willing to trust and obey You. In Jesus' name, Amen!

And the Lord restored the fortunes of Job when he had prayed for his friends. Job 42:10

Sometimes I dream the weirdest dreams which make no sense. A person whom I have not seen or even thought about in a long time comes up in the dream and make me wonder. Even people who I barely know show up in my dream out of nowhere.

When this occurs, we must not ignore it as just a dream (or a nightmare). It is God's way of bringing a person to our attention because they are in a need of prayer. God places them in our mind to intercede on their behalf as they may be fighting a physical or spiritual battle and are not able to pray for themselves. We do not need to know the details about what is going on in their life or what they need prayers for, we just need to lift them up to the LORD in prayer whatever they may be dealing with. God loves to listen to our prayers made on behalf of others and He is quick to respond when offered sincerely. Therefore, let us pray for others more than we pray for ourselves.

If we confide in each other with a prayer request, we should honor our commitment and pray for each other with a burden in our heart. Additionally, we must remain faithful to keep it between our self and God. There should not arise any need to start the gossip mill by sharing our concern about the individual to others.

If God has placed us in a position to pray, we must pray as His prayer warriors and fight on our knees for those who cannot fight for themselves. The blessing is all ours, so let us pray for others!

Dear LORD, may I not take it lightly when thoughts of people come to my mind or when I feel a heavy burden in my heart towards someone. May I feel that nudge from You to pray for them as if I am praying for my own. Thank you for giving us the blessing to pray for each other, so please help us to do so faithfully. In Jesus' name, Amen!

Don't just pray - November 20

'Lord, when did we see you hungry or thirsty or a stranger or needing clothes or sick or in prison, and did not help you?' He will reply, "'Truly I tell you, whatever you did not do for one of the least of these, you did not do for me." Matthew 25: 44-45

Oftentimes, we tend to look for a simple way out when we offer our help to someone in need. One of the easiest things we do or say is "I'll pray for you". While prayer is vital, there are still other things that we can do to help and show our support. In addition to praying for others, we can also do some physical work such as visit the sick when permitted, comfort those who are mourning, give worn out family members a break by filling in for them when possible, offer to give a ride as needed, bring a meal, help clean up the house, babysit, etc.

God has called us not only to pray for others and think that our job is done, but also to be His hands and feet to do things for those in need. God says, whatever you do for these children of mine, you have done it unto me. By helping others selflessly, we in turn do things directly for God. He uses us to get His work done on earth. Therefore, we must have a willing heart to serve Him and others. It is not only our thoughts that count but also how we love and treat people.

Dear LORD, please reveal to me any persons in my family, church, work, school or neighborhood who can use a helping hand. Please give me a heart to serve them in whichever way I am capable of. May I not just bless with my words but show it by deed also. In Jesus' name, Amen!

416

Memory lane - November 21

Forget the former things; do not dwell on the past. See, I am doing a new thing! Now it springs up; do you not perceive it? Isaiah 43:18-19a

My husband loves to keep things while I love to throw them out. He sees everything as memorabilia and assumes that one day we would have a need for it. I look at it as clutter, and chances are that we would never need it again, so I prefer to get rid of it. He calls me "Hurricane Cleris" as he nervously watches me sweep the house away. Sometimes I end up throwing some valuable things out without even thinking about it while I am on a rampage to clean. On the other hand, He often goes through the trash and takes them out because he just cannot let it go, so I call him "Sanford and Son". Eventually I just wait till trash day and throw it out on that morning to get rid of it permanently. Many times, he does not even notice it has gone and hardly ever has a need for it.

We can relate this to what we do with our past experiences. Some of us like to hold on to everything from the past, even the bad things and keep reminding ourselves of the poor choices that we had made and how bad we were. We know that God has forgiven us and does not hold it against us any longer however, we keep falling for the devil's scheme who keeps reminding us of our past mess ups and makes it harder for us to forgive ourselves and let go.

It is true that we cannot erase the memories from our mind, but we can change our outlook towards it. We can take the valuable lessons that we learned from our mistakes and use them to better ourselves moving forward. God uses our past to sharpen our present and future for our good. So, if God has removed it, then we do not need to go back digging for it and keep feeling sorry about it. Once it's gone, it gone! God has forgiven and forgotten and so should we. Therefore, let it go and make room for new blessings to come.

Dear LORD, when I find myself walking down the memory lane of my past, please help me not to reminisce over my sins but remember Your grace and forgiveness. Thank you for pulling me out of the miry clay which I was stuck in and saving me. Help me to look forward and not behind. In Jesus name, Amen!

If your right eye causes you to sin, pluck it out and throw it away. For it is better that you lose one of your members than the whole body to be thrown into hell. Matthew 5:29

A couple of Bible verses in Chapter 5 of the book of Matthew talk about plucking out the eye, hand, leg, or any other body part which causes us to sin. This does not literally call us to tear out our eyeball or pull out our hand or leg. But Jesus used this as an expression to basically tell us that we should do whatever it takes to stop ourselves from sinning. If we catch ourselves looking at someone lustfully or enviously then we should be quick enough to realize what we are doing and immediately shut off the thought. If our hand causes us to steal and our fingers to flip to inappropriate channels, magazines, or mobile apps, then we need to recall if our actions are God-honoring and stop our hand from touching it. If our feet cause us to walk into a place where we should not be, we should be strong enough to resist the temptation and walk in the other direction.

Basically, it comes down to discipline and how serious we are about our relationship with Jesus. If we desire to live eternally with Him in heaven, then we should not be ignorant of our actions but rather discern the difference between right and wrong and quickly react to pull ourselves away before we fall deeper into sin.

So, if anything or anyone causes us to sin, we should "pluck" it out of our life because we can afford to live without it but not without Jesus.

Dear LORD, give me Your wisdom to know the intent of my eyes, ears, mouth, hands, feet, mind and heart. If there is any impurity in me that brings You dishonor, please pluck it out of my life. May my physical and spiritual body be kept holy and be a dwelling place for You. In Jesus' name, Amen!

Follow the law - November 23

Let every person be subject to the governing authorities. For there is no authority except from God, and those that exist have been instituted by God. Romans 13:1

We generally do not like rules and wish we could do whatever we please. We feel limited when our boundaries are set. But what a chaos and disorder it would be if there were no rules and we had all the freedom? Everything would fall apart if we were not bind to authorities and guidelines so thank God for the rules.

Our actions and choices not only affect us, but the people in our surrounding as well. Therefore, rules have been set forth by authorities to keep us in line. For example, the white lines between a parking spot in the parking garage help us to park our cars in an orderly fashion so that we do not park too close to other cars and avoid hits and dents. They are also meant for easy access to get in and out. The double lines between two parking spots gives us a little "wiggle" room to maneuver our car and park it in between our boundaries.

God gives us rules because we need them and are meant for the benefit of all. He gives us a little wiggle space to make our own decisions, but we must remain within the lines otherwise we end up paying for the consequences. Our limited life eventually has an end so we must stay within the boundaries which God has set for us to enjoy an infinite life.

Dear LORD, please help me to understand that the rules and regulations which You have set are meant for my good. May I not cheat or use shortcuts to override the rules but know that they are there to protect and keep me safe. So please help me to respect Your authority and the authorities of the world and be obedient to the regulations. In Jesus' name, Amen

---

Jesus replied, "What is impossible with man is possible with God.". Luke 18:27

When hardships come in life and we feel like there is not much we can do anymore and have hit rock bottom, God is the rock that we can stand on.

As humans we weigh things from our perspective and limit GOD by our thinking, but GOD is not bound by any limits, situations, or time. He works in ways that our minds cannot comprehend. He thinks differently than we do, and He is aware of our past, present, and future. He may allow certain hardships to come our way because He wants us to grow from them and learn to depend on God rather than rely on our own strength. He works in ways that are overall for our own good and not harm.

When there seems to be no way or we feel that we are losing hope, we need to hold on to God even tighter because while we may be tossed around by the storm around us, He is the anchor who holds us fast. Remember that when things seem IMpossible, God says "I am possible".

So, let us give our impossible situations into God's hands and let Him make them possible in His infinite wisdom.

Dear LORD, thank you that I have You to rely on when things do not go my way. There are many things which I cannot make sense of and do not understand how to fix them, but it does not mean that You cannot either. Please help me to realize that I am limited but You are a limitless God. Your thoughts and plans are so much bigger than I could ever imagine with my limited mind, so I submit my thoughts into Your hands and trust You with my life. In Jesus' name, Amen!

Thank you! - November 25

Bless the LORD, O my soul, and forget not all his benefits. Psalm 103:2

Normally, Monday mornings are probably the worst part of our week. By Sunday evening, we start dreading going to work the next day, children start whining about going to school and come up with excuses to not go. But for most of us, our Monday mornings were not like any other during the Covid-19 pandemic. We wished it were a routine Monday and had to wake up for job, school or any other activity. Many of us saw and experienced for the first time in our lives what it's like to stay home forcefully, not being able to go out to the mall, restaurants, be able to hang out with friends, family and be limited on how many supplies we could buy.

We do not realize the value of something until it is taken away from us. We often take God's blessing for granted and easily forget His goodness towards us. As much as we do not like going to work or school, we need to be grateful that if it were not for these, we could not sustain with our physical needs and enjoy luxuries of life. We take our freedom for granted and use our time, money and talents all for our own benefits and pleasures instead of giving some of it back to God who is the giver of everything.

We need to reflect on our blessings and understand how good we have it. All our blessings, big and small are from God and every one of these have been given to us not because we deserve or have earned these but due to God's grace and love for us. Our God knows what we need and gives it to us in different measures, so instead of complaining and grumbling over matters which we take lightly, let us turn it into praise and gratefulness.

Dear LORD, thank You for Your provision of all necessities and more which You give us. Please help me to not take these for granted and overlook my blessings but be appreciative of all that You do. Please help me to trust in You that I shall not lack anything because You are my Jehovah Jireh, my provider. In Jesus' name, Amen!

What God has done for me - November 26

But in your hearts revere Christ as Lord. Always be prepared to give an answer to everyone who asks you to give the reason for the hope that you have. 1 Peter 3:15

Many have mistaken Christianity as a lifestyle and focus on the moral and ritualistic changes that should take place when we become Christians. We end up focusing more on ourselves and how we present ourselves as "Christians" to others. Our time and energy are spent on changing our way of living, thinking, behaving, etc. to be more "Christ-like" while deprioritizing the one who is the reason for our change.

Yes, Christianity is about living by the standards taught to us in the Bible, but it is foremost about Jesus Christ and understanding who He is and what He has done for us. Christianity is not about how much and what we do for God, but it is all about what God has done for us. There is nothing we can do to match up to His love and sacrifice. The only thing we can do is be thankful for His grace. Once we understand the value of the cross and the power of Jesus' resurrection, we would come to realize that our religion is not important, but our relationship with Jesus is. And this fact should affect our lifestyle to be more Christ-like.

We do not need to worry about making Christianity our lifestyle but focus on our personal relationship with Jesus, the rest will follow supernaturally. And when people ask us about our faith, we should have only one answer "It's all about Jesus"!

Dear LORD, help me not to worry about showing You how good I am and how well I follow the Christian principles. I am sorry, LORD, for the thing that I have made it, when it is all about You, Jesus. Please help me to have a heart of worship and keep You in the center of my life. In Jesus' name, Amen!

Undelivered - November 27

Behold, I stand at the door and knock. If anyone hears My voice and opens the door, I will come in and dine with him, and he with Me. Revelation 3:20

When there is a registered mail delivery for us at home but we are not there to sign and receive it, the post office sends us a few more notifications to come pick it from the post office within certain timeframe, otherwise it gets send back to the sender as "mail undeliverable".

In the same way, God has sent us His free gift of salvation but we keep turning Him away because we are too busy to open the door of our heart and receive it. He keeps sending us reminders through His word and through other people to come and get this free gift, but we keep declining the notifications.

One day, it will be too late when our timeframe is over, and the opportunity will be lost. We will find the doors closed and no longer can be opened because we chose to ignore the messages God kept sending us.

So, before it is too late, let us not delay in opening the door of our heart to receive the precious free gift before it goes back to God as undeliverable.

Dear LORD, I pray for my family and friends who have not accepted You as their personal Lord and Savior. You have made it so easy and brought the free gift of salvation right to the door of our hearts, yet many of us are arrogant, lazy or too busy to open the door for You. Please help us to realize that without this gift, we cannot enter Your kingdom so may we receive it while we still have time on this earth. In Jesus' name, Amen!

Keep trying - November 28

It's not that I have already reached this goal or have already become perfect. But I keep pursuing it, hoping somehow to embrace it just as I have been embraced by the Messiah Jesus. Philippians 3:12

We regularly receive short-messages and bible verses reminding us how to be good and not do certain things such as getting angry, speaking lies, not worrying and being happy. It is good to read and hear the encouraging messages, but the truth is that it is exceedingly difficult to be good. It's not easy to hold our tongue when someone speaks against us, hold our temper when we feel wronged, not worry when we are in trouble, be filled with pride when we have something to show off, and take revenge for our mistreatment.

We are born with an evil nature so only evil comes out naturally. Therefore, in order to remain a godly person and do good, it takes a lot of effort. It requires hard work to go against the natural flow. It does not happen automatically just because we desire to become better, or even when we pray about it. With prayer, comes the work. In every given moment and situation, we need to make a conscious decision on how we behave and handle it. We need to train our mouth to keep it shut when we feel the urge to speak back, shut the thought off immediately when it starts to wander, and remain calm and walk away when provoked.

All these require self-control and discipline on our part. More often though as much as we try, we end up failing like Paul who said, "I don't do the things I'm supposed to do but end up doing the things I don't want to do". We will never reach the state of perfection in this lifetime but that should not stop us from trying. We must strive for good! God is God of multiple chances and it is by His grace that we can keep going no matter how many times we fail.

So, if God keeps giving us chances, why not take them and aim for perfection each time!

Dear LORD, Your word gives me encouragement that although the righteous fall seven times, the LORD picks him up. Thank you for giving me so many chances to keep trying even when I keep failing. Please help me not to give up on myself as You do not give up on me. In Jesus' name, Amen!

The LORD detests double standards. Proverbs 20:23

As a swing sways back and forth, so do many of us as Christians. We may call ourselves Christians, but our actions prove otherwise in many cases. We often base our Christian walk according to the atmosphere, mood, or situation that we are in. We go with the flow and our behavior depends on where we are at or who we are with. On Sundays in church or at any other religious events, we behave more holy and proper. But as soon as we leave the "godly" arena, we go back to our usual self which is much more different than what we portray ourselves amongst other Christians. When we are amid our friends or others who are nonbelievers, some of us tend to lower our Christian standards and act like everyone else just to fit in, because it's convenient and don't want to disappoint or spoil the fun for others. Or simply because we also want to enjoy the pleasures of the world, and so we put our godliness aside for a while.

But being a Christian is not about flexibility or convenience. It is a one-time decision to follow Jesus and no matter where we are or who we are with, nobody should influence to sway. We cannot choose Jesus for some things and leave Him out of others. Once we have made up our mind and accepted Jesus, we must follow Him all the way, even if it means to give up of our worldly pleasure for His sake.

Dear LORD, may I be rooted in You and not live with double standards. Help me to make up my mind that I belong to You and no matter what others tell me to do or what situation I am in, let me not be moved. I have decided to follow Jesus so please help me to never turn around. In Jesus name, Amen!

It's on the way - November 30

The LORD is my strength and my shield; my heart trusts in him, and he helps me. My heart leaps for joy, and with my song I praise him. Psalm 28:7

When we keep praying about a matter over and over, it is often because we doubt whether God has heard our prayer yet, and thus we keep asking Him for it with anxiousness. We prove our lack of faith when we continue to pray in a doubtful manner.

Instead of requesting the same thing over and over to God continuously as if he has not heard us, we need to turn our request into thanks. We ought to tell God what we need once and then start thanking Him for hearing our prayer and begin to believe that the answer is on its way. By doing this, we bring our request to God's attention and at the same time we show Him that we trust Him to have already answered us.

By thanking God in advance for the answered prayer, we prove our trust in Him. But when we keep praying for it over and over, we prove our insecurity in His ability. God hears us the first time we call out to Him. His memory does not fade, and He does not ignore our prayer. God knows ahead of time what we need so He is already at work on it before we even ask. So, let us continue to bring our requests to God but learn to bring them with thanksgiving for it has already been answered.

Dear LORD, thank you for working on my prayer before I even request You. Please increase my trust in You so that when I am praying, I am believing. Please take away my anxiety and fill me with Your peace knowing that my God will supply all my needs according to the riches of His glory. In Jesus' name, Amen!

December

Proven again - December 1

Trust in the Lord with all your heart, and do not lean on your own understanding. In all your ways acknowledge him, and he will make straight your paths.
Proverbs 3: 5-6

Have we experienced that on our way through life's journey, we may have come across a huge mountain in front of us and didn't know how we would ever get to the other side of it as it seemed unsurmountable to cross? We do not know how but God did what seemed impossible for us then and made a way. We either passed straight through the mountain or the mountain was just moved for us. If we have experienced this firsthand before then why is it, we feel afraid or doubt God when we come across another mountain? Has God's ability diminished? Has His hand become too short to save us this time?

If God did it once, He will do it again! His promise to help us through every struggle in life will never be broken. He was faithful yesterday, is faithful today, and will remain the same tomorrow. We may become restless and faithless but God's faithfulness towards us never changes. The size of the mountain in front of us might bring out the fear in us but when we factor God in it, it does not matter how big the mountain of sickness, worry, fear or any other problem might be, God's power can remove all fear and cancel out every obstacle from our path.

Therefore, when we come across yet another mountain, let us see it through the eyes of God. A mountain is nothing but a mole hill for God to trample over. Instead of being discouraged by looking at it, let us see it as another opportunity for God's power to display as He moves the impossible situation out of the way.

Dear LORD, please help me to remember Your goodness from the past and have faith that You will deliver me once again as You always have. Instead of worrying and looking for new solutions, may I bring them to You who already has the answers to my problem. In Jesus' name, Amen!

Calling the shots - December 2

I press toward the goal for the prize of the upward call of God in Christ Jesus.
Philippians 3:14

To basketball players, every shot is crucial. They have a goal in their mind to make every shot possible. Some shots are made, and some are missed. But in either case, there is a lesson to be learned from each shot. When the ball is thrown right into the basket, it boosts up the players' confidence and helps them to get better at it every time. But when it is missed, it gives them an opportunity to learn from it and try harder the next time.

Similarly, like basketball players, we too have a desire to make every shot which we have set the "baskets" in life. We plan out the course of our lives and expect to succeed in each one as we go along. But not all shots are meant to be made! The successful shots encourage us to move on and become better. And the missed ones help us to reanalyze our failure and make corrections where we messed up. When we miss some shots, we need to understand the reason behind it. Maybe it is that we are out of God's will or we are too confident in our own ability. Instead of being humble and giving God the glory for blessing us with the success, we puff up with pride and give ourselves credit. Often also, we go about our business as if it is none of God's business to interfere in. We call the shots of our life and tell God what we will do. But when we turn arrogant, God causes us to "miss our shot" to humble us and realize our need for God's help.

So whether we win or lose, we need to remember that God is in control and each shot of life only helps us to become stronger in Him as we give God the glory for our success, and to try again when we miss it.

Dear LORD, please help me to submit my goals into Your hands and then give my best in all that I do. Whether I win or lose, I give You praise for it as each success and failure teaches me to become a better person in You. So, help me to accept it and wait for You to teach me what You need me to learn. In Jesus' name, Amen!

God of Angel Armies - December 3

He who dwells in the secret place of the Most High, shall abide under the shadow of the Almighty.² I will say of the Lord, "He is my refuge and my fortress; My God, in Him I will trust."³ Surely He shall deliver you from the snare of the fowler and from deadly pestilence.⁴ He shall cover you with His feathers, and under His wings you shall take refuge. Psalm 91: 1-4

On our trip to Egypt recently, our tour bus was escorted by Police vans from the front and the back. In addition, we had two security guards in the bus with us, fully equipped with their weapons to guard us wherever we went. Although danger may be lurking around us, we did not feel threatened at all but roamed around freely without any worry or fear as we knew the armed guards were looking out for us. As long as we stayed within their sight and followed their safety instructions, we were safe and secure.

We live in this world where we are surrounded not only by physical dangers but spiritual threats also. Everywhere we turn, the devil is ready to attack and harm us spiritually. But God the Holy Spirit, is like our bodyguard who protects us from all evil. He goes before us, walks with us, and stands behind us as we walk through this journey of life. We may be surrounded by harm and danger all around us, but we can rest assured that God is with us and He will not allow us to be harmed. We can walk through the valley of danger and come out unharmed to the other side as God comes along our side and hems us under His wings. It is only if we choose to walk away from His watchful eye and go off on our own, we put ourselves in harm's way.

If we feel like we may be in physical or spiritual danger, know that God's presence is always with us. He is the God of angel armies and there is nothing or no one more powerful whom God cannot fight against. So, trust God and feel safe and secure in His arms, He is always there!

Dear LORD, as You are with me, may I not be afraid even amongst danger. Help me to stay within Your watchful eye and find refuge in You. Thank you for the tight hedge of Your protection and guarding my life so that no evil that comes against me can prosper. In Jesus' name, Amen!

Fierce and fearless - December 4

For you did not receive the spirit of slavery to fall back into fear, but you have received the Spirit of adoption as sons, by whom we cry, "Abba! Father!"
Romans 8:15

It is easy to rejoice and praise the LORD when everything in life is smooth sailing. When things are going well, it is easy to believe in God and have faith. But our faith quickly turns into doubt the moment we are hit with a crisis. It becomes difficult to trust God because our fear of the unknown outcome is greater than our faith. We allow fear to consume our thoughts, emotions, and our daily living because that is all we can think about, which takes away our peace and leaves no room for faith.

Fear comes from the devil who puts all sort of negative thoughts in our mind so that we become discouraged and lose hope in God. But God helps us overcome our fear with faith if we look for Him amid our trials. The Bible says that God has not given us a spirit of fear but of power and love. He has given us the power through Jesus Christ to rebuke the devil to leave and fill our heart and mind with faith instead of fear.

Therefore, if we feel overcome by fear, know that God is more powerful than what we think or give Him credit for. Let us open the eyes of our heart and see God at His best, fearless and fierce. If God is with us, whom shall we fear?

Dear LORD, when the enemy puts thoughts into my mind which cause me to worry, feel frustrated, angry and afraid, please help me to submit them to You and allow You to fight my battles for me. Please take away all my fear and anxiety and fill me with your peace and power. In Jesus' name, Amen!

Angels in Disguise - December 5

Do not forget to show hospitality to strangers, for by so doing some people have shown hospitality to angels without knowing it. Hebrews 13:2

When we imagine Angels, we picture them as bright white, cute beings floating in the clouds with wings and a halo. This can be a description of heavenly angels but there also exits earthly angels in human form such as You and me who God uses as His hands and feet to get things done on earth. We may not even think about it, plan it or realize it, but God orchestrates us to be there at the exact time and place where someone needs us, or we need them.

For example, a man with his snow plow sitting in a parking lot ends up giving a ride to someone who happened to be stuck in the blizzard; a person at work finishes off all of your tasks while you were struggling with it; or while waiting in the waiting room to see the primary doctor, a specialists "happens" to be there who offers you His specialized treatment that can cure you. These folks might be ordinary people in an ordinary situation, but God planned it for them to be there in that exact place so that He can help us through them in time of trouble. In the same way, God uses each one of us at some point to help someone in need.

Therefore, we should not take it lightly when God nudges us to be in a specific place and calls us to help somebody in need. We should be willing and prepared as God may be using us as angels in disguise to show hospitality to each other.

Dear LORD, may I not ignore those nudges from You when You ask me to do something for a person in need. I could be the angel whom You send to answer a prayer. Please help me to always be hospitable and have a willing heart to help as I could be serving angels whom you send to me. In Jesus' name, Amen!

Warrior, not a worrier - December 6

"Therefore I tell you, do not worry about your life, what you will eat or drink; or about your body, what you will wear. Is not life more than food, and the body more than clothes?" Matthew 6:25

People worry at different levels for different reasons. There are some people who do not let anything get to them and are worry-free. They usually do not rely on anyone and figure things out on their own, good or bad. Then there are folks like me who worry about every little thing. I know I pray about it and tell God that I trust Him, yet I cannot help myself but to still feel tensed. Many times, the worry is not even real and is about unnecessary things which end up not being a big deal anyhow; but I drive myself crazy over-thinking and replaying the problem in my mind over and over.

On one hand we say that we trust God but on the other hand we worry, so by doing this we basically cancel the trust factor out. Trust and worry do not go together. If we say that we trust God, then we should completely hand the situation over to the LORD. That does not mean that we shouldn't even think about it and ignore the situation, but as we deal with the circumstance, we need to remember and acknowledge that God is in control and He has the best plan for us in His mind. We should pray about every little thing that matter to us and let Jesus have it all, not give Him some and keep some for our self. He can do much better with it then we can.

Dear LORD, help me not to be a worrier, but a warrior – a prayer warrior! Teach me to pray about everything even if its insignificant. If it matters to me, it matters to You also so when worry grips my heart, help me to overcome it with prayer and trust. In Jesus' name, Amen!

Walk on water - December 7

But blessed is the one who trusts in the LORD, whose confidence is in him.
Jeremiah 17:7

We behave like the Israelites many times who came to the Red Sea and thought that it was the end of them. They didn't see any hope in front of them until God did a miracle and parted the sea for them to get across.

We too come to a dead end situation in life many times and ask God to part the sea for us so that we can walk across. But what if instead of parting the sea, God called us to walk on water to get us to the other side? Would we still trust God or start to drown like Peter?

Real trust in God is to be confident that when God has said, "Let's go to the other side", that He will get us to the other side. Sometimes God parts the sea and makes a straight path for us to walk on, but sometimes He asks us to go through the storm to get to the other side. In either scenario, our faith must be strong enough to do what God says, knowing that He who promised is faithful and will see us through.

We need to check our trust level and see where we stand in our faith with God. Do we believe in God only when He does a miracle and parts waters for us or, do we still believe Him even if He does not?

———————————————

Dear LORD, please help me to trust You even in impossible situations. It might be impossible for me, but everything is possible for You so may I do as You say, not on my ability but by Your power in me. In Jesus' name, Amen!

———————————————

Sphere of influence - December 8

Show yourself in all respects to be a model of good works, and in your teaching show integrity, dignity. Titus 2:7

All of us are influenced by people in our daily lives. Especially young adults generally make decisions based on who is around them, what others have to say, and what seems to be the "norm" of the surrounding. If everyone in the surrounding uses foul language then they also use such language thinking that since everyone does it, it is normal and must be ok.

People are likely to engage in activities which seem to suit the environment rather than what is right. And these days, right and wrong is defined by what the overall society says instead of defining it according to God's moral standards.

Christians face a huge challenge in the world today as they are surrounded by the things of the world but are expected to live beyond the influence of the world. It is difficult, especially for the children growing up currently to understand the difference between right and wrong because right is overpowered by most wrongs that is acceptable and ruling our society. As hard as it may be, if we keep our focus on Jesus and are determined to follow Him, God helps us through it all. He gives us the strength to step away from negative influences and the courage to resist temptation. He gives us wisdom to understand what is good and bad in His sight and make the right choice.

But the final decision falls on us individually to choose whose influence we fall under -the influence of the world (friends, peers, social media) or of God! God has called us to live in the world but not be partakers of the world. The purpose of our living is to glorify God through our life and so our focus should be on God and how He wants us to live. In the end it is not going to matter how well we lived our life but how and for whom we lived it. The things of the world may seem good temporarily, but nothing can compare to the permanent happiness that lies with God.

Dear LORD, please show me who is in my sphere of influence—who am I influenced by and who am I influencing? Help me not to follow the patterns of the world but be firm in following You. Instead of being a follower, may I be a leader who influences others to follow You. In Jesus' name, Amen!

Team Player - December 9

For as in one body we have many members, and the members do not all have the same function, so we, though many, are one body in Christ, and individually members one of another. Romans 12:4-5

Millions of people tune in to watch about twenty-two players play a game of championship football. While these players work extremely hard to put on a good game and entertain us, the rest of us sit either in the stadium or in front of a TV, cheering or criticizing their every move. It is easy for us to just sit and watch, but these players have worked hard the entire season.

Many of us think of the church in the same way. Most of us go in as spectators while there are only a few who work hard and perform the duties of maintaining the church building, its activities and lookout for the welfare of its congregation. Some just like to go to church to receive the spiritual food for the week and have nothing else to do with the operation of it.

We need to realize that church is not like a football field. Some of us are not called to be spectators, just to sit, watch and criticize; all of us are called to be a part of the team. Each one of us has God-given talent that the church can use to build up God's kingdom. Some of us are called to be up front on the stage to preach and sing, while some are called to work behind the scenes such as serving in the kitchen, cleaning, teaching Sunday school, controlling the media room, organizing outreach events, etc. Even if it is as simple as smiling and greeting people with a genuine heart, God uses ushers in the church to make others feel welcomed.

The church team needs our participation to win souls for Christ so instead of attending church as a spectator, we must become a player.

Dear LORD, show me my role in the church where I can serve You with the best of my ability. May I not be an observer to sit in the pews and just watch the team but be a part of it and do what You have called me to do. Help me to keep my eyes on my own play and not worry or compare to anyone else. May we recognize and allow each other to function to our full potential in the team for Christ. In Jesus' name, Amen!

God's helper - December 10

And I will ask the Father, and he will give you another Helper, to be with you forever. John 14:16

There is a story of a man who was stranded in the middle of the sea. He was firm in his faith and believed that God would come to save him. So, when a boat, helicopter, and a ship passed by and tried to help him, the man declined saying he does not need their help as God would come to save him. When he did not make it and died, the man asked God why He did not come to his rescue and God said, "I did! I sent you the boat, helicopter and the ship to rescue you but you denied my help".

We often wait for God to speak to us or help us in some majestic, miraculous way. We expect Him to come out of a and perform some magic like a genie to awe us by His powers. But God does not operate in such way. He works in subtle ways and uses people to do His work on earth. He works through us to accomplish His task. God sends us help in different forms such as advice of a friend, medical treatment, assistance from others, and more importantly by guiding us through His word, the Bible.

So when we are in need, let us keep our spiritual eyes open to see the help God sends for us, our ears attentive to God's words spoken to us by others and the Bible, and keep our hearts in tune with God to recognize His hand at work in form of people and things.

Dear LORD, as I wait for your help and answers, may my heart recognize it as You send it to me through other people who come alongside me to help, speak a word of encouragement, pray with me and for me. Thank you particularly for Your Helper, the Holy Spirit whom you have sent as my guide and aide in all aspects of life. In Jesus' name, Amen!

Unsinkable - December 11

He replied, "You of little faith, why are you so afraid?" Then he got up and rebuked the winds and the waves, and it was completely calm. Matthew 8:26

A boat is meant to float on water. Sometimes the waves can become turbulent and cause the boat to sway and become unsteady. But if the boat can stay above the water, it can withstand the winds and waves and overcome the storm that rages around it. Only if water gets into the boat, will it start to sink.

Our faith works like a boat. Sometimes situations in life can shake us up and make us panic and tremble with fear. But if we can learn to trust in God and know that He is with us and will take care of the storm that we are going through, we remain unsinkable. It is only when we allow our mind and heart to be infiltrated with doubt, fear and worry, we begin to drown.

So when we find ourselves caught in a storm such as an illness, financial crisis, family matter, career issue, spiritual downfall, or anything that forces us to sink, we need to fill our boat with God's presence by spending additional time in prayer, reading more of God's word, singing and listening to worship songs and messages which build up our faith. By doing so, we fill ourselves with more of Jesus so that there is no room for doubt and fear to come in our boat and cause us to sink.

Dear LORD, when You are with me in the boat, there is no wave high enough or wind strong enough to make me sink, so help me to keep my eyes above the waves and continue to sail as You rebuke the storm back into still waters. In Jesus' name, Amen!

Family name - December 12

For God so loved the world that he gave his one and only Son, that whoever believes in him shall not perish but have eternal life. John 3:16

We can come up with multiple reasons why God should not love us any longer when we mess up. The devil searches for reasons to turn us away from God and makes up lies about God's unfailing love. He puts doubts by telling us that we have failed at not meeting God's criteria and no longer should be considered as part of God's family.

But we need to understand that the only criteria that needs to be met is our faith in Jesus. If we acknowledge Jesus as our God, believe in His death and resurrection, then that is all there is to it. It does not matter who we are or what we have done. Once we have accepted Jesus as our Savior from sin, nothing else can separate us from God's love or take away our place from the family of God.

When children are born, they are given the family name and loved by the parents regardless of what they have done. There is nothing they can do which can take away the love and affection the parents feel for their children or disown them from the family.

In the same way, God loves each one of us dearly and when we accept Him as our God, He gives us His name and we eternally become a part of His family. Therefore, we must not pay attention to the devil and allow him to tell us otherwise. There is nothing the devil can do to keep us away from God and there is nothing we can do wrong that God cannot forgive. Once we have been accepted into God's family, we have received the inheritance of eternal life in Jesus.

Dear LORD, I come to You just as I am with all my sin and shame. I repent of my sins and in need of Your forgiveness. Thank you for cleansing me with Your precious blood and accepting me into Your family. I accept You as my LORD and give You praise for who You are. In Jesus' name, Amen!

And many of the Samaritans of that city believed in Him because of the word of the woman who testified, "He told me all that I ever did." John 4:39

Often, we try to hide our sin, even from God due to our feeling of shame and guilt. We feel as if God who is sinless and perfect would not want to associate with us, the sinful, dirty person therefore, we try to keep our distance from Him.

Jesus knew everything about the Samaritan Woman's sins. He told her things about her that maybe none other than she and Jesus would have known. Regardless of who she was or what she had done, it did not stop Jesus from befriending the woman from Samaria and offered His love and forgiveness. As sinful as she may have been, Jesus drew her to Himself, and drew many people to Him through the Samaritan Woman.

Regardless of whether we tell Him or not, God knows everything about us. He can tell us things about us that only we know alone. He is aware of our secret sins and knows where we fall short. Yet He sympathizes with us and does not look down on us for all the times we fall into sin. As much as we try to keep our distance, Jesus draws closer to offer His forgiveness and friendship. We may feel as if we have let ourselves and God down, but God's love for us is unconditional. His love for us does not depend on how good we are, nor do God's good plans for us alter based on our sins or righteousness. God can use us–the sinful us nonetheless, to testify for Him. He can make living waters of eternal life flow in us and through us when we draw near to Him.

Dear LORD, thank you for coming after me even when I try to run away from You. There is nothing that can be hidden from You so please help me not run and try to conceal it from You. You have invited me to come You Just as I am, even with my sins and faults, so here I am LORD. Turn me and mold me into who You have desired for me and may my life be a testimony about Your goodness. In Jesus' name, Amen!

Words of wisdom - December 14

A perverse person stirs up conflict, and a gossip separates close friends.
Proverbs 16:28

Perverse people are those who are stubborn and self-righteous. Some are so strong willed that no matter what, they do not change their opinion but fight even harder in order to prove themselves right. They argue to their last breath but never admit that they are wrong. These folks just love to be the opposite of everything and always look for reasons to argue. They may be wise in their own eyes, but according to the Bible, they are considered a fool and it gives us warning to stay away from people like these. A truly wise person knows when to speak up and when to remain silent. Speaking less and listening more is the sign of wisdom which brings about a peaceful situation rather than a conflict.

Everyone loves a good gossip and we all are guilty of this. Some Christians have a nicer way of gossiping. They call it "prayer request" and use this as an excuse to go around telling others about a person's situation. They may act deeply concerned and tell others to pray for them while in reality, they themselves do not have much concern or intention of praying for others; they just like to spread news and happenings of others people's lives in a "caring" way.

We may take it lightly and not think much of it when we talk about others behind their backs but by doing so, we prove ourselves to be untrustworthy. We betray some one's trust when we share something about someone who has confided in us and trusts us to keep it confidential. Once that trust is gone, it is hard to re-gain it and become a loyal friend again.

If we cannot agree with someone on a matter, it is better to remain quiet and let the other person be the fool rather to argue and be a fool also. And if we can only say something about a person behind their back but not to their face, then we better not talk at all.

These are words of wisdom from the Bible and wise is he who abides by these!

Dear LORD, set a watch over my mouth and guard the door of my lips so that I do not gossip and engage in conversations which are offensive and hurtful to others. Give me wisdom to recognize those folks who are slanderers and help me to stay away from them so that I too do not become one as Your word says, bad company corrupts good character. In Jesus' name, Amen!

God's museum - December 15

The sun rises, and the sun goes down, and hastens to the place where it rises.
Ecclesiastes 1:5

We like to go to museums to see old artifacts and learn about historical events. There are many Biblical Museums that feature things from the Bible that were discovered from the past. But besides these, there are so many things still in existence that we are surrounded by in this present day which are not found in any museum—such as the SUN. The sun that we see every day is the same Sun that God created in the beginning of the universe to give us light. It is the same exact heavenly ball of fire that Adam, Noah, Abraham, Moses, David, John, Jesus, Peter and Paul saw that we see today and get light and energy from.

God's proof of existence is all around us. He reminds us every day of His presence by showing us such things which we know that no one else but God can create. It is up to us to acknowledge it and give God the credit rather than wasting time proving His non-existence.

As we go about our business every day and enjoy the sunlight without giving it much thought, let's take a moment to actually gaze at the SUN and see how bright, effective, and powerful it is today as it has been since the beginning of creation. And while we ponder at the SUN, let us not forget the SON who is the light of the world.

Dear LORD, thank you for giving us proof of Your existence and creation in every little thing that we see and feel. I stand in awe of Your power and majesty; in Your gentleness and kindness; in Your humility and love. May I never forget how great thou art! In Jesus' name, Amen!

Don't do it again - December 16

As a dog returns to its vomit, so a fool repeats his foolishness. Proverbs 26:11

I f we have been admitted in the hospital for a sickness and ready to get discharged after we feel well, the doctor gives us instructions on how to better take care of ourselves and what to eat and avoid. Because the experience was so painful and we know the hardship that we went through, we take care of ourselves, exercise, take our medications regularly, and discipline ourselves to ensure that we never have to go through that again. But as months and years go by, some of us find ourselves slipping away from the disciplined regime and go back to our old eating habits and lifestyle.

We all have given up something from the past and vowed to never go back to it. It could be an addiction or some internal sin which made us sick to our core, so we decided to puke it out of our life. But after a while, we find ourselves running back to the same old sin which we said we would not return to.

When a dog vomits, it forgets that the vomit is nothing but the junk that it had eaten earlier that made it sick. The dog forgets the pain and discomfort that the unhealthy stuff it had devoured earlier brought upon it and still goes back to it. As disgusting as it sounds for a dog to do this, we too behave similarly with our sin. Even when we know that our sin had made us sick and we vomited it out of our lives, our behavior is no better than the dog if we go back to it.

God has told us that once we know the truth about our sin and have repented of it, we must leave it once for all and sin no more. So, if we find ourselves returning to it, we need to ask God to remind us of our spiritual sickness we once were in and move forward with the new life that He has given us.

Dear LORD, once I have been convicted of my sin and sworn to give it up, please help me to keep that vow and not return to it no matter how tempting it may be. Help me to remember the pain that it had caused me and You and may it stop me from doing it again. Give me a hatred for my sin that I am repulsed by it and will not return to the same pit again. In Jesus' name, Amen!

Co-driver - December 17

"Behold, I am the Lord, the God of all flesh. Is anything too hard for me?
Jeremiah 32:27

It is as simple as that–If God is with us, what can happen to us that is beyond His power? Is there anything too difficult for God? Is there a question that He cannot answer? Is there anything broken that God cannot mend? Everything is possible with God but the only way we can testify to this personally is to allow God to do so and move out of His way.

Most often we tell God what the problem is but also at the same time, we tell Him how to solve it. If its broken, we give God the bandage and show Him where and how to apply it; we tell God how to answer our own question. We may say that God sits in the Driver's seat of our life but we come and sit on His lap and steer the wheel, creating an illusion for us and others that God is in control, while in reality He's just there and we are the ones driving. And when something goes wrong and we get in trouble, we quickly jump back to the passenger seat and let God take the wheel. Oftentimes, we even blame God for the mess that we have made.

We cannot be co-drivers with God if we entrust our life in His hands. We must allow God to take full control and enjoy the ride peacefully as He drives us to where He wants us to be.

Dear LORD, do as You please with my life. I surrender my life into Your hands and give You control. Help me to trust as You lead me according to Your will. With You as the driver of my life, I cannot fail so help me to move aside and not come in Your way. In Jesus' name, Amen!

Looking in the wrong places - December 18

You will seek Me and find Me when you search for Me with all your heart.
Jeremiah 29:13

Often when I am in any trouble or under stress, I pray to God for help and tell Him that I trust Him to handle the matter. However, at the same time, I frantically run around trying to fix my own problem. And while I am waiting for God, I begin to doubt His presence as He seems to take too long to answer, and I do not know if He will show up to help. But the truth of the matter is how can I hear God or know that He is there to help me if I'm searching for God in the wrong places amongst my other million fearful thoughts that run through my mind. When my heart paces with anxiety and I am on my own problem-solving spree, the chances are I am too occupied to see God at work, and so He seems distant. God is always near, but I put barricades between us that hinders Him from reaching me. He is always willing to help but we become too busy for His help and in turn blame Him for not coming to our aid.

God says in order to reach Him, we must reach out to Him with all our heart. Before we jump to conclusions and look for our own solutions, we need to come close to God and draw His attention. We need stay clear of our anxious thoughts and give God room to work. So that He can come in and fill our mind with wisdom, strength to tackle the problem that we are facing and give us peace that He is there for us. We will find Him if we look for God and in the right places.

Dear LORD, when I am feeling anxious and fearful, I search for You in the wrong places. Make me to realize that You are not found in my anxiousness, fear, worry or discouragement. I need to rid of these from my heart first so that I can find You in the right places. Help me to look and find You in my trust, faith and hope. In Jesus' name, Amen!

It's beyond me - December 19

Since ancient times no one has heard, no ear has perceived, no eye has seen any God besides you, who acts on behalf of those who wait for him. Isaiah 64:4

People say that there is no limit to imagination. But the reality is that there is a limit to it. We can imagine our wildest or weirdest thoughts but then there is an end as to how far our mind can think. Our mind can only think of things or twist our imagination made up of only what our physical eyes have seen, and ears have heard.

But there is more to it than our natural understanding. It is beyond our human capability to imagine how and what God does. We think of God's capability by putting Him in our natural shoes instead of us putting ourselves in His supernatural shoes. We limit the power of God to do things only up to that what our mind can comprehend. If it is beyond our human capability, we assume that God cannot accomplish it either and thus put an end to His omnipotence.

In order to understand God, we must open our spiritual eyes. We must believe by faith in things beyond our sight, thoughts, education and intellect. We should not let the ability of God be limited to what our natural eye can see, or mind can understand. God operates on a supernatural level and we operate on physical level. Therefore, when things don't make sense in the natural realm for us, we must remember that God is up to something bigger which He will manifest to us when we choose to trust Him above our comprehension and wait for Him.

Dear LORD, You are much bigger and powerful than what I can understand so please give me eyes to see supernaturally with faith and not by my physical sight. Increase the understanding of my mind to comprehend Your greatness and a heart to feel Your immense love. In Jesus' name, Amen!

The heavens proclaim the glory of God. The skies display his craftsmanship.
Psalm 19:1

Millions of people came out to witness the solar eclipse that took place recently. When we see something like this, we cannot help but acknowledge the one who made it happen. The God who created the sun and moon can turn morning into night and night into day. God has put the universe in place and set it in motion to function just the way He designed it. He has given us limited knowledge to figure out how these things work based on our human understanding and so we cannot imitate and recreate what God has created.

The same God who is so powerful to change the course of day and night, is the same God who can change the course of our life instantaneously. He can turn our sorrow into joy and our darkness into morning. It may seem impossible to us, but we are witnesses that nothing is impossible with God. The God who holds the universe in His hand is the same God who holds us individually in the palm of His hand also.

If our circumstances seem to last forever and if we have lost hope, think about the eclipse and remember that we belong to a God who holds time in his Hands, and He can do things beyond our imagination. The eclipse of sorrow and pain too can pass at God's command just the way He commands the sun and moon where to go. If we belong to a mighty God whom the sun and moon submit to, then who and what do we have to be afraid of?

Dear LORD, how majestic is Your name in all the earth! You created the heavens and earth and all that is in it by the power of Your spoken word, then how can I not trust You to take care of my needs? I believe with all my heart that You can change my circumstances. so, just say the word, LORD, and it will be well. In Jesus' name, Amen!

Make me blush - December 21

Are they ashamed of their disgusting actions? Not at all—they don't even know how to blush! Jeremiah 6:15

To blush is to develop a pinkish color on the face when we feel embarrassed. We usually blush when we do not know how to react to an uncomfortable situation and it just naturally becomes evident on our face.

Our sins should make us uncomfortable enough that it shows up on our face. When we sin, it should cause us to feel ashamed and a need to hide our face. But most often, we continue to sin without any remorse or regret. Sinning comes naturally to us and so we do not do anything to stop ourselves. We look at the sinful world around us and make ourselves right at home in it. We justify our sin by measuring it with someone else's and assume that ours is not as bad, or since everyone is doing it, it is acceptable and if no one knows about it, it is not a big deal.

But no matter what we think of sin, God calls it as it is and calls us out on it. He convicts us by His Holy Spirit to let us know when we have done something wrong. But it is up to us to act on the conviction. If we truly are righteous and want to live a godly life, we ought to accept our sin instead of excusing it. It must create a sense of guilt and embarrassment within us that we have hurt God, ourselves, others, and must have an urgent need to be forgiven rather than flaunt our sin.

Dear LORD, when I commit a sin, may Your conviction be so heavy on me that it shows up on my face. May I become weary and restless that I must confess and get rid of it from my life. Thank you for Your forgiveness and please help me not to commit those sins again. In Jesus name, Amen!

Light at the end of the tunnel - December 22

No temptation has overtaken you except such as is common to man; but God is faithful, who will not allow you to be tempted beyond what you are able, but with the temptation will also make the way of escape, that you may be able to bear it. 1 Corinthians 10:13

C hesapeake Bay Tunnel in Virginia is one of the longest tunnels in America. When we pass through this 20-mile-long tunnel, we may feel like it is a never-ending tube, and the end seems nowhere near when we pass through it. But like any underpass, there is always a light at the end of the tunnel.

In the same way, when we are faced with temptation, it may feel so intense and so strong against us that we feel as if we will not be able to resist it and get out of it. But if we stay focused and keep our eyes towards the destination, we will see the light at end of the tunnel. We are not meant to remain stuck inside of it but come through on the other side. No matter how many things the devil throws against us to tempt and fall in sin, God also provides a way for us to get out of it. The devil knows what our weak points are, and he uses those to tempt us. But God knows our strength and He equips us with those to stand against the temptation.

So, while we go through tempting situations in life, if we stay on course, God will guide us through the dark tunnel and get us out safely and on the other side. God always makes a way where there seems to be no way. So, let us trust God and follow His directions as we go through tunnels of temptation.

Dear LORD, thank you for providing a way out of the tempting situations that I deal with. Help me not to give up and give into the temptation but walk out of it through the way that You provide for me. In Jesus' name, Amen!

Do it for the LORD - December 23

And whatever you do, in word or deed, do everything in the name of the Lord Jesus, giving thanks to God the Father through him. Colossians 3:17

I t is no fun to do something good when no one's there to notice and see us for a job well done. Mostly in everything we do, we like to be seen and our work to be noticed so that we receive the compliments and rewards from people. We work harder on our jobs when we know that our boss is watching us, hoping to get a promotion or bigger bonus. Or in school, some students do extra just to be noticed or get a good report by the teacher or the coach. Even in church, some folks engage in more activities to prove something, as if to the LORD but it's more for people to see and praise them rather than God.

Praise God if we do not fall in this category, but many of us do and don't even realize it. If no one was around to see it or if our work was never acknowledged, would we still give our best or would do a whatever job just for the sake of getting it done?

Whether people notice or not, God sees everything that we do and with what type of attitude we do it. Therefore, in all our duties whether at work, school, home, church, or any community, we ought to give it our best and do it without the expectation of acknowledgement and without complaining or grumbling. We must be humble and sincere in all that we do, big or small, behind the scene or up front, as God is the ultimate boss whom we are working for and He rewards us according to what and how we do.

Dear LORD, it is You alone whom I need to impress and not anyone else so please help me to do my work with all diligence and give my best in everything that I do. Thank you for entrusting me to be Your faithful servant, may I represent You through my service. In Jesus' name, Amen!

All that I have - December 24

Do not despise these small beginnings, for the LORD rejoices to see the work begin. Zechariah 4:10a

A lot of events are categorized as successful or unsuccessful based on the size of the audience. The more people that attend, the more we feel that we accomplished our goal. But if only a handful show up, we easily get discouraged and maybe even quit without giving it another chance. But the Bible clearly teaches us to hang in there and not get disappointed when our effort does not seem to go too far right away. When we are certain of what God wants us to do, our focus should be on the task and not on the outcome. The audience should not be our target but our performance for the LORD. Our duty is to faithfully continue to do what He asks and let God worry about its results. He uses our performance to touch the lives of others and accomplish His purpose through us.

Just the way Jesus used the lunch of a little boy with two fish and five loaves of bread to feed thousands, God can use our "little" work which we offer to Him and multiply it beyond our imagination. We may not want to come forward to offer our "little lunch" by looking at the size of the crowd, but God can work with whatever we give Him. So, we should not hold back our "two fish and five loaves" from God assuming that it is will not be sufficient and will not go far. God sees our faith and miraculously turns our little into much when we give Him all that we have. Our small start can result in grand finale when our goal is to only please God and not our self or others from beginning till end.

Therefore, let us not despise small beginnings but trust it to the LORD and watch it multiply.

Dear LORD, many times I am afraid to bring You my worship and service as I feel that it is nothing compared to others. But to You, it does not matter how much of it I bring. So, I am giving You with faith all that is of me, LORD! Accept it and multiply it to hundred-fold for Your glory. In Jesus' name, Amen!

The best gift ever - December 25

In this is love, not that we have loved God but that he loved us and sent his Son to be the propitiation for our sins. 1 John 4:10

When it is our fault in hurting somebody's feelings or causing a problem for someone, often we ask, "What can I do to make it up to you?" In order to receive forgiveness and be right with the person, we are willing to do something extra so that the other person is no longer mad at us. This is what Propitiation means–to offer sacrifice to God in order to turn Him away from His anger so that we do not get punished for our wrongdoing.

We often ask God what we can do to make it up to Him for our sins and try offer sacrifices like how they would do in the Old Testament and do the "work" so that God forgives us. But there is no service, sacrifice, or gift that we can offer that can satisfy His perfect justice. The only satisfaction, or propitiation, that could be acceptable to God had to be made by God Himself. For this reason, God the Son, Jesus Christ, left his heavenly kingdom and came into the world in human flesh to be the perfect sacrifice for sin and be the "propitiation for the sins of the people".

True love is what God did for us. He himself is the offended one but He is the one who became the sacrifice to make up for our sin. God did not demand anything from us, rather He supplied His own sacrifice. It is like me being angry at my husband for some wrong he did, and when he asks "what can I do to make it up to you?", instead of me telling him to take me out to dinner, I take him out to a fancy restaurant, pay for it, and then no longer be mad at him and consider it as if he "made it up to me".

You see, we have no reason to boast in ourselves about being good and earning or deserving forgiveness; it is nothing that we did to receive this precious gift. It is only due to God's love and grace.

Dear LORD, I realize that there is nothing I can do to make it up to You for Your gift of love. I do not deserve it or can earn it by any means. There was only one solution and You already took care of it. Thank you for the gift of Jesus who came into this world to die so that I can live. I owe it all to You! In Jesus' name, Amen!

Finest teacher - December 26

Teach me to do your will, for you are my God; may your good Spirit lead me on level ground. Psalm 143:10

We all have the title of a Teacher. We mostly think of a teacher as someone who teaches in a school by Profession. But each one of us plays a role of a teacher. Parents, Sunday School teachers and leaders, Siblings, and Bosses are also teachers. These are the instructors who mostly bring positive influence in our lives and equip us to do good and succeed. But there is also other type of teachers in our lives who are of negative influence such as our cell phones, TV, Movies, Music, Video games, Internet, and company of bad friends. We all are surrounded by people and things that either teach us what is good and upright or bad and corrupt. It is up to us to decide whom we learn from. It can build us up or tear us down. Therefore, it is important to choose well who teaches us at every stage of our life.

But the greatest teacher of all is God who is Omniscient, and He is the one who has set the standards for right and wrong. There is no better teacher than Jesus, who is the living word himself. We can argue with Him in our own understanding and try to prove Him wrong, but He is the ultimate authority who has the final say. So, what better teacher to learn from then directly from God himself! He has given us His textbook, the Bible, that educates us in all that we need to know for this life and beyond.

Dear LORD, please help me to be careful about whom I allow to influence me in order to live a godly and righteous life. I open my heart to You and am teachable, please impart Your wisdom in me so that I can use it to make better choices in life. Let everything that I do and say be a witness about Your influence in me. In Jesus' name, Amen!

Horizontal love - December 27

My child don't reject the Lord's discipline, and don't be upset when he corrects you. For the Lord corrects those he loves, just as a father corrects a child in whom he delights. Proverbs 3: 11-12

While going somewhere recently, we took the wrong exit. We had to drive about ten miles in the wrong direction to take the next exit to turn around. Then we needed to drive back again for ten miles in order to be on the right road. We eventually did end up on the correct path, but one wrong turn cost us additional toll, fuel and twenty minutes of extra time which made us late to where we needed to be.

Committing a sin is like taking a wrong turn and going in the opposite direction of where God wants to go. We may realize that we did something wrong and turn around, but often we do have to face our sin's consequences. God does not charge or condemn us for taking the wrong turn. He readily forgives if we are repentant, but we must face the consequences such as when a person commits a crime, God forgives them for what they did but they do have to serve their time in prison for their action.

The reason for consequence is for us to realize what we did wrong and pay the price in some form of punishment for our wrongdoing. God is a just God who forgives and will never hold it against us, but He does teach us a lesson through it to make us a better person. He wants us to learn from our mistake and to be careful the next time. If He did not discipline us, we would be spoiled, not take God or our actions seriously and end up in worse situations.

Therefore, whom God loves, he punishes also for the betterment of us.

Dear LORD, when I do something wrong, help me to accept Your chastisement as a form of Your love and care for me. Teach me to be faithful to my consequence and may it serve as a reminder of Your forgiveness and grace to have another opportunity to get it right with You and with those whom I have offended. In Jesus name, Amen!

But if you suffer as a Christian, do not be ashamed, but glorify God that you bear this name. For it is time for judgment to begin with the family of God; and if it begins with us, what will the outcome be for those who disobey the gospel of God? 1 Peter 4:16-17

God has given each one of us specific talents so that through those talents, God can accomplish the purpose He has established for us. Using our talents for God's work is a serious business but often we take it lightly and choose not to walk in our own calling but rather of someone else's. We try to make other people's gift our own gift and present that offering to God, forcefully bestowing it on Him. While we may feel good about our offering, God is not pleased with an offering that is not genuine but brought to Him with conceit and for self-glorification.

When we as Christians, step on each other's toes to work for God's kingdom and compete to get up first on the heavenly bound ladder, we block the way for others who genuinely are trying to seek God and for those who have a true burden for lost souls. We hinder God's work by causing them to stumble and thus oppress God's own children.

If we who are known by God's name, persecute each other internally, like a parent who is stricter on His own child, God's judgment will come heavily on His own first. As a family of God, we need to ensure that we do not cause each other to stumble and suffer for the sake of our own selfishness. We bear Christ's name, so it is our duty to uphold God's integrity by living a life of righteousness from within and not put on a façade for others.

Jesus was mocked for His righteousness; then we as Christians should not give a reason to be mocked for our unrighteousness.

Dear LORD, whatever I do for your Kingdom, may it be through the ability and talents that You have given me, and not an extension of anyone else's. Remove from me pride, envy and self-righteousness that comes in the way of others who are serving You. Help me to serve You with faithfulness and humility. In Jesus' name, Amen!

Forgiving myself - December 29

And because you belong to him, the power of the life-giving Spirit has freed you from the power of sin that leads to death. Romans 8:2

Many times, when we mess up, we can say sorry and ask for forgiveness from whom we have hurt, but we linger around with the guilt of it and do not easily forgive ourselves. And when we cannot forgive our self, we assume that it is too big for God to forgive also, and so we do not even attempt to ask Him. We may eventually let it go and pardon our own sin but if it is not brought to God, there is no true forgiveness.

The highest authority that we need forgiveness is from God. It is He who has the final right for our forgiveness. Therefore, it does not matter then whether we are forgiven by others, our self, or any law. If Christ declares us free, freedom is ours if we accept His forgiveness and no longer walk in the same sinful path. Once we repent from our sin and ask for forgiveness from Jesus, He cleanses us from all our unrighteousness and frees us from the bondage of sin and death. Before we are in Christ, we live under the authority of the devil and abide by his laws of sin which eventually leads to our death. But once we belong to Jesus, He becomes our authority and gives us free life. Being a Christian means that we are united to Jesus Christ by faith. There remains no guilt or shame for our sin once we belong to Him. It is in Christ alone that our hope of eternal life is found and no guilt in life or power of hell can pluck us away from His mighty hand.

So, if the Son sets you free, you are free indeed!

Dear LORD, I indeed am free because You have set me free. Please help me to not go back into the prison whose doors You have already opened wide for me. May I not allow the devil to pull me back into bondage. Thank you for saving and rescuing me from my guilt and blame. In Jesus' name, Amen!

Christian by choice - December 30

The Lord says: "These people come near to me with their mouth and honor me with their lips, but their hearts are far from me. Their worship of me is based on merely human rules they have been taught. Isaiah 29:13

I f you ask some children why they go to church, many say "Because my parents make me". Many of us go to church, read Bible, say prayers, take communion, and give offerings because that is how we were trained by our parents. We follow the rituals of being a Christian but never have a personal relation with Jesus. Our closeness to Him goes as far as reading His word and saying a prayer in His name, but never fully understanding how powerful this name is, who Jesus Christ is, and our need for salvation through Him.

We need to understand that Christianity is not just a religion that one decides to follow like any other religion. Being a Christian means that we are a Christ-follower, a disciple of Jesus. Once we accept Jesus as the true LORD and Savior, our worship of Him comes naturally from the heart and not due to human traditions that we have been taught. Our going to church, praying, and reading more from His word becomes a desire and not a dread. Instead of feeling forced to do so, we do all that we can for His service with a gladness in our heart and for God's name to be glorified.

No one can make us a Christian; we are one by our own decision. Therefore, we need to ask ourselves if we are a Christian by birth or by spiritual re-birth which comes by accepting Jesus as our Savior.

Dear LORD, although my parents may have forced me to go to church in my childhood, I thank you for it now as through the years, I came to know You and experienced You for myself to accept You as my own, personal LORD and Savior. I have decided to follow You so hold my feet firm to Your path no matter what obstacles come my way. In Jesus' name, Amen!

One way only - December 31

Jesus answered, "I am the way and the truth and the life. No one comes to the Father except through me. John 14:6

A bypass surgery of the heart is a procedure that restores blood flow to the heart by diverting the flow around the section of a blocked artery. It is an alternative route for blood to flow, bypassing or going around the blocked passage. This procedure, if performed successfully is like a new heart placed in the body as the blood is now able to flow freely and without pain. It is a great procedure for the physical heart for those who need it but can be dangerous if we attempt to do the same spiritually. Many of us try to apply the same principal to our soul and try to bypass our way to God by different means. We seek alternate paths to heaven by coming up with reasons or excuses for our sin. Or we attempt to win God over by our charity or good works.

Many world religions believe that there are multiple ways to heaven and so if one passage is blocked, we can try some other route. But the Bible clearly says that there is only one way to heaven and that is through Jesus Christ. If we desire to live eternally with God, we must believe in Jesus Christ as our Savior from sin, confess our sin and ask for His forgiveness. Instead of re-routing through any other direction, we must allow Jesus to cleanse us and unclog our sins. Our religious efforts must be removed and replaced with a personal relationship with Jesus which block the flow of His love and the work of the Holy Spirit in us. When Jesus performs this procedure by our consent, He removes our old, stubborn stony heart and puts in us His spirit and gives us a new heart to live for Him.

A bypass surgery gives new life to the heart, but a bypass surgery of the soul leads to eternal life. Therefore, let us allow Jesus to unblock the arteries of our soul by cleansing us within instead of bypassing.

Dear LORD, I acknowledge that You are the one and only way to heaven. Please help me not to seek any other means to get to You. May I be a living witness of this truth to those around me. Cleanse my heart so that the blood of Jesus can flow fully and freely in my life and I can live an abundant life in You. In Jesus' name, Amen!

A Personal Word

We have been facing unheard of, trying times lately. As a human we may feel overwhelmed and fearful, but during these times we need to acknowledge the power of our God Jesus Christ. He has promised to never leave us nor forsake us, therefore, we must learn to rely on Him and trust God to make provisions for our needs. These are times when one can also realize a need for a Savior from sin. And that Savior is none other than Jesus Christ who not only provides for physical needs but forgives us and gives us hope for eternal life. It is Jesus who gave His life on the cross for ours sins and it is through his name, we can be forgiven and have access to eternity. The Bible says *"if you confess with your mouth the Lord Jesus and believe in your heart that God has raised Him from the dead, you will be saved. For whoever calls on the name of the Lord shall be saved." Romans 10:9 & 13.* If you feel that you need forgiveness from your sins and would like to invite Jesus into your life, you can simply say a prayer as below:

Dear LORD,

You sent your only begotten Son Jesus Christ to die on the cross for my sins. I confess my wrongdoings and repent of my sins. Please forgive my sins and cleanse me from all unrighteousness. Teach me to live a life that pleases you and honors your name. I invite you in my heart to be my LORD and Savior. I pray this in the sweet and loving name of Jesus Christ. Amen!

If you prayed this prayer and are willing to walk forward with a new life in Jesus, please join a Christ-worshipping church and seek pastoral guidance.

We would be thrilled to hear about your repentance so please let us know if you have accepted Jesus through email or our Facebook page.

Please like our **Zion Devotions** Facebook page.
Subscribe to our **Zion Devotions** YouTube channel.
You may also reach us at: **ziondevotions@gmail.com**

About the Author

I, Cleris Christian am a happily married wife of Mr. Jodrejoy Christian for 22 years. Together we are blessed with our two beautiful children, Joshua and Rebecca who are our most precious gifts from God. I was born and raised in a devout Christian family by my parents, Samuel and Ruth Christian who are my godly role models. My life revolves around God and family who are my priority and whom I love dearly. Although I am a full-time employee in the business world, my passion is not about climbing the career ladder but rather new heights for God's kingdom. I cherish my time with God in quiet time of praying and reading Bible through which I find my strength and courage to serve Him wherever He calls.

"But you are a chosen people, a royal priesthood, a holy nation, God's special possession, that you may declare the praises of him who called you out of darkness into his wonderful light". 1 Peter 2:9, NLT

CPSIA information can be obtained
at www.ICGtesting.com
Printed in the USA
BVHW071939240321
603021BV00002B/2